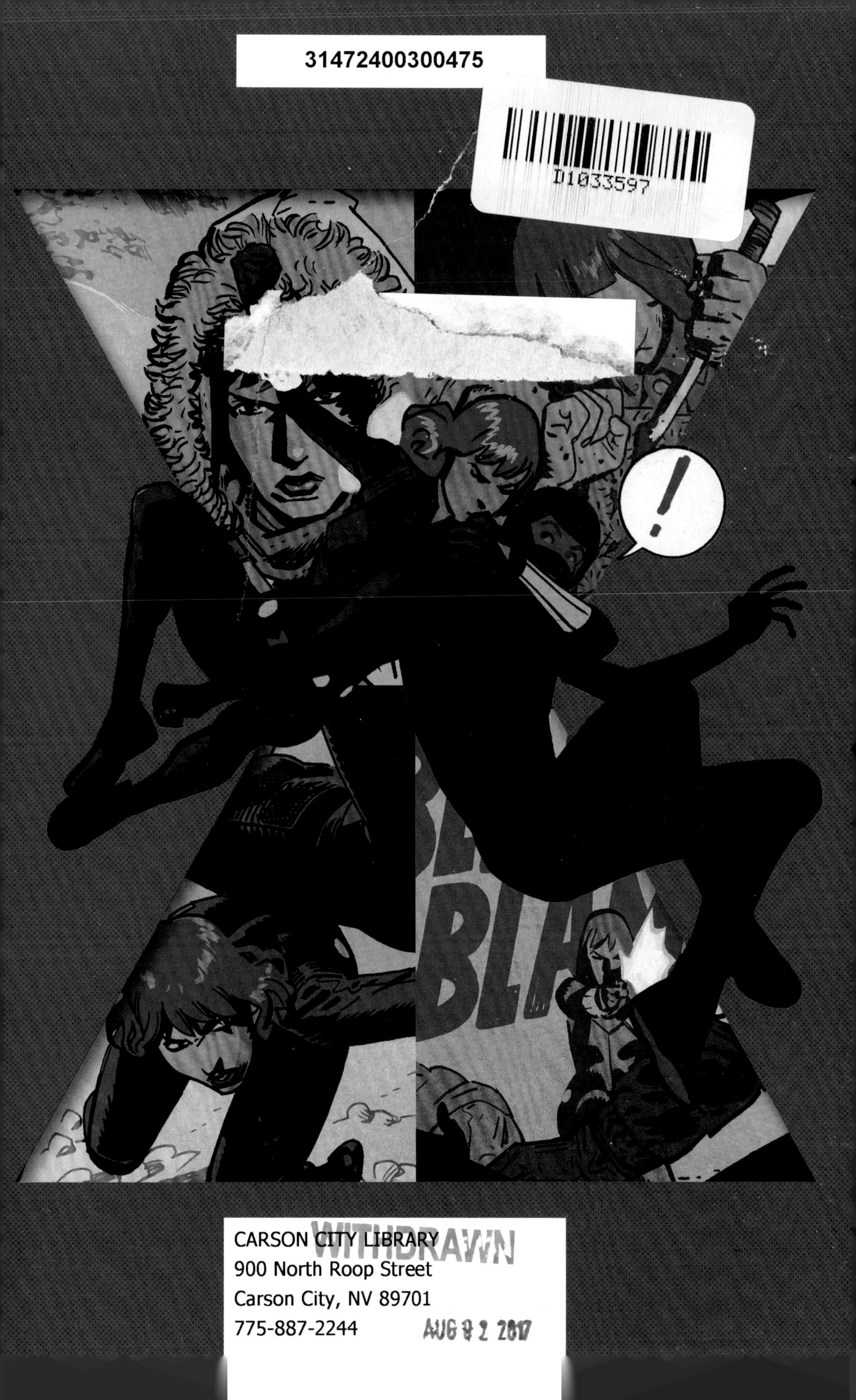
!

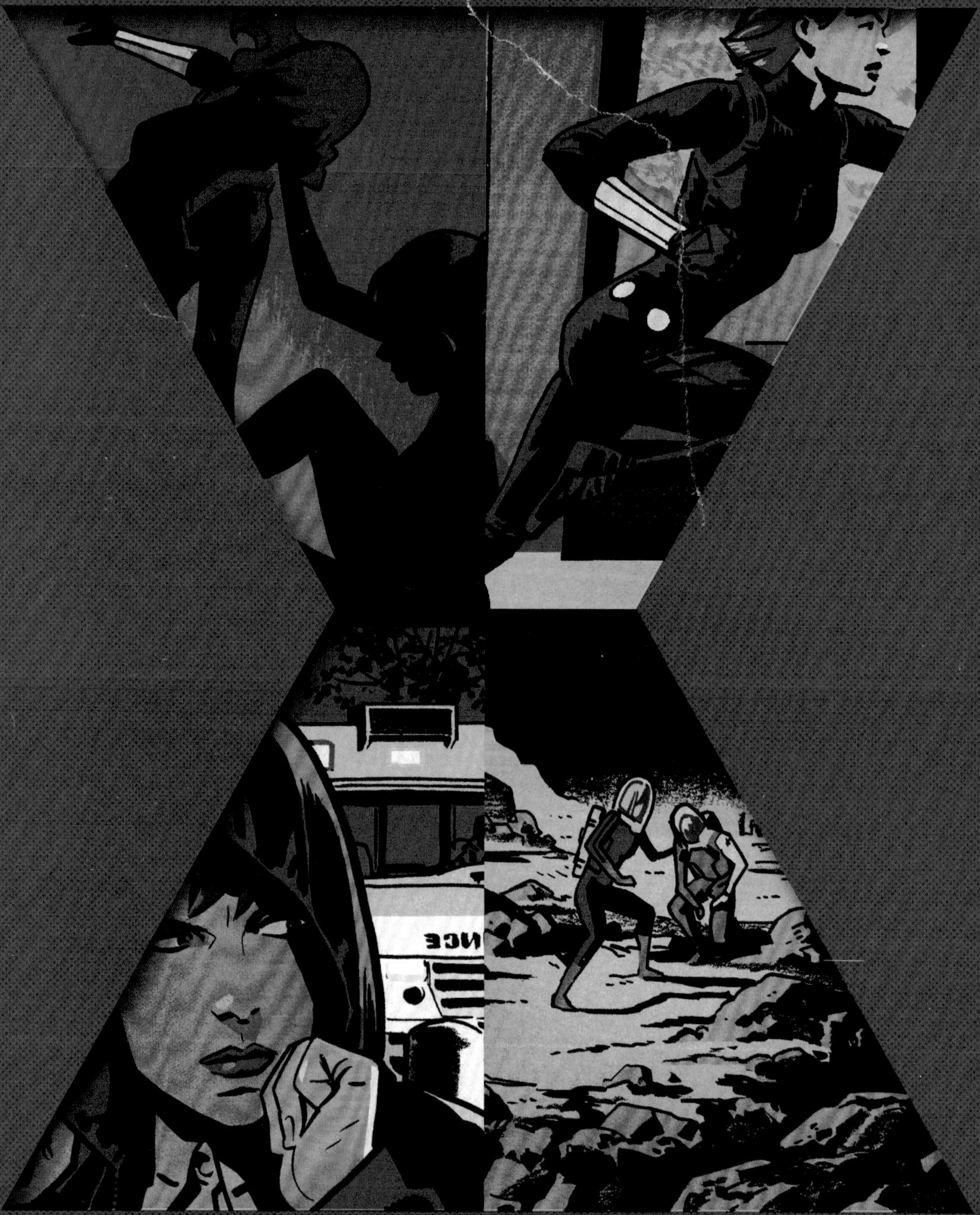

# BLACK WIDOW

## NO MORE SECRETS

**MARK WAID & CHRIS SAMNEE**
WRITERS

**CHRIS SAMNEE**
ARTIST

**MATTHEW WILSON**
COLOR ARTIST

**VC's JOE CARAMAGNA**
LETTERER

**CHRIS SAMNEE & MATTHEW WILSON**
COVER ART

**KATHLEEN WISNESKI**
ASSISTANT EDITOR

**JAKE THOMAS**
EDITOR

---

COLLECTION EDITOR **JENNIFER GRÜNWALD**
ASSISTANT EDITOR **CAITLIN O'CONNELL**
ASSOCIATE MANAGING EDITOR **KATERI WOODY**
EDITOR, SPECIAL PROJECTS **MARK D. BEAZLEY**

VP PRODUCTION & SPECIAL PROJECTS **JEFF YOUNGQUIST**
SVP PRINT, SALES & MARKETING **DAVID GABRIEL**
BOOK DESIGNER **ADAM DEL RE WITH JAY BOWEN**

EDITOR IN CHIEF **AXEL ALONSO**
CHIEF CREATIVE OFFICER **JOE QUESADA**
PRESIDENT **DAN BUCKLEY**
EXECUTIVE PRODUCER **ALAN FINE**

**BLACK WIDOW VOL. 2: NO MORE SECRETS.** Contains material originally published in magazine form as BLACK WIDOW #7-12. First printing 2017. ISBN# 978-0-7851-9976-2. Published by MARVEL WORLDWIDE, INC., a subsidiary of MARVEL ENTERTAINMENT, LLC. OFFICE OF PUBLICATION: 135 West 50th Street, New York, NY 10020. Copyright © 2017 MARVEL No similarity between any of the names, characters, persons, and/or institutions in this magazine with those of any living or dead person or institution is intended, and any such similarity which may exist is purely coincidental. **Printed in Canada.** DAN BUCKLEY, President, Marvel Entertainment; JOE QUESADA, Chief Creative Officer; TOM BREVOORT, SVP of Publishing; DAVID BOGART, SVP of Business Affairs & Operations, Publishing & Partnership; C.B. CEBULSKI, VP of Brand Management & Development, Asia; DAVID GABRIEL, SVP of Sales & Marketing, Publishing; JEFF YOUNGQUIST, VP of Production & Special Projects; DAN CARR, Executive Director of Publishing Technology; ALEX MORALES, Director of Publishing Operations; SUSAN CRESPI, Production Manager; STAN LEE, Chairman Emeritus. For information regarding advertising in Marvel Comics or on Marvel.com, please contact Vit DeBellis, Integrated Sales Manager, at vdebellis@marvel.com. For Marvel subscription inquiries, please call 888-511-5480. **Manufactured between 3/3/2017 and 4/4/2017 by SOLISCO PRINTERS, SCOTT, QC, CANADA.**

10 9 8 7 6 5 4 3 2 1

NATASHA ROMANOFF IS AN EX-KGB ASSASSIN, AN EX-AGENT OF S.H.I.E.L.D.,
AND A SOMETIME AVENGER. SHE HAS TRIED TO USE HER UNIQUE SKILL SET
TO ATONE FOR HER PAST, BUT ATONEMENT IS NOT ERASURE. SOONER OR
LATER, THE PAST COMES PROWLING BACK.

# BLACK WIDOW

THE WEEPING LION, WHO GATHERS SECRETS THROUGH PSYCHIC EAVESDROPPING,
BLACKMAILED BLACK WIDOW INTO WORKING FOR HIM, UNTIL SHE FAILED A TASK
AND HER SECRET WAS RELEASED...CAUSING THE LION TO LOSE HIS LEVERAGE.
NATASHA TRACKED DOWN AND DEFEATED THE LION.
NOW BLACK WIDOW INTENDS TO USE HIM AGAINST OLD ENEMIES:
THE FORMER RED ROOM HEADMISTRESS AND HER DAUGHTER, RECLUSE,
WHO FOUNDED THE DARK ROOM, A NEW SCHOOL FOR CHILD ASSASSINS.
THE WIDOW WON'T ALLOW MORE GIRLS TO SHARE HER OWN FATE.

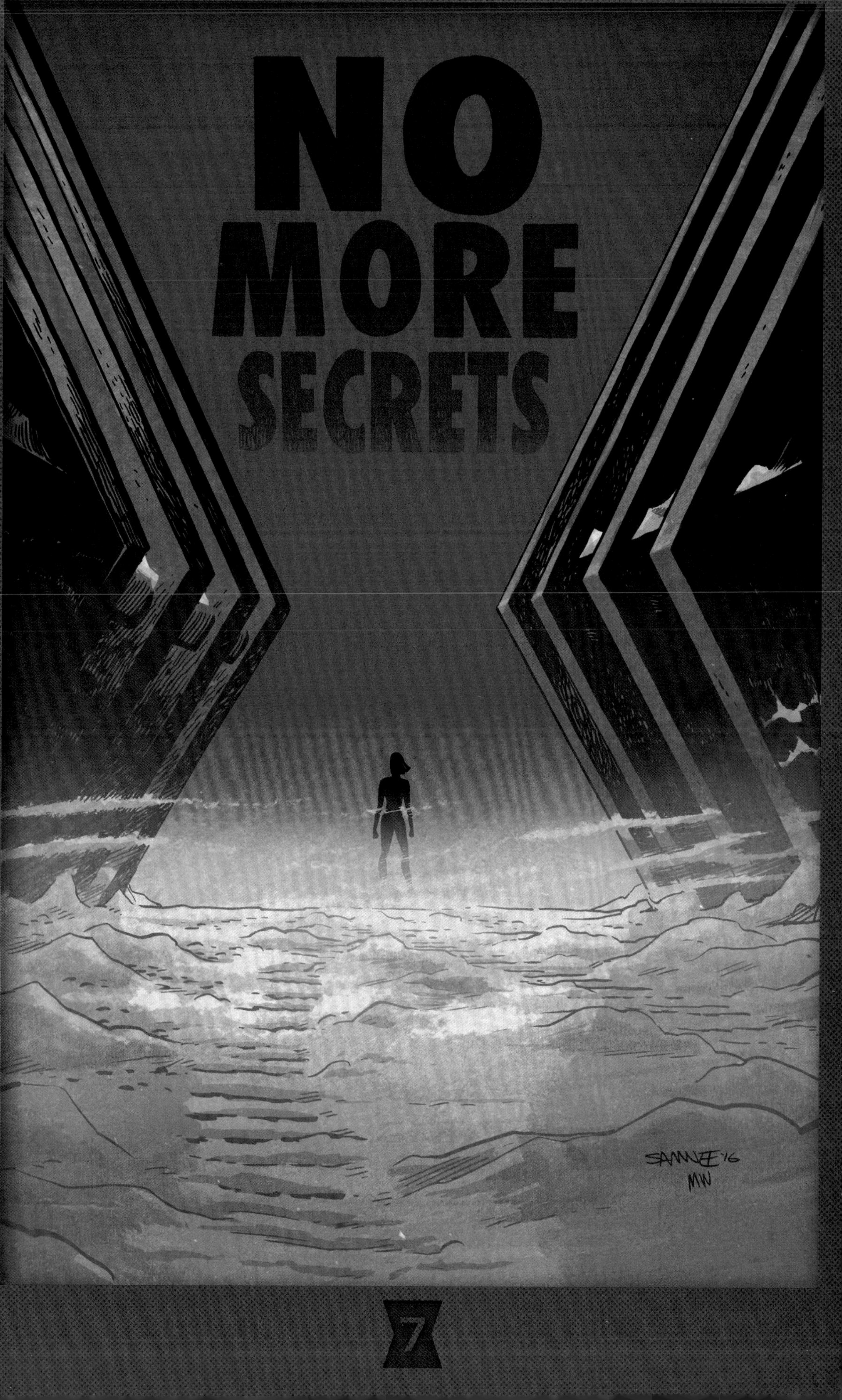
NO
MORE
SECRETS
SAMNEE '16
MW
7

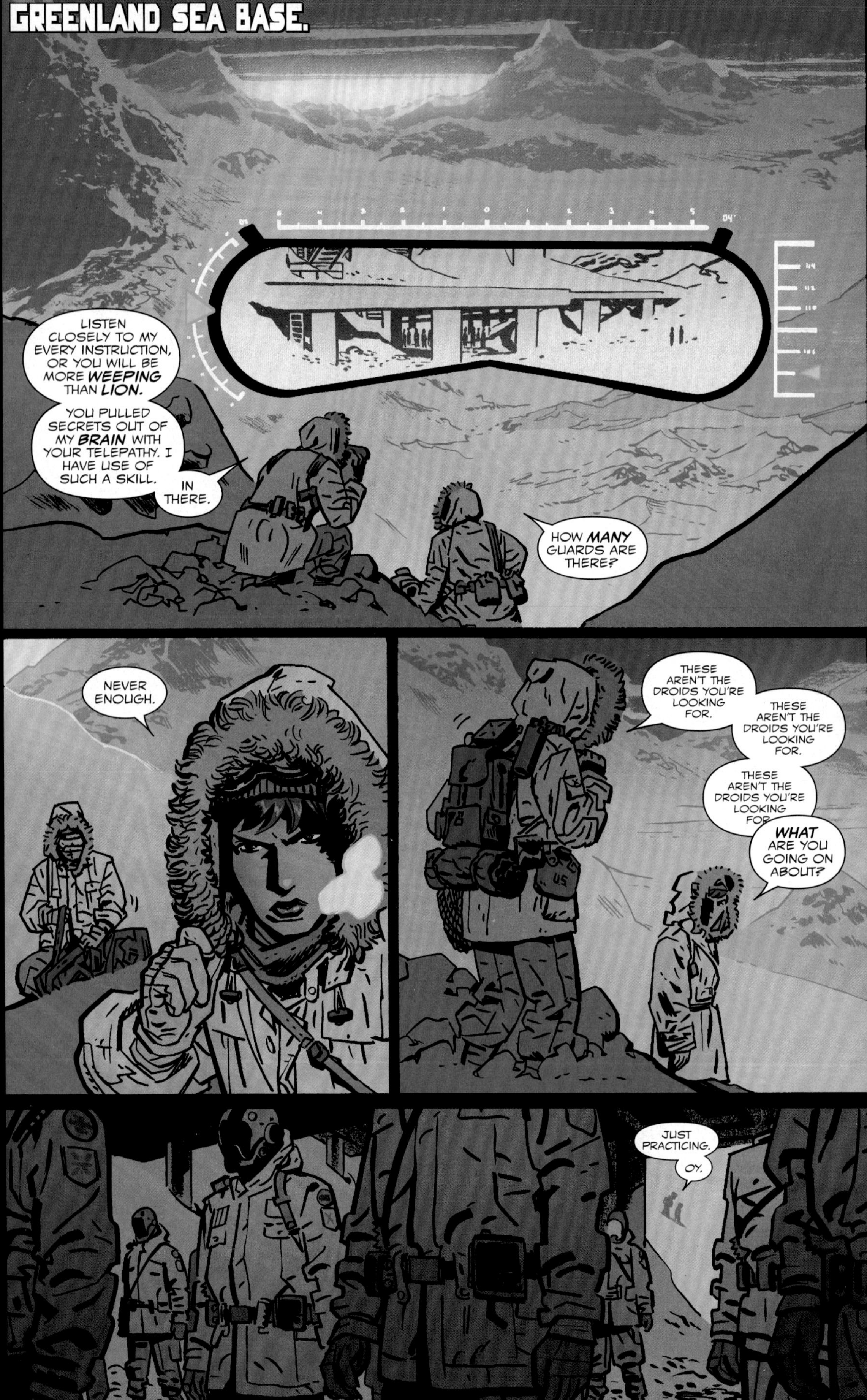
GREENLAND SEA BASE.
LISTEN CLOSELY TO MY EVERY INSTRUCTION, OR YOU WILL BE MORE WEEPING THAN LION.
YOU PULLED SECRETS OUT OF MY BRAIN WITH YOUR TELEPATHY. I HAVE USE OF SUCH A SKILL.
IN THERE.
HOW MANY GUARDS ARE THERE?
NEVER ENOUGH.
THESE AREN'T THE DROIDS YOU'RE LOOKING FOR.
THESE AREN'T THE DROIDS YOU'RE LOOKING FOR.
THESE AREN'T THE DROIDS YOU'RE LOOKING FOR
WHAT ARE YOU GOING ON ABOUT?
JUST PRACTICING.
OY.

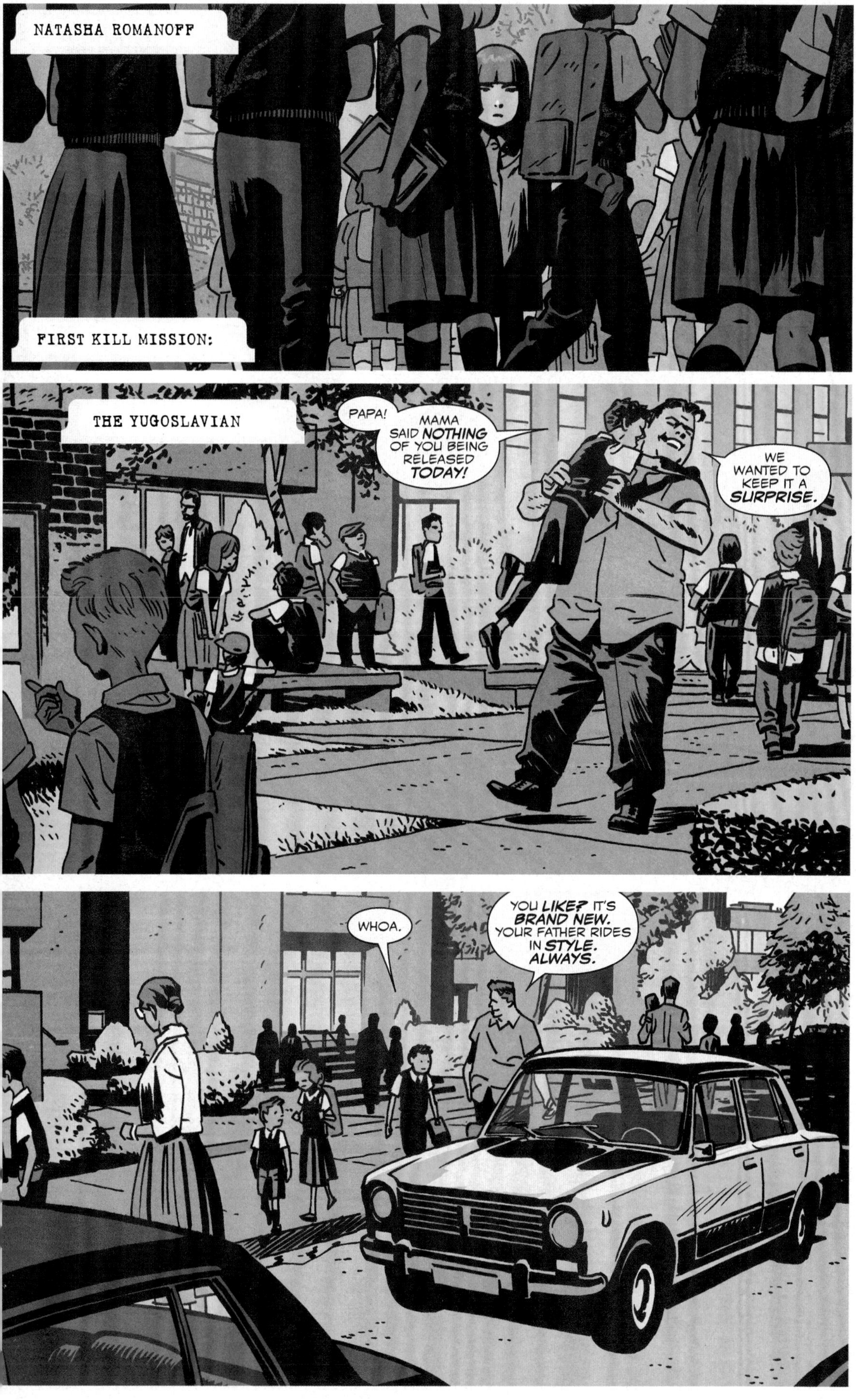
NATASHA ROMANOFF
FIRST KILL MISSION:
THE YUGOSLAVIAN
PAPA!
MAMA SAID NOTHING OF YOU BEING RELEASED TODAY!
WE WANTED TO KEEP IT A SURPRISE.
WHOA.
YOU LIKE? IT'S BRAND NEW. YOUR FATHER RIDES IN STYLE. ALWAYS.

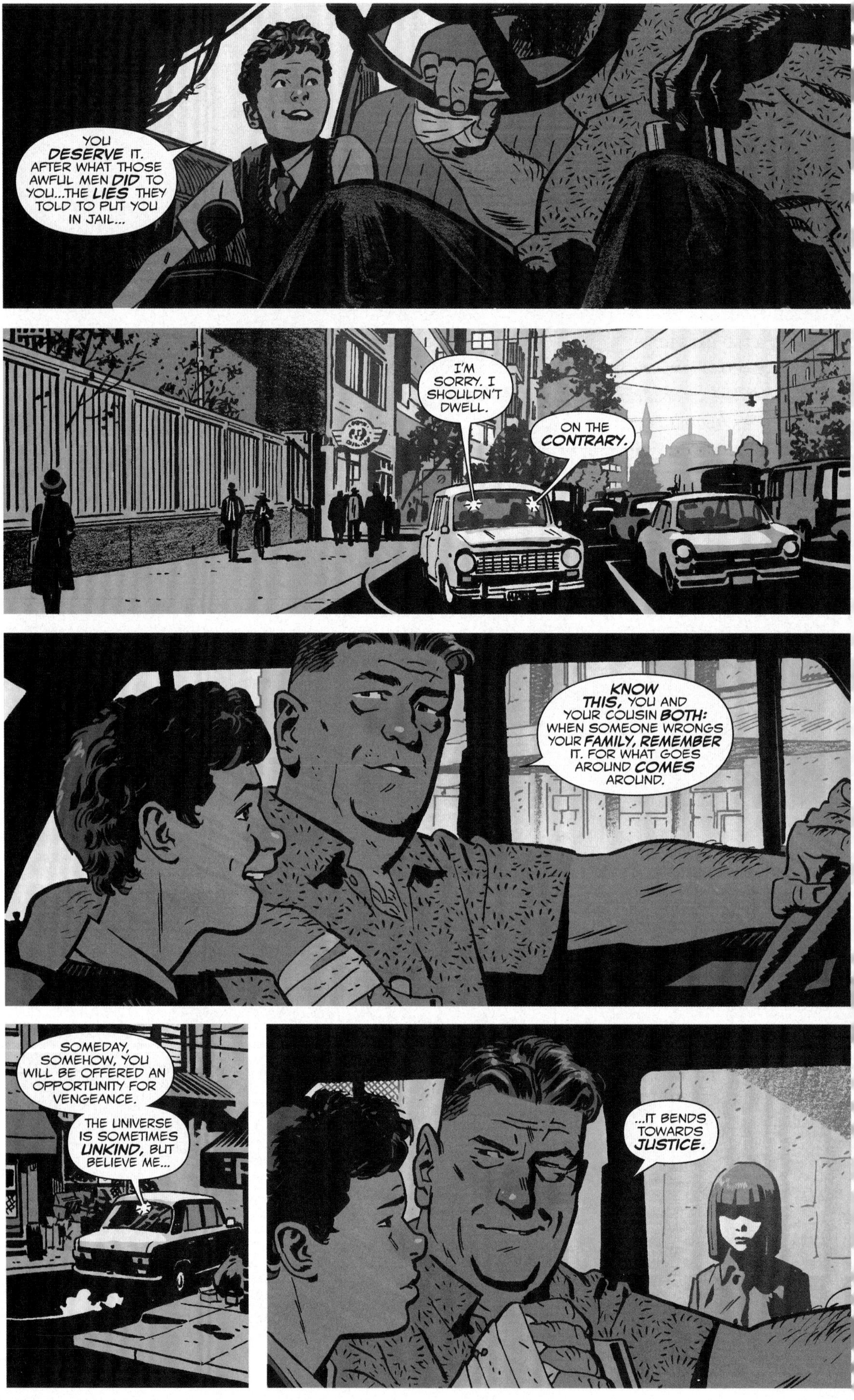
YOU DESERVE IT. AFTER WHAT THOSE AWFUL MEN DID TO YOU...THE LIES THEY TOLD TO PUT YOU IN JAIL...
I'M SORRY. I SHOULDN'T DWELL.
ON THE CONTRARY.
KNOW THIS, YOU AND YOUR COUSIN BOTH: WHEN SOMEONE WRONGS YOUR FAMILY, REMEMBER IT. FOR WHAT GOES AROUND COMES AROUND.
SOMEDAY, SOMEHOW, YOU WILL BE OFFERED AN OPPORTUNITY FOR VENGEANCE.
THE UNIVERSE IS SOMETIMES UNKIND, BUT BELIEVE ME...
...IT BENDS TOWARDS JUSTICE.

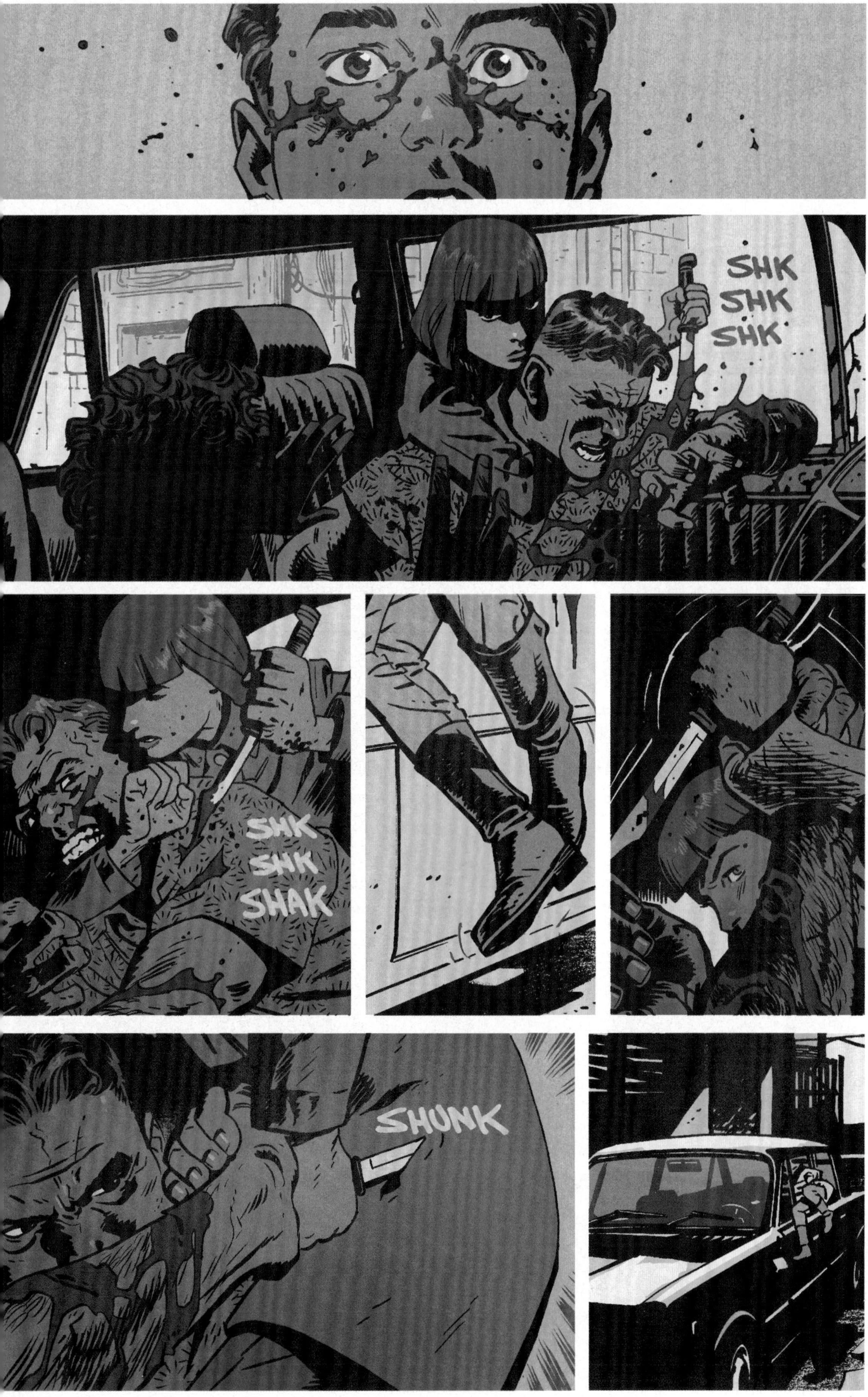
SHK
SHK
SHK
SHK
SHK
SHAK
SHUNK

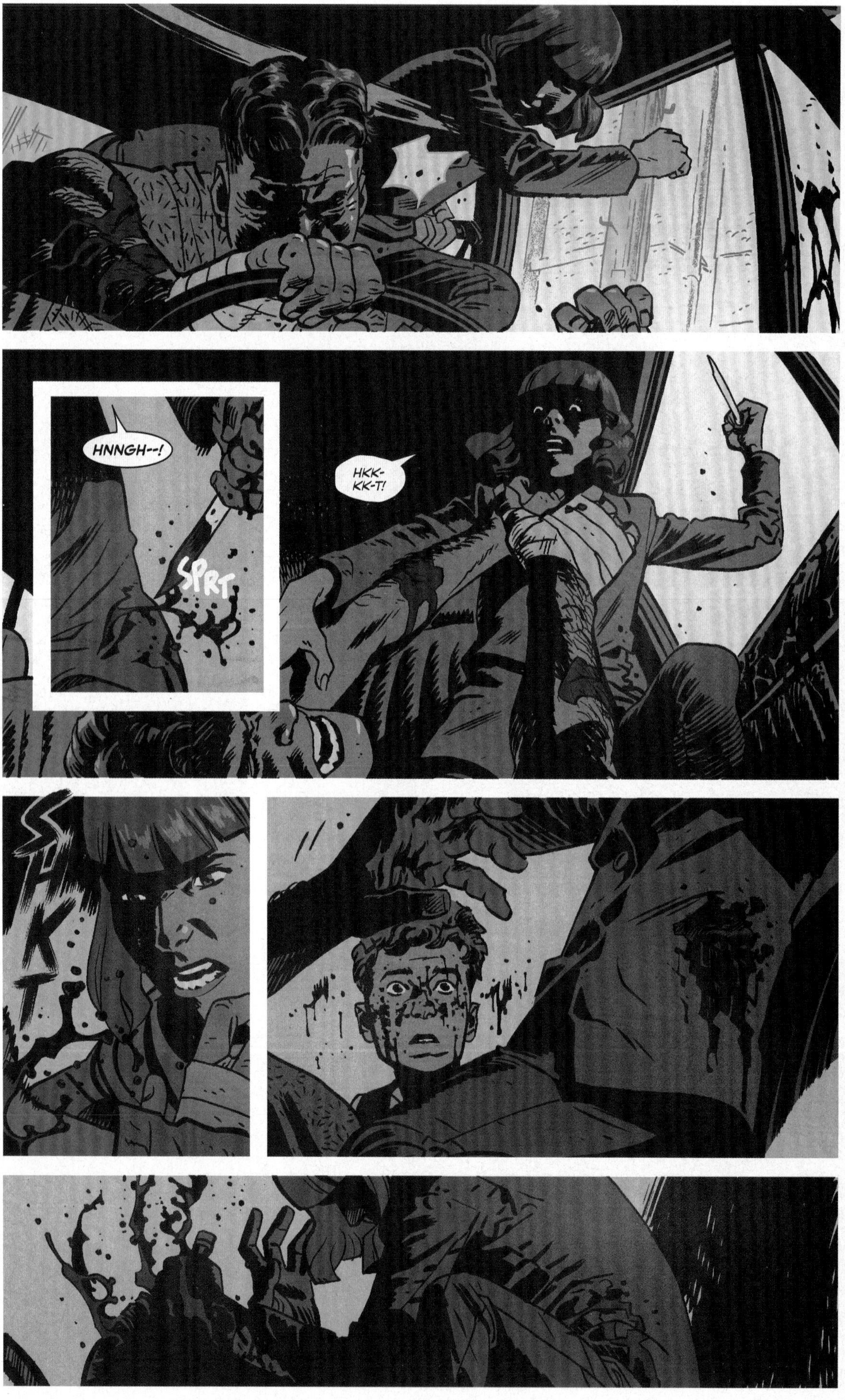
HNNGH--!
SPRT
HKK-
KK-T!
SHKT

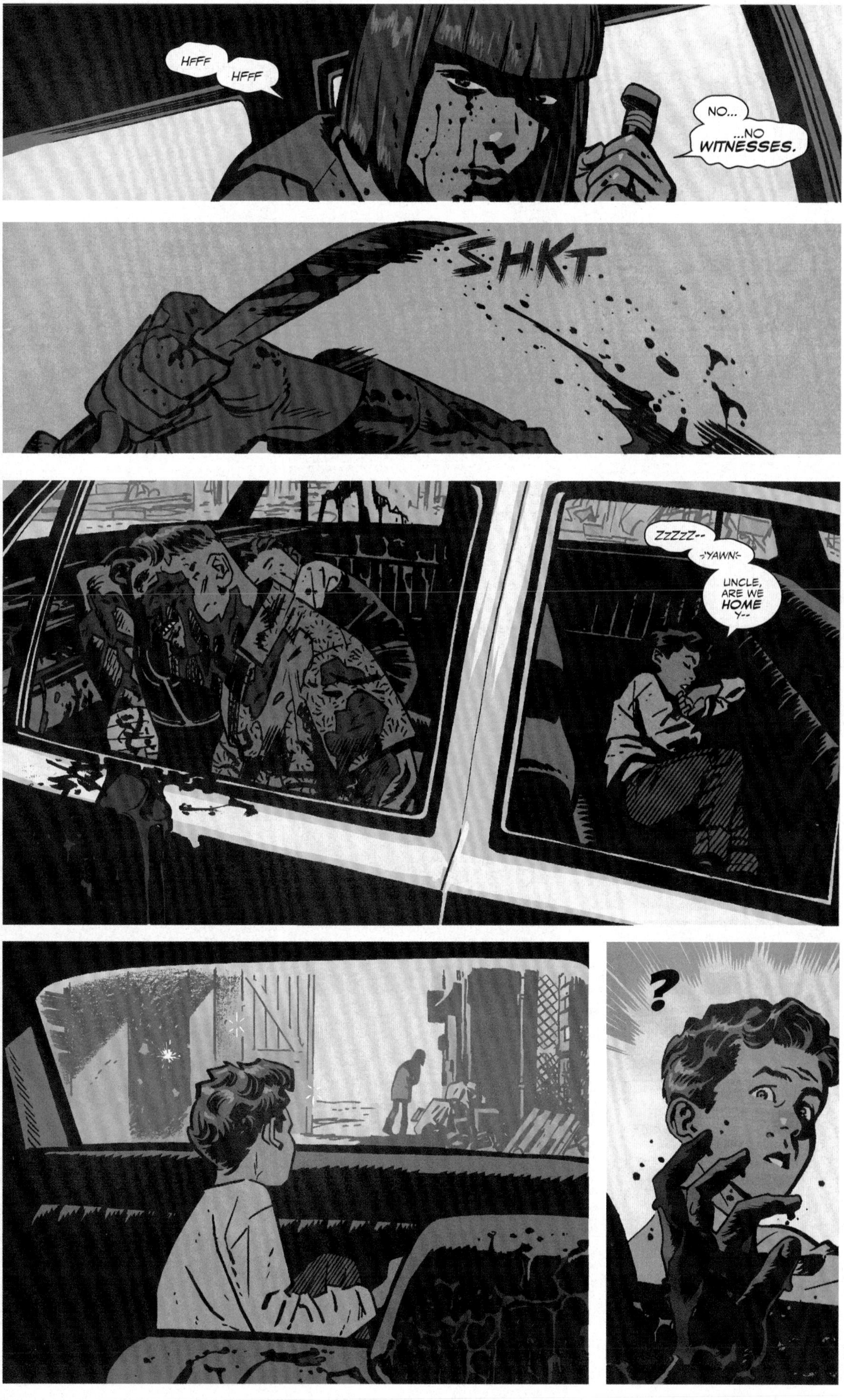
HFFF
HFFF
NO...
...NO WITNESSES.
SHKT
ZZZZZ--
YAWN
UNCLE, ARE WE HOME Y--
?

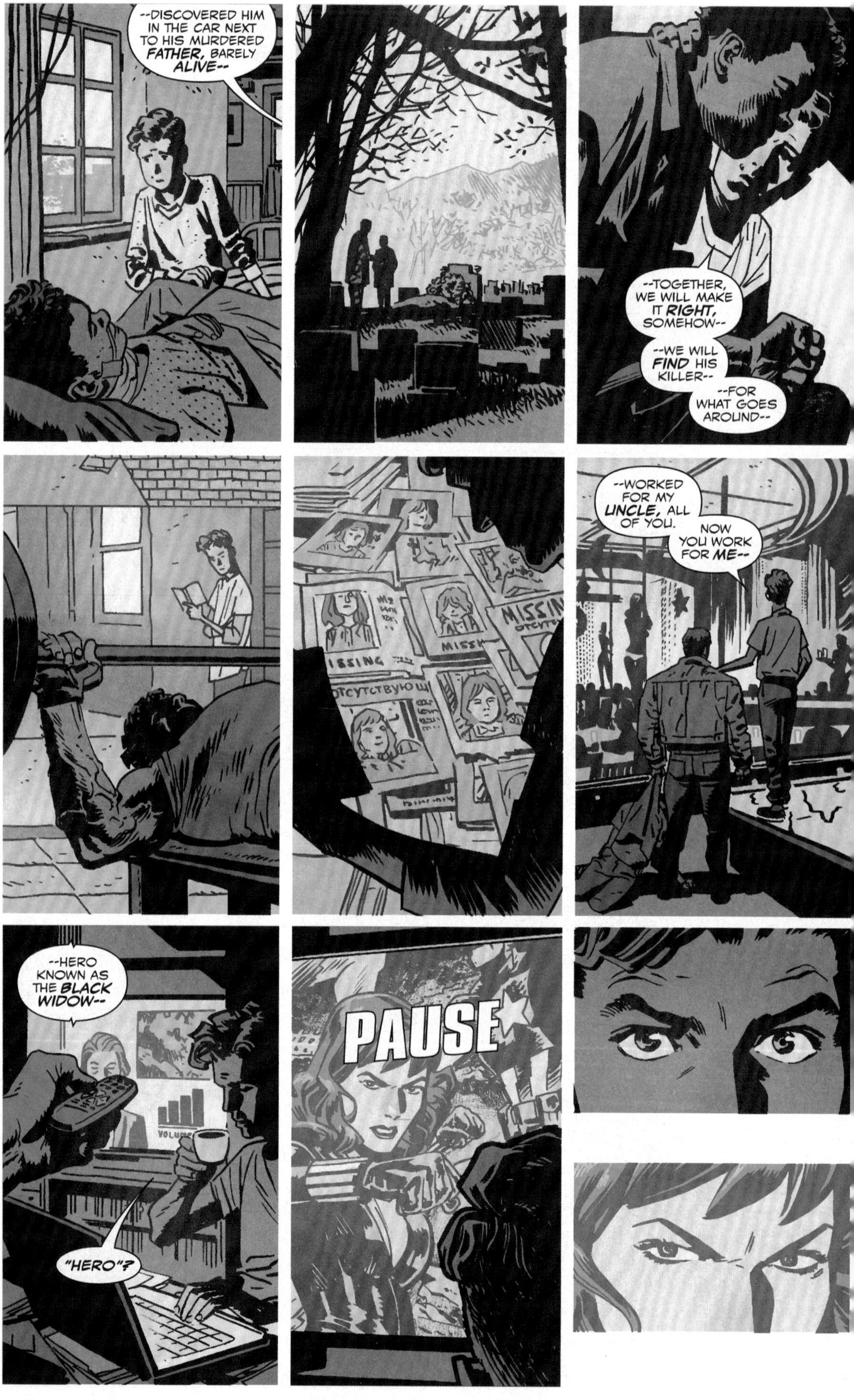
--DISCOVERED HIM IN THE CAR NEXT TO HIS MURDERED FATHER, BARELY ALIVE--
--TOGETHER, WE WILL MAKE IT RIGHT, SOMEHOW--
--WE WILL FIND HIS KILLER--
--FOR WHAT GOES AROUND--
--WORKED FOR MY UNCLE, ALL OF YOU.
NOW YOU WORK FOR ME--
--HERO KNOWN AS THE BLACK WIDOW--
"HERO"?
PAUSE

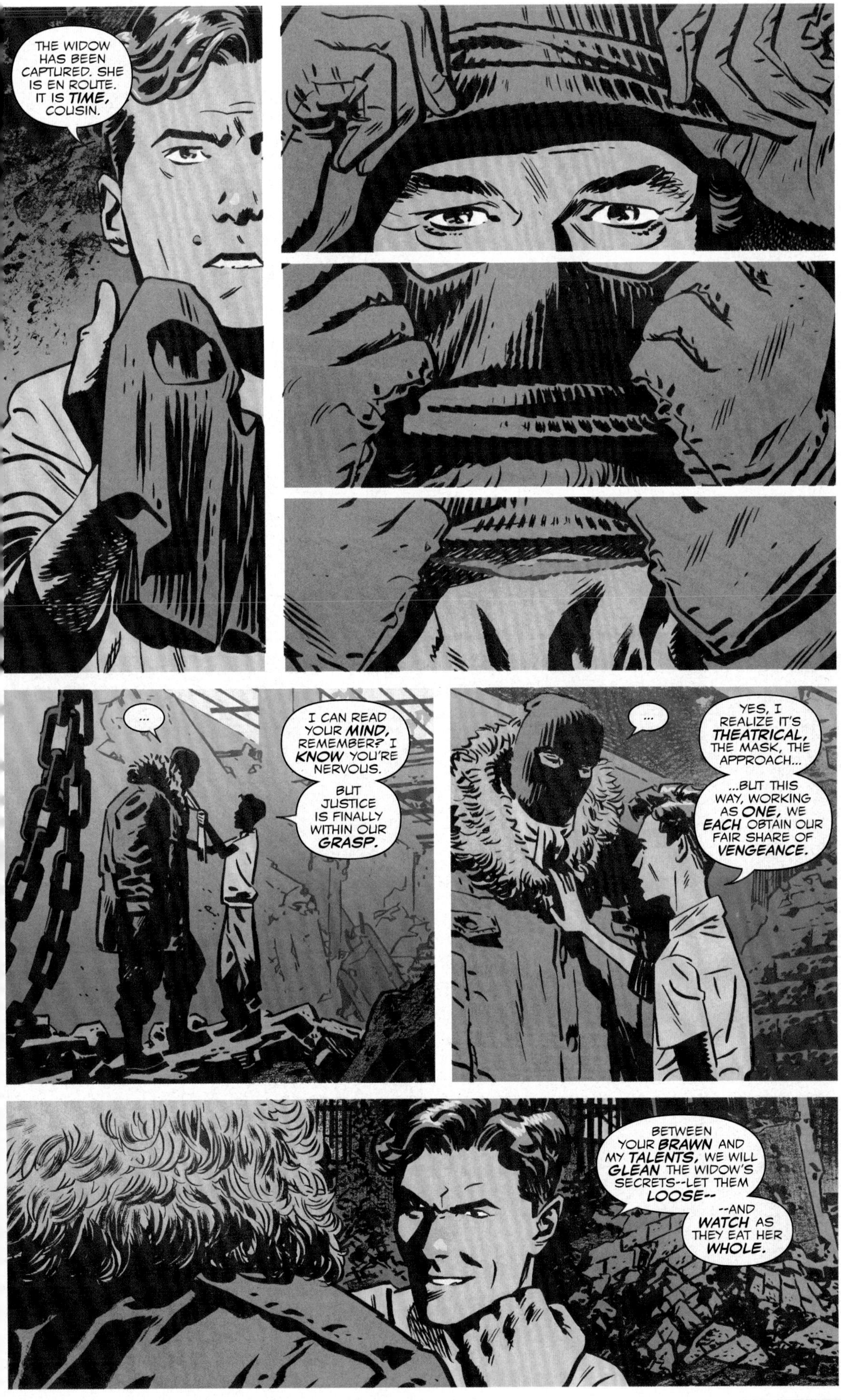
THE WIDOW HAS BEEN CAPTURED. SHE IS EN ROUTE. IT IS TIME, COUSIN.
...
I CAN READ YOUR MIND, REMEMBER? I KNOW YOU'RE NERVOUS.
BUT JUSTICE IS FINALLY WITHIN OUR GRASP.
...
YES, I REALIZE IT'S THEATRICAL, THE MASK, THE APPROACH...
...BUT THIS WAY, WORKING AS ONE, WE EACH OBTAIN OUR FAIR SHARE OF VENGEANCE.
BETWEEN YOUR BRAWN AND MY TALENTS, WE WILL GLEAN THE WIDOW'S SECRETS--LET THEM LOOSE--
--AND WATCH AS THEY EAT HER WHOLE.

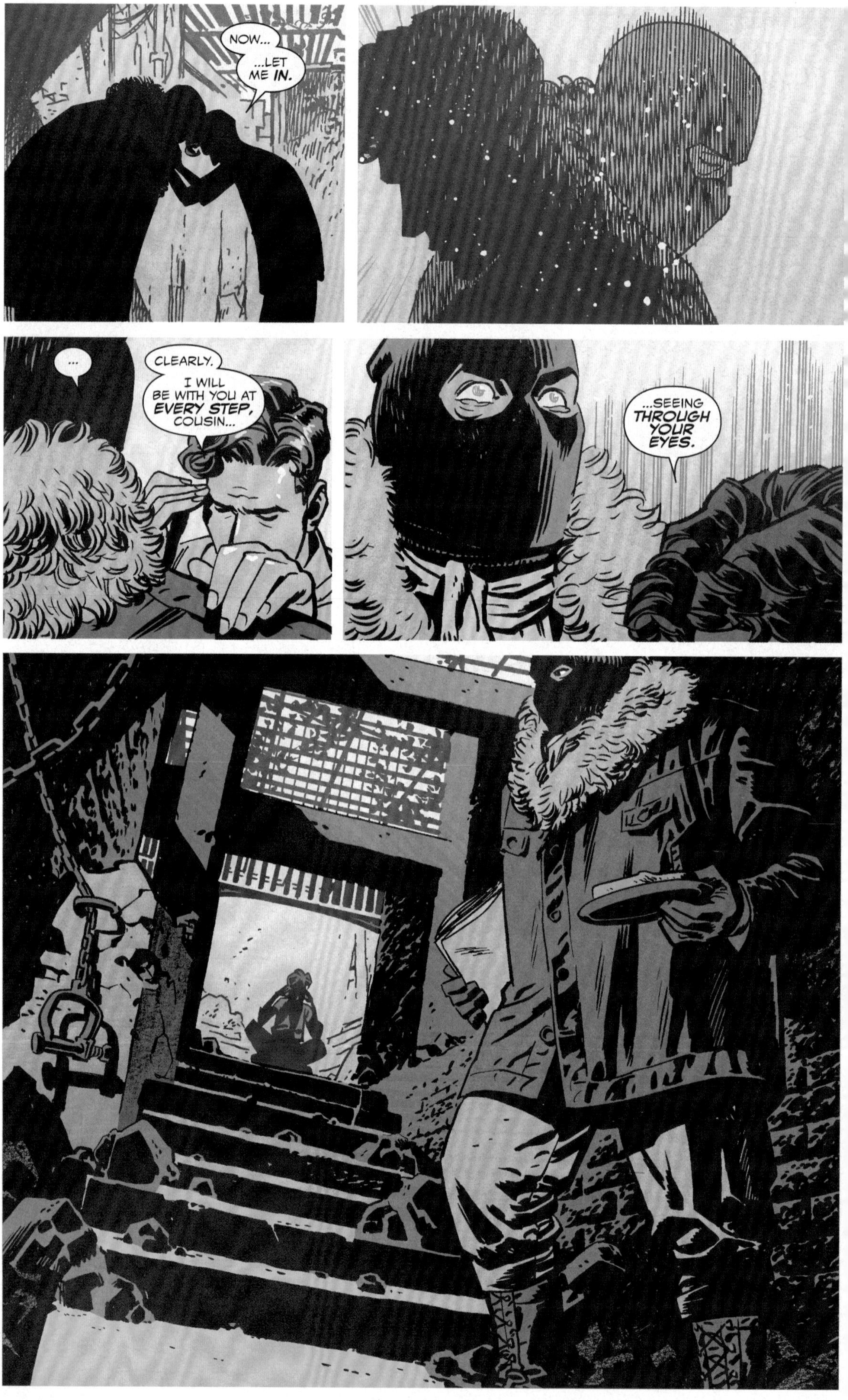
NOW...
...LET ME IN.
...
CLEARLY.
I WILL BE WITH YOU AT EVERY STEP, COUSIN...
...SEEING THROUGH YOUR EYES.

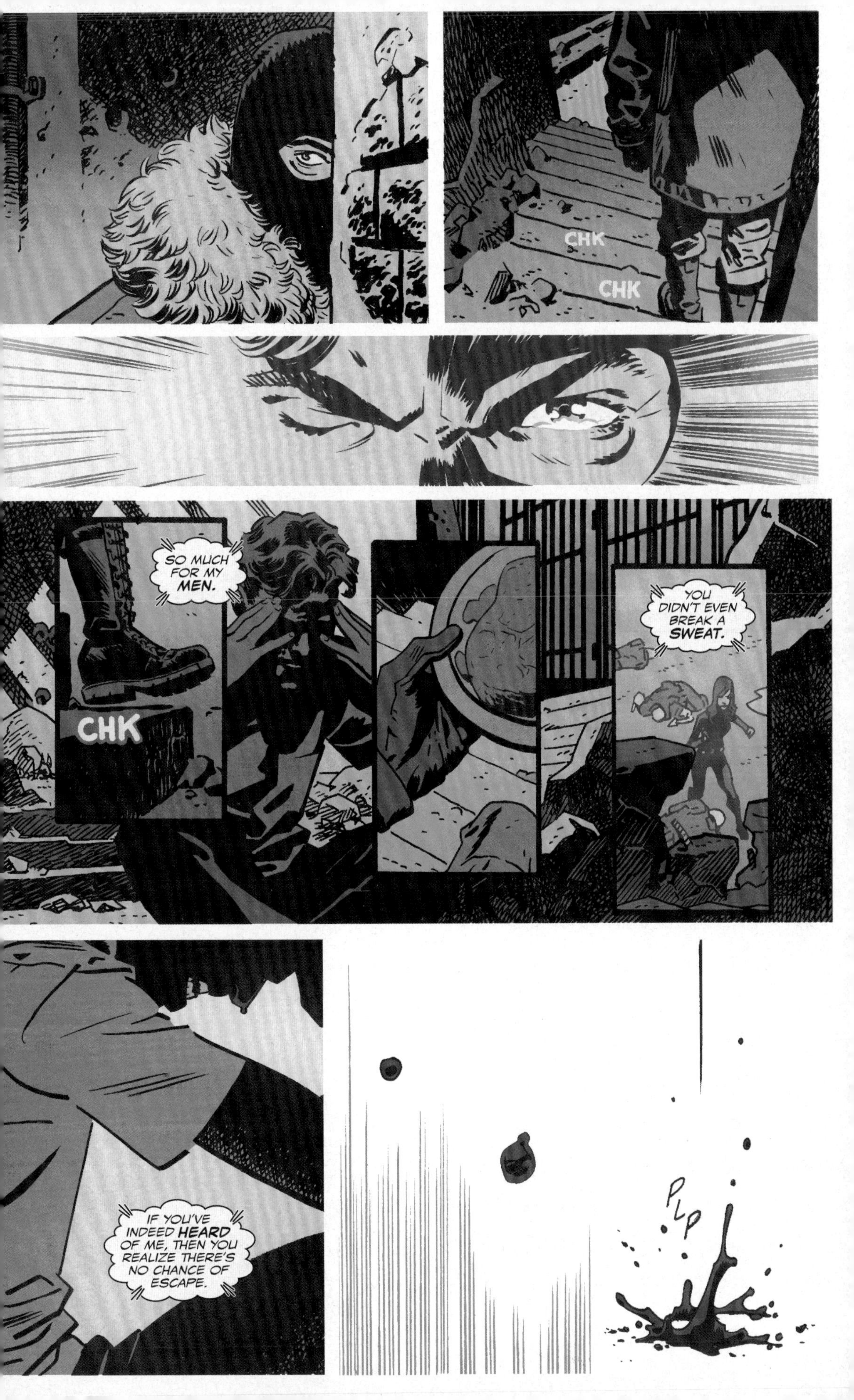
CHK
CHK
CHK
SO MUCH FOR MY MEN.
YOU DIDN'T EVEN BREAK A SWEAT.
IF YOU'VE INDEED HEARD OF ME, THEN YOU REALIZE THERE'S NO CHANCE OF ESCAPE.
PLP

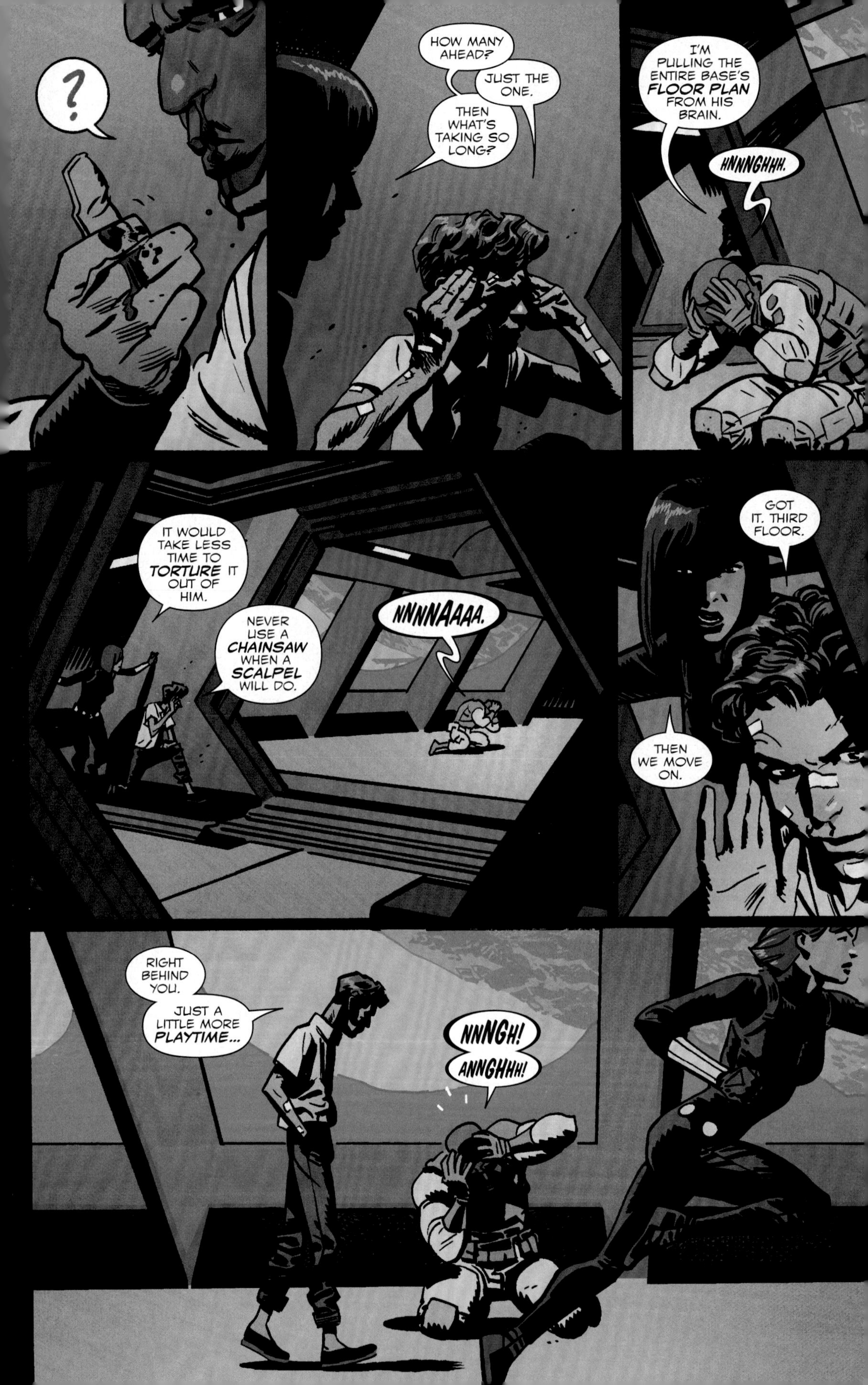
?
HOW MANY AHEAD?
JUST THE ONE.
THEN WHAT'S TAKING SO LONG?
I'M PULLING THE ENTIRE BASE'S FLOOR PLAN FROM HIS BRAIN.
HNNNGHHH.
IT WOULD TAKE LESS TIME TO TORTURE IT OUT OF HIM.
NEVER USE A CHAINSAW WHEN A SCALPEL WILL DO.
NNNNAAAA.
GOT IT. THIRD FLOOR.
THEN WE MOVE ON.
RIGHT BEHIND YOU.
JUST A LITTLE MORE PLAYTIME...
NNNGH!
ANNGHHH!

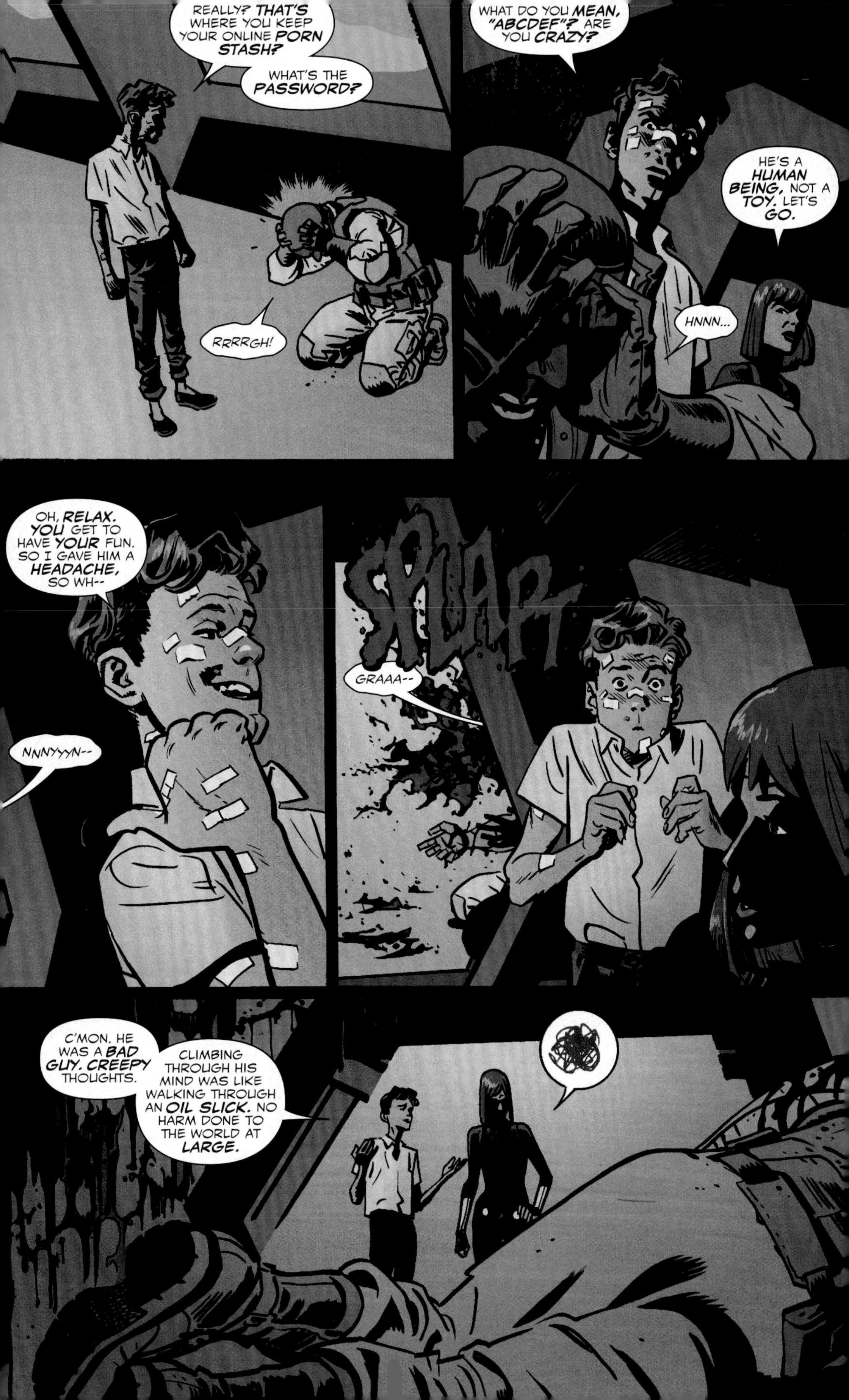

REALLY? THAT'S WHERE YOU KEEP YOUR ONLINE PORN STASH?
WHAT'S THE PASSWORD?
RRRRGH!
WHAT DO YOU MEAN, "ABCDEF"? ARE YOU CRAZY?
HE'S A HUMAN BEING, NOT A TOY. LET'S GO.
HNNN...
OH, RELAX. YOU GET TO HAVE YOUR FUN. SO I GAVE HIM A HEADACHE, SO WH--
NNNYYYN--
SPLAT
GRAAA--
C'MON. HE WAS A BAD GUY. CREEPY THOUGHTS.
CLIMBING THROUGH HIS MIND WAS LIKE WALKING THROUGH AN OIL SLICK. NO HARM DONE TO THE WORLD AT LARGE.

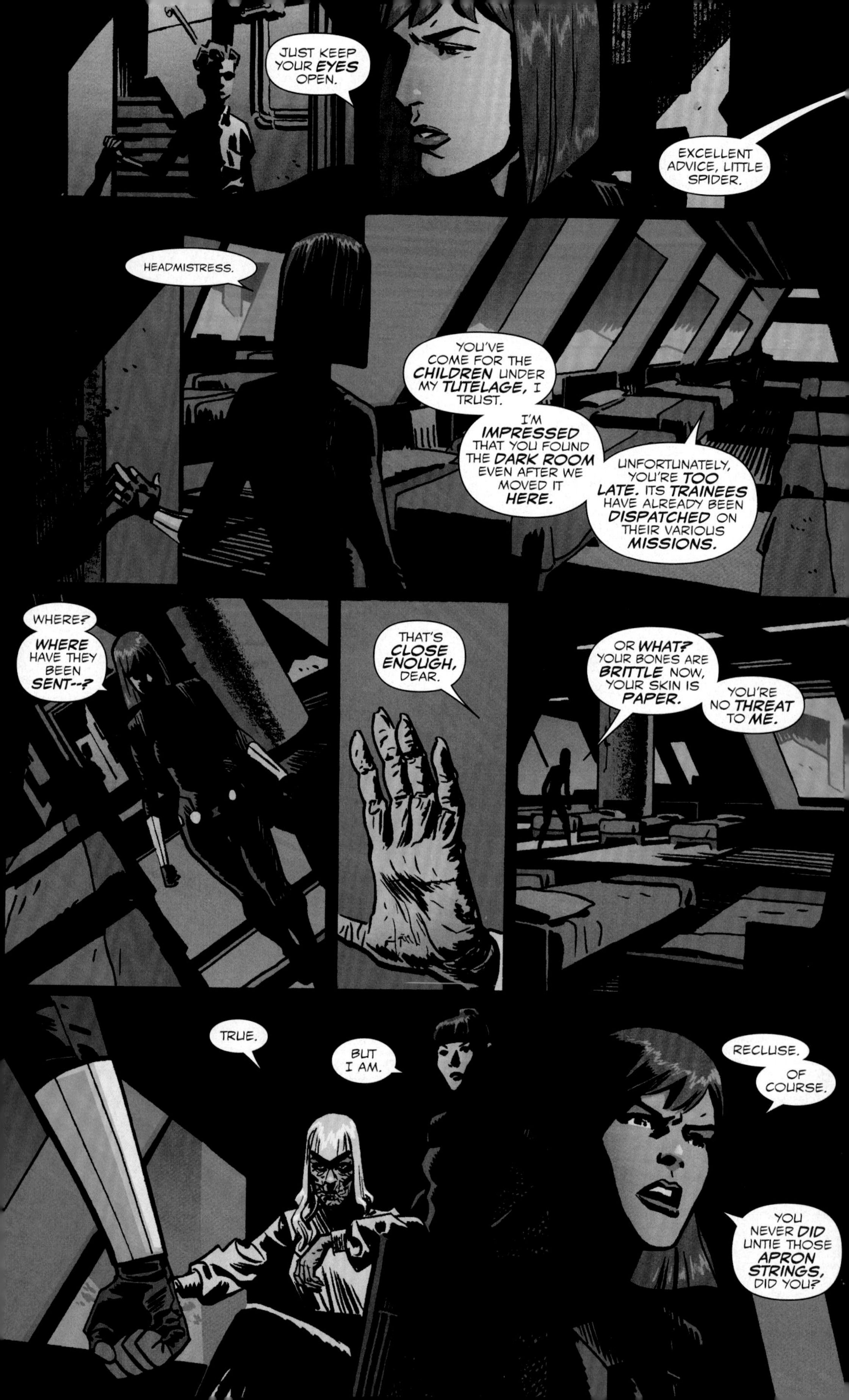
JUST KEEP YOUR EYES OPEN.
EXCELLENT ADVICE, LITTLE SPIDER.
HEADMISTRESS.
YOU'VE COME FOR THE CHILDREN UNDER MY TUTELAGE, I TRUST.
I'M IMPRESSED THAT YOU FOUND THE DARK ROOM EVEN AFTER WE MOVED IT HERE.
UNFORTUNATELY, YOU'RE TOO LATE. ITS TRAINEES HAVE ALREADY BEEN DISPATCHED ON THEIR VARIOUS MISSIONS.
WHERE? WHERE HAVE THEY BEEN SENT--?
THAT'S CLOSE ENOUGH, DEAR.
OR WHAT? YOUR BONES ARE BRITTLE NOW, YOUR SKIN IS PAPER.
YOU'RE NO THREAT TO ME.
TRUE.
BUT I AM.
RECLUSE.
OF COURSE.
YOU NEVER DID UNTIE THOSE APRON STRINGS, DID YOU?

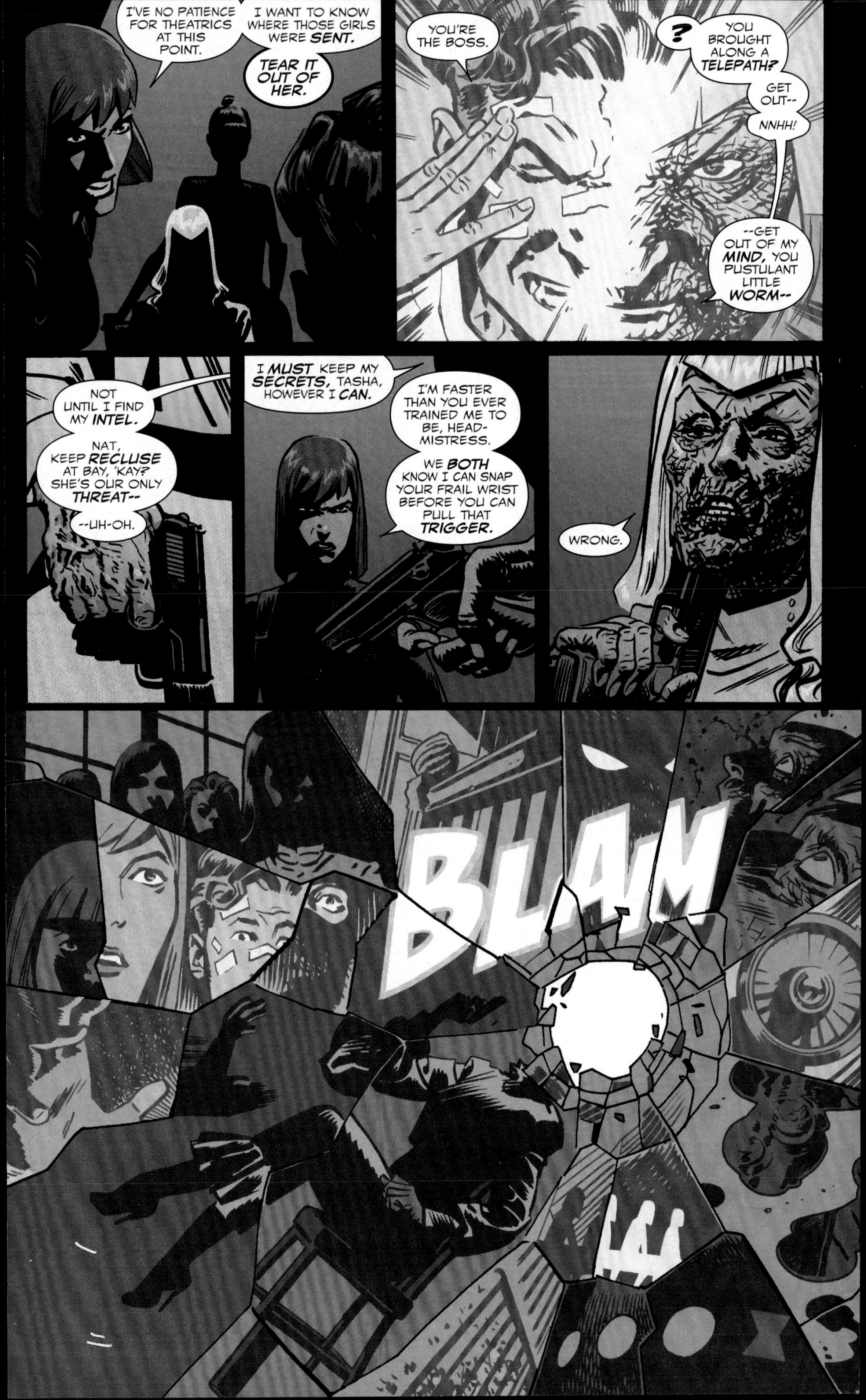
I'VE NO PATIENCE FOR THEATRICS AT THIS POINT.
I WANT TO KNOW WHERE THOSE GIRLS WERE SENT.
TEAR IT OUT OF HER.
YOU'RE THE BOSS.
? YOU BROUGHT ALONG A TELEPATH?
GET OUT--
NNHH!
--GET OUT OF MY MIND, YOU PUSTULANT LITTLE WORM--
NOT UNTIL I FIND MY INTEL.
NAT, KEEP RECLUSE AT BAY, 'KAY? SHE'S OUR ONLY THREAT--
--UH-OH.
I MUST KEEP MY SECRETS, TASHA, HOWEVER I CAN.
I'M FASTER THAN YOU EVER TRAINED ME TO BE, HEAD-MISTRESS.
WE BOTH KNOW I CAN SNAP YOUR FRAIL WRIST BEFORE YOU CAN PULL THAT TRIGGER.
WRONG.
BLAM

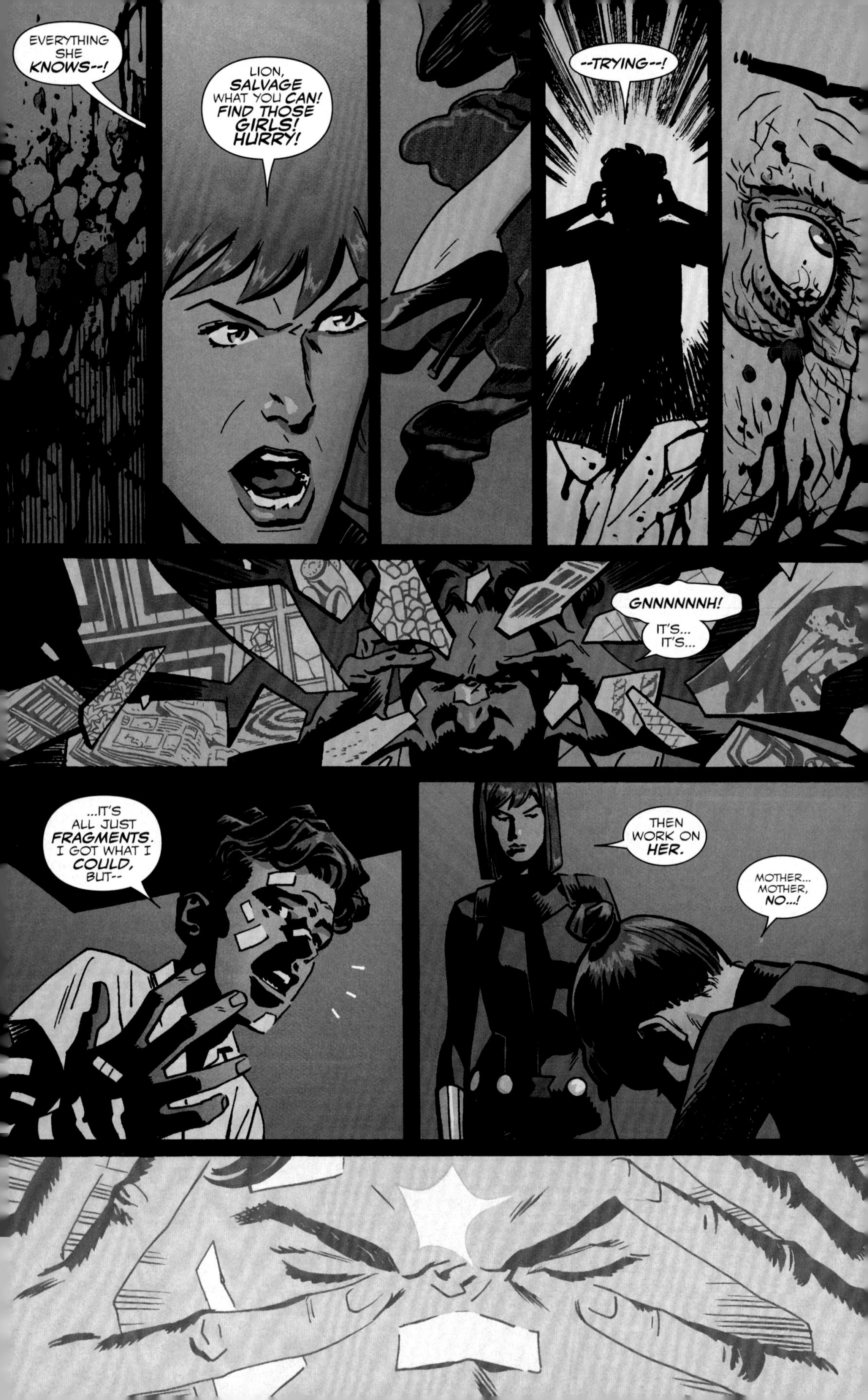
EVERYTHING SHE KNOWS--!
LION, SALVAGE WHAT YOU CAN! FIND THOSE GIRLS! HURRY!
--TRYING--!
GNNNNNNH!
IT'S... IT'S...
...IT'S ALL JUST FRAGMENTS. I GOT WHAT I COULD, BUT--
THEN WORK ON HER.
MOTHER... MOTHER, NO...!

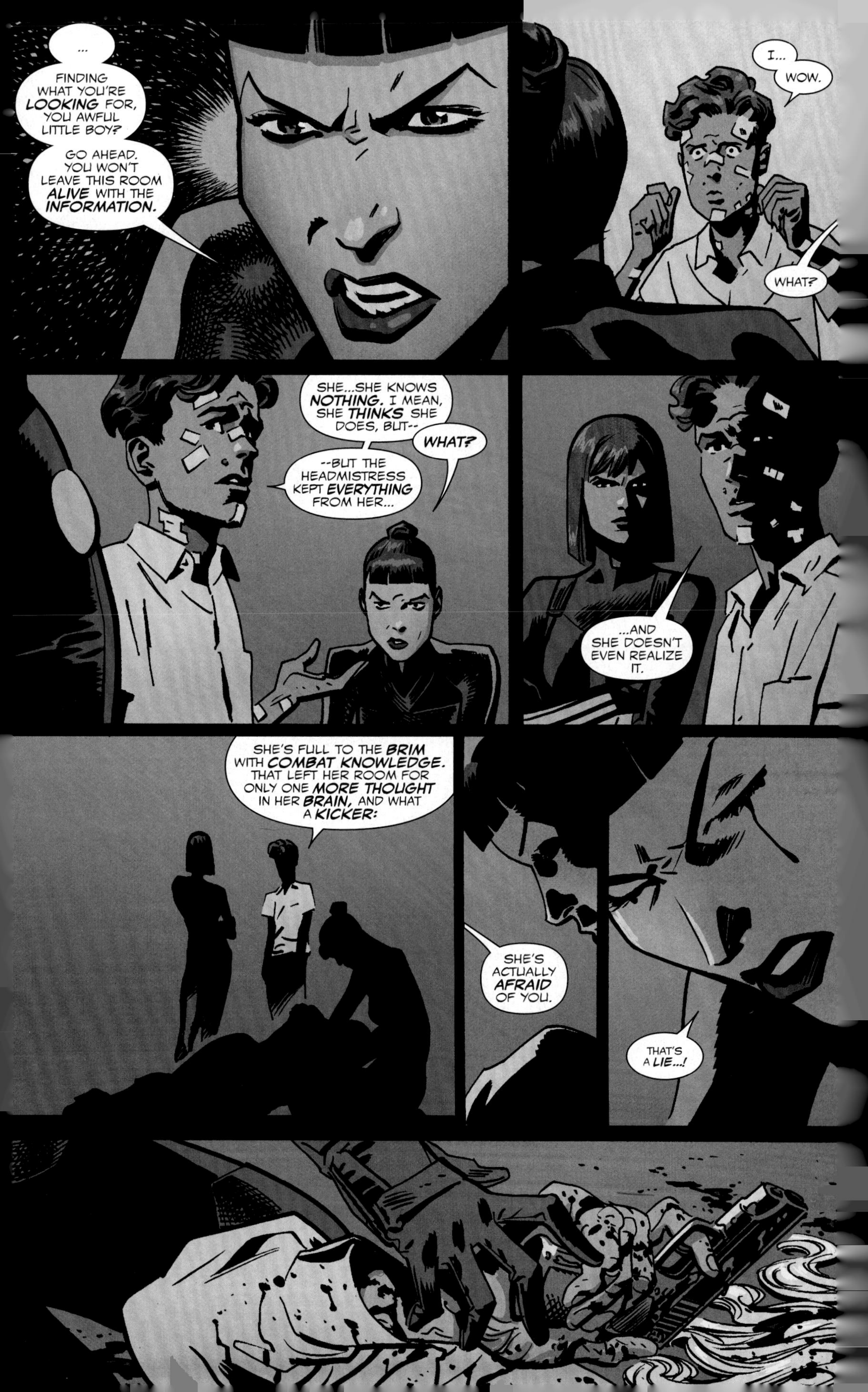
...
FINDING WHAT YOU'RE LOOKING FOR, YOU AWFUL LITTLE BOY?
GO AHEAD. YOU WON'T LEAVE THIS ROOM ALIVE WITH THE INFORMATION.
I...
WOW.
WHAT?
SHE...SHE KNOWS NOTHING. I MEAN, SHE THINKS SHE DOES, BUT--
WHAT?
--BUT THE HEADMISTRESS KEPT EVERYTHING FROM HER...
...AND SHE DOESN'T EVEN REALIZE IT.
SHE'S FULL TO THE BRIM WITH COMBAT KNOWLEDGE. THAT LEFT HER ROOM FOR ONLY ONE MORE THOUGHT IN HER BRAIN, AND WHAT A KICKER:
SHE'S ACTUALLY AFRAID OF YOU.
THAT'S A LIE...!

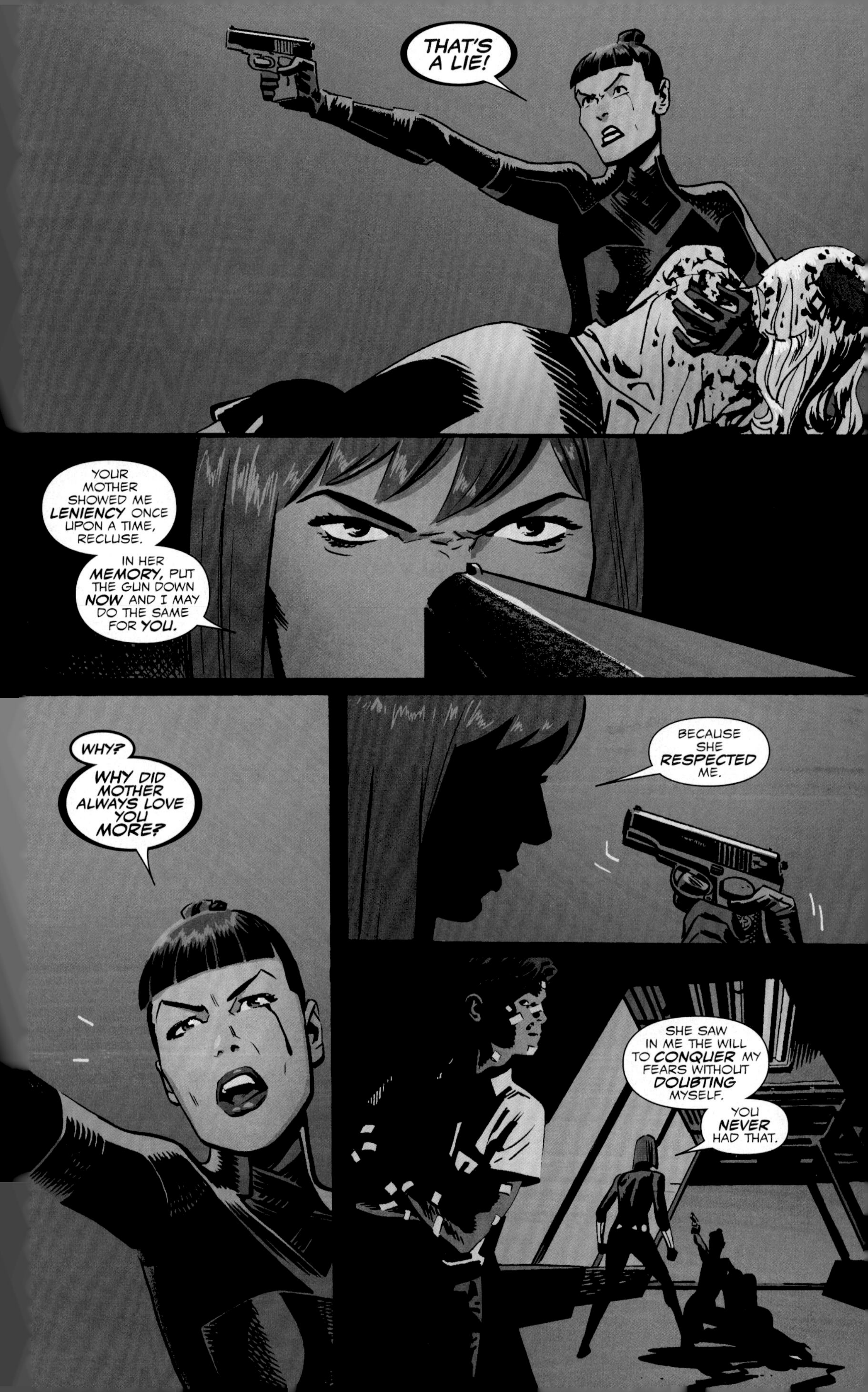
THAT'S A LIE!
YOUR MOTHER SHOWED ME LENIENCY ONCE UPON A TIME, RECLUSE.
IN HER MEMORY, PUT THE GUN DOWN NOW AND I MAY DO THE SAME FOR YOU.
WHY?
WHY DID MOTHER ALWAYS LOVE YOU MORE?
BECAUSE SHE RESPECTED ME.
SHE SAW IN ME THE WILL TO CONQUER MY FEARS WITHOUT DOUBTING MYSELF.
YOU NEVER HAD THAT.

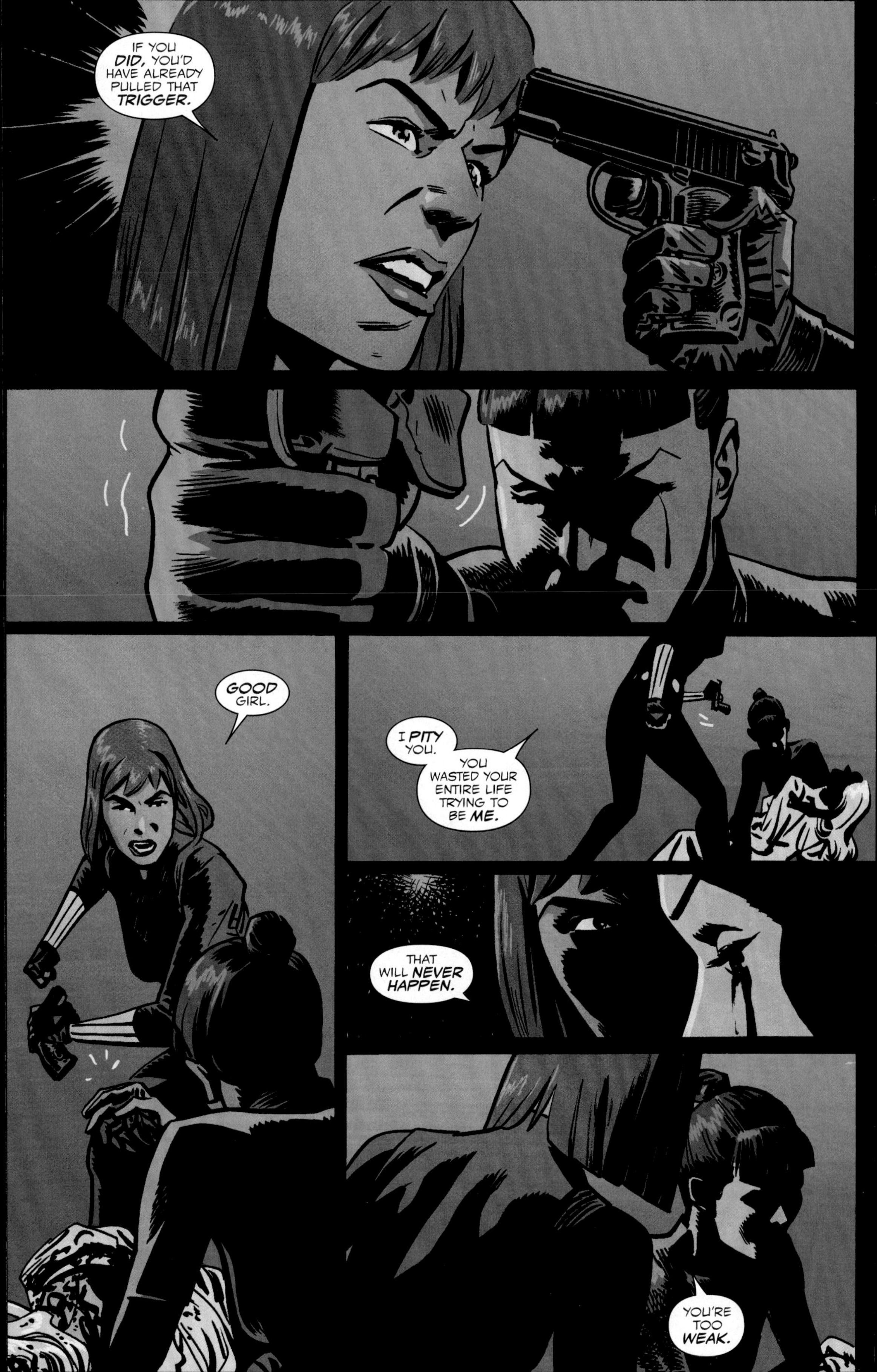
IF YOU DID, YOU'D HAVE ALREADY PULLED THAT TRIGGER.
GOOD GIRL.
I PITY YOU.
YOU WASTED YOUR ENTIRE LIFE TRYING TO BE ME.
THAT WILL NEVER HAPPEN.
YOU'RE TOO WEAK.

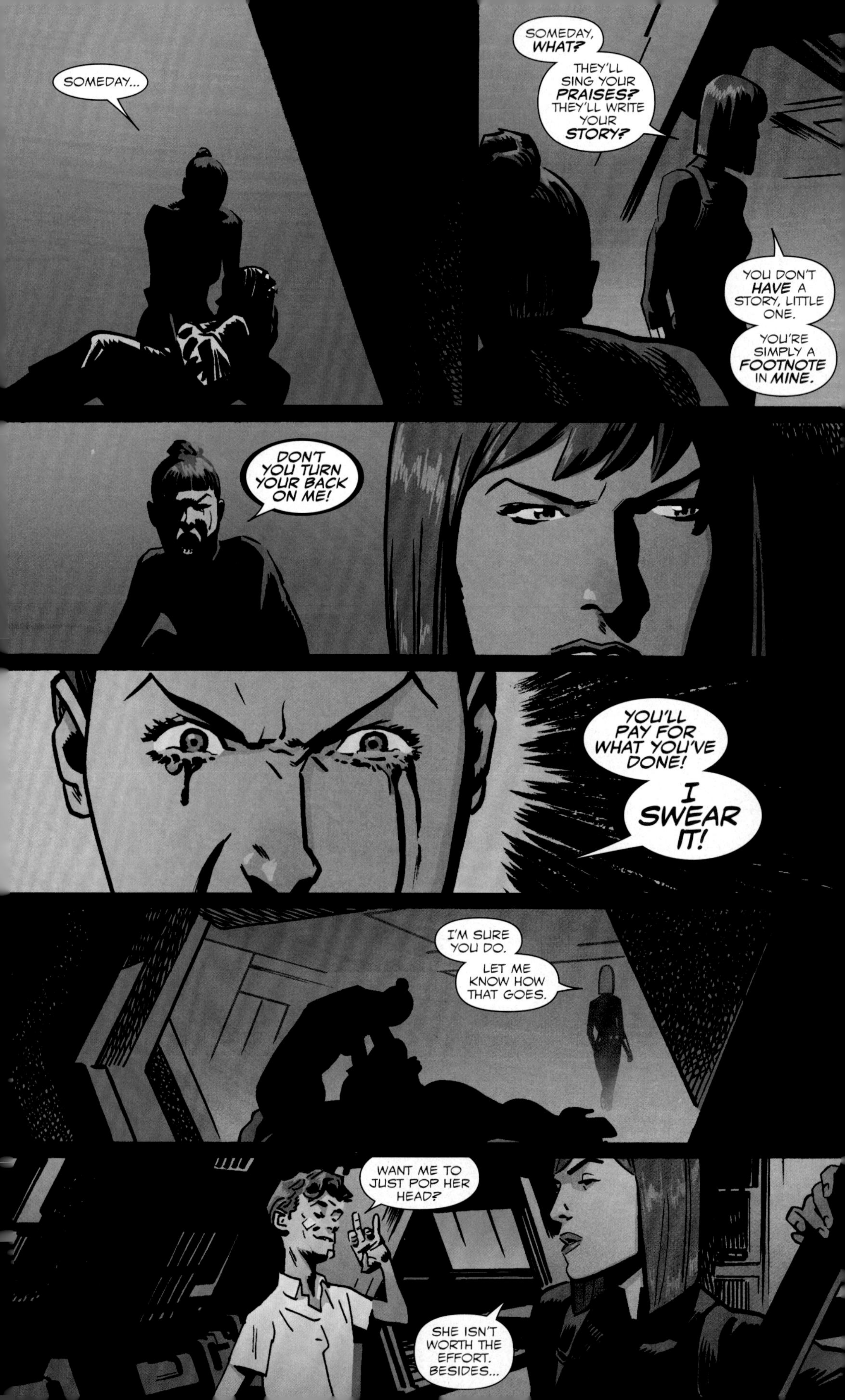
SOMEDAY...
SOMEDAY, WHAT?
THEY'LL SING YOUR PRAISES? THEY'LL WRITE YOUR STORY?
YOU DON'T HAVE A STORY, LITTLE ONE.
YOU'RE SIMPLY A FOOTNOTE IN MINE.
DON'T YOU TURN YOUR BACK ON ME!
YOU'LL PAY FOR WHAT YOU'VE DONE!
I SWEAR IT!
I'M SURE YOU DO.
LET ME KNOW HOW THAT GOES.
WANT ME TO JUST POP HER HEAD?
SHE ISN'T WORTH THE EFFORT. BESIDES...

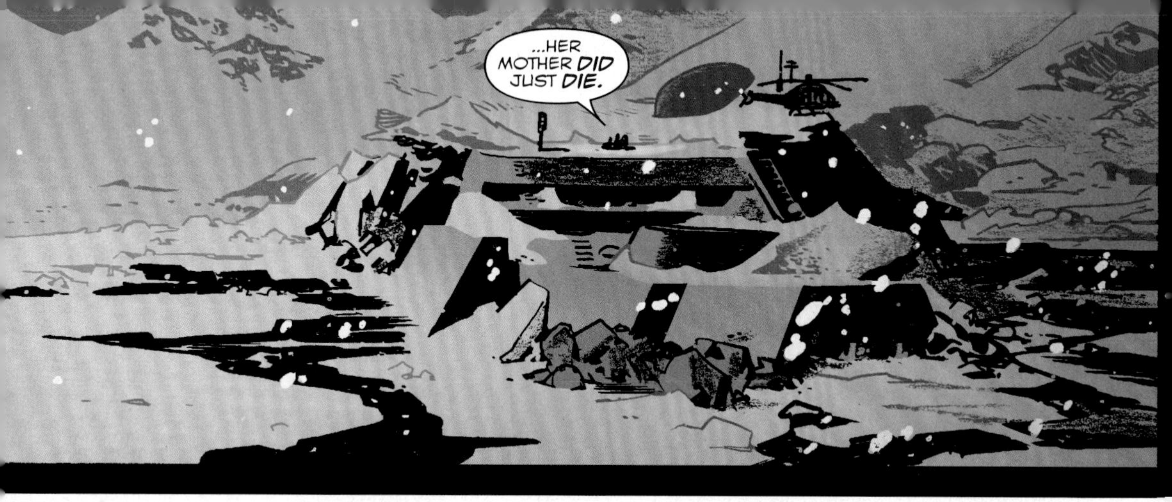
...HER MOTHER DID JUST DIE.

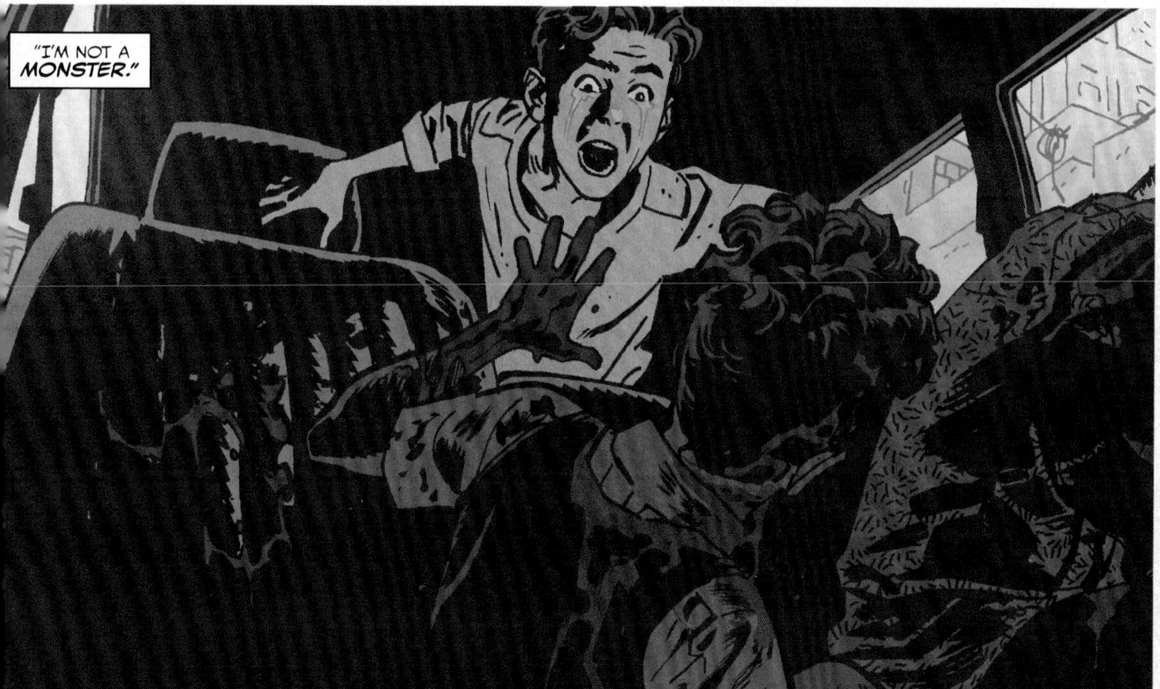
"I'M NOT A MONSTER."

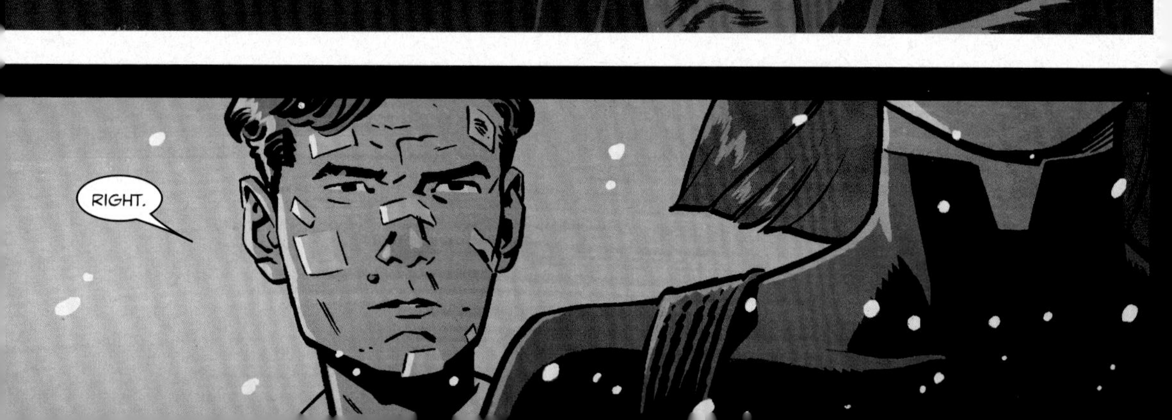
RIGHT.

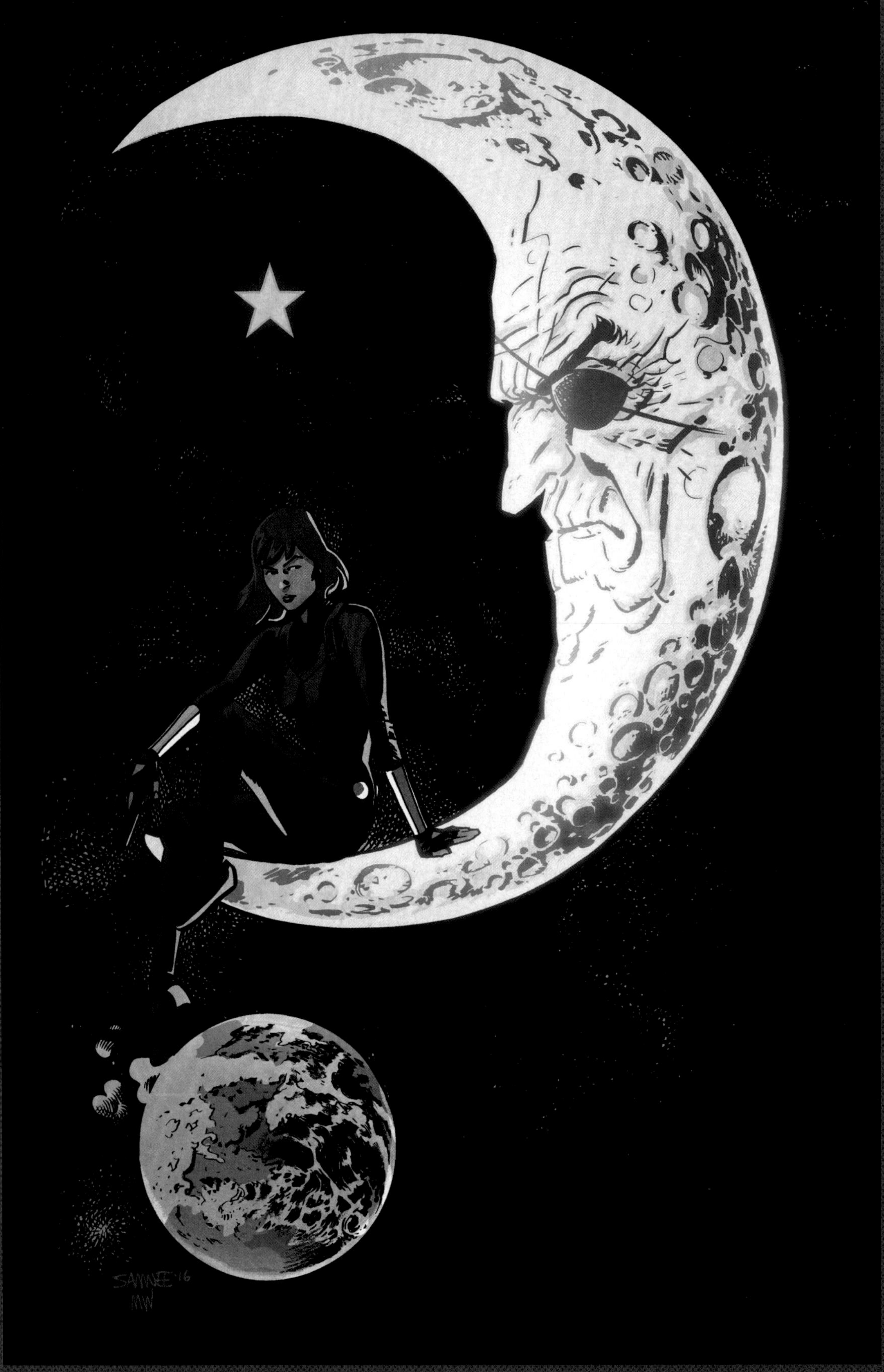
SAMNEE '16
MW

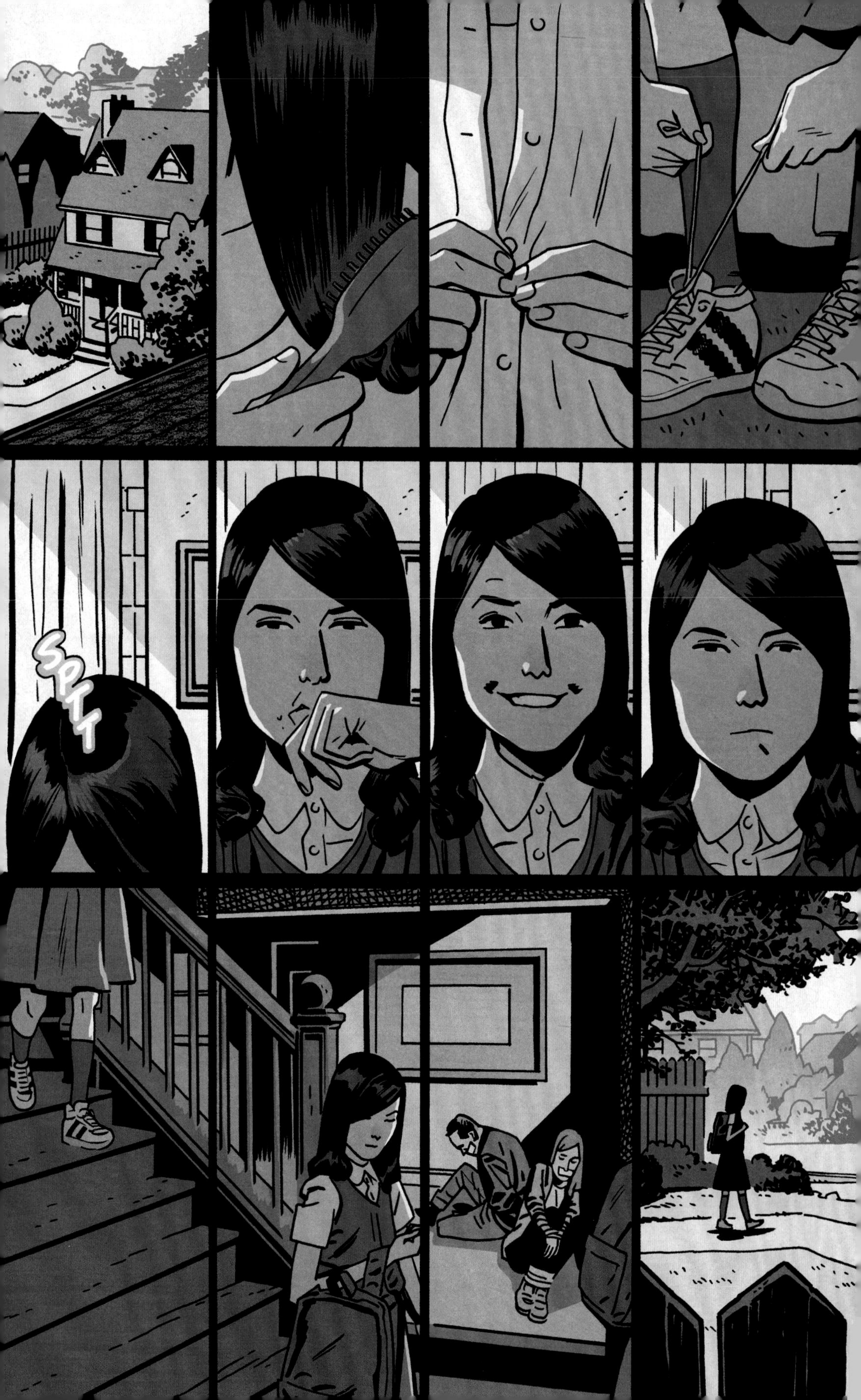
SPTT

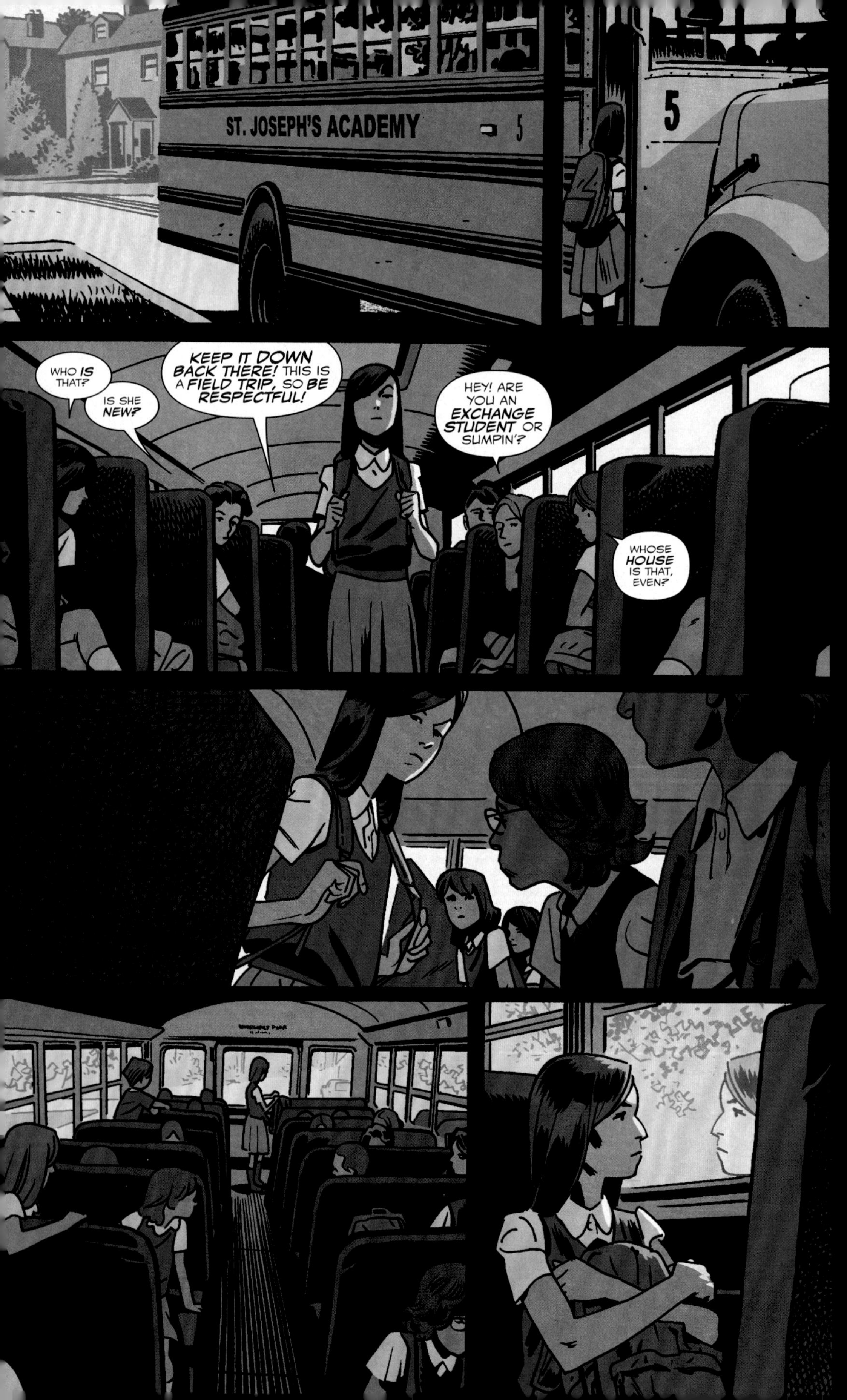
ST. JOSEPH'S ACADEMY
5
5
WHO IS THAT?
IS SHE NEW?
KEEP IT DOWN BACK THERE! THIS IS A FIELD TRIP, SO BE RESPECTFUL!
HEY! ARE YOU AN EXCHANGE STUDENT OR SUMPIN'?
WHOSE HOUSE IS THAT, EVEN?

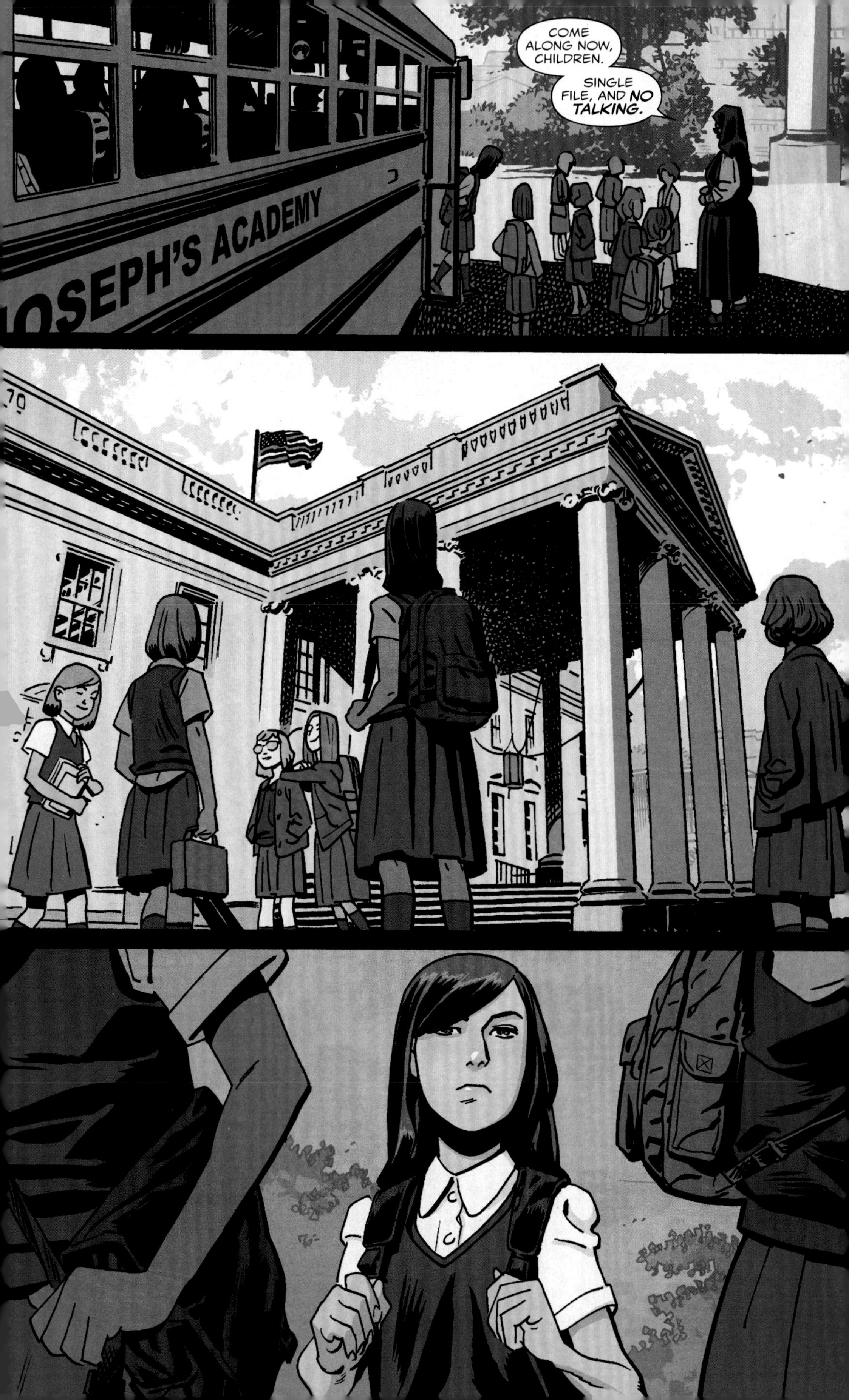

COME ALONG NOW, CHILDREN.
SINGLE FILE, AND NO TALKING.
OSEPH'S ACADEMY

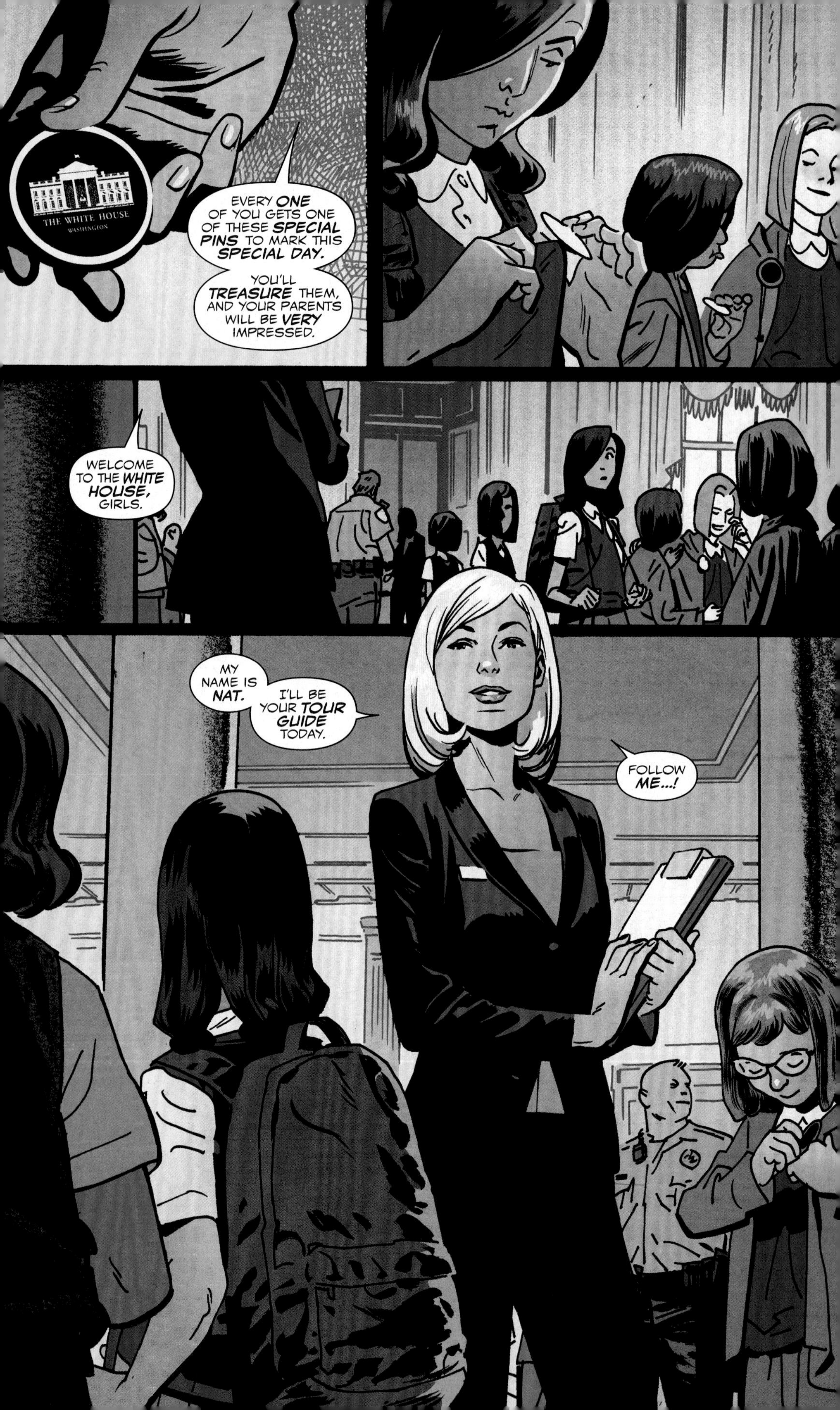
THE WHITE HOUSE
WASHINGTON
EVERY ONE OF YOU GETS ONE OF THESE SPECIAL PINS TO MARK THIS SPECIAL DAY.
YOU'LL TREASURE THEM, AND YOUR PARENTS WILL BE VERY IMPRESSED.
WELCOME TO THE WHITE HOUSE, GIRLS.
MY NAME IS NAT.
I'LL BE YOUR TOUR GUIDE TODAY.
FOLLOW ME...!

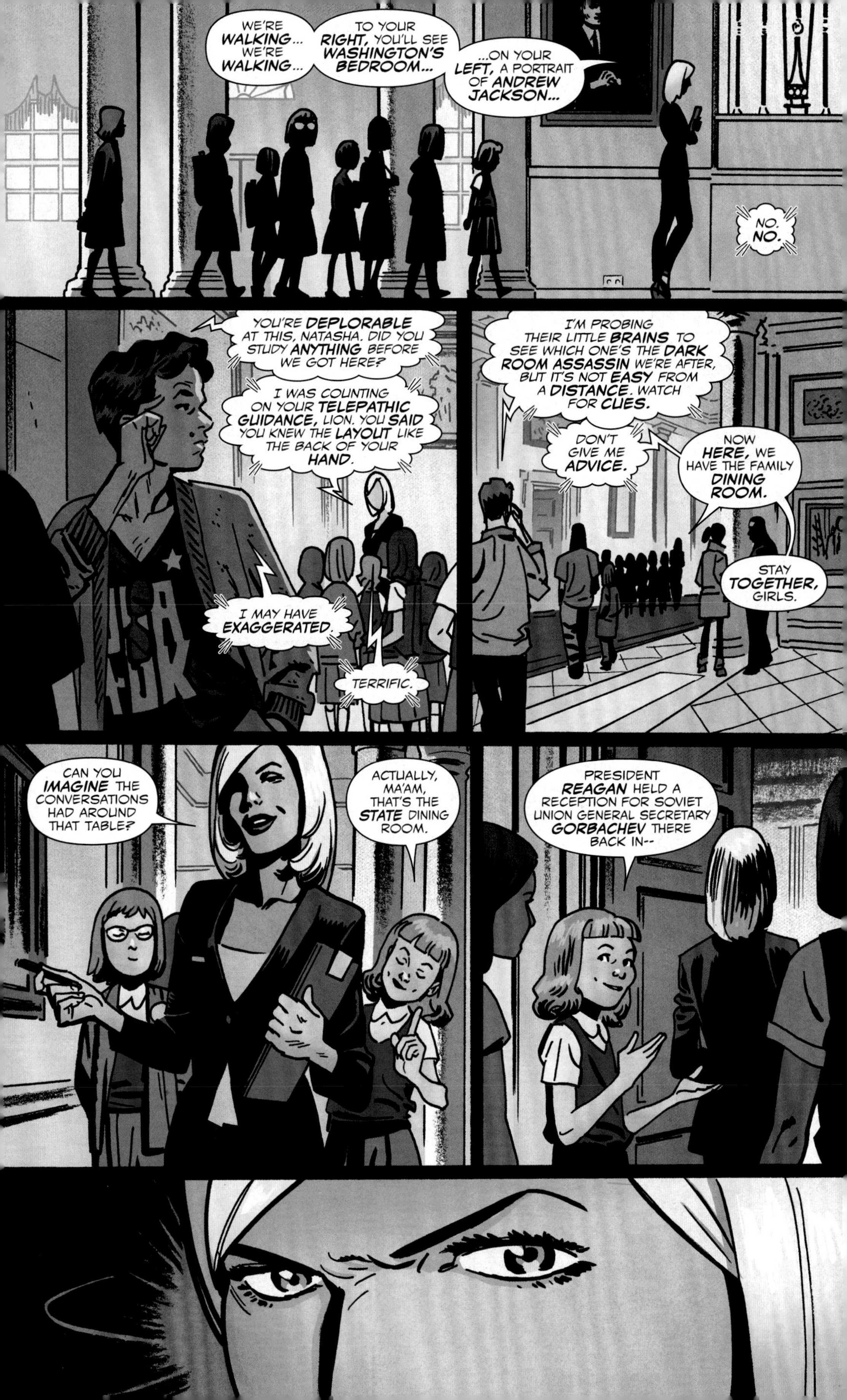

WE'RE WALKING... WE'RE WALKING...
TO YOUR RIGHT, YOU'LL SEE WASHINGTON'S BEDROOM...
...ON YOUR LEFT, A PORTRAIT OF ANDREW JACKSON...
NO. NO.
YOU'RE DEPLORABLE AT THIS, NATASHA. DID YOU STUDY ANYTHING BEFORE WE GOT HERE?
I WAS COUNTING ON YOUR TELEPATHIC GUIDANCE, LION. YOU SAID YOU KNEW THE LAYOUT LIKE THE BACK OF YOUR HAND.
I MAY HAVE EXAGGERATED.
TERRIFIC.
I'M PROBING THEIR LITTLE BRAINS TO SEE WHICH ONE'S THE DARK ROOM ASSASSIN WE'RE AFTER, BUT IT'S NOT EASY FROM A DISTANCE. WATCH FOR CUES.
DON'T GIVE ME ADVICE.
NOW HERE, WE HAVE THE FAMILY DINING ROOM.
STAY TOGETHER, GIRLS.
CAN YOU IMAGINE THE CONVERSATIONS HAD AROUND THAT TABLE?
ACTUALLY, MA'AM, THAT'S THE STATE DINING ROOM.
PRESIDENT REAGAN HELD A RECEPTION FOR SOVIET UNION GENERAL SECRETARY GORBACHEV THERE BACK IN--

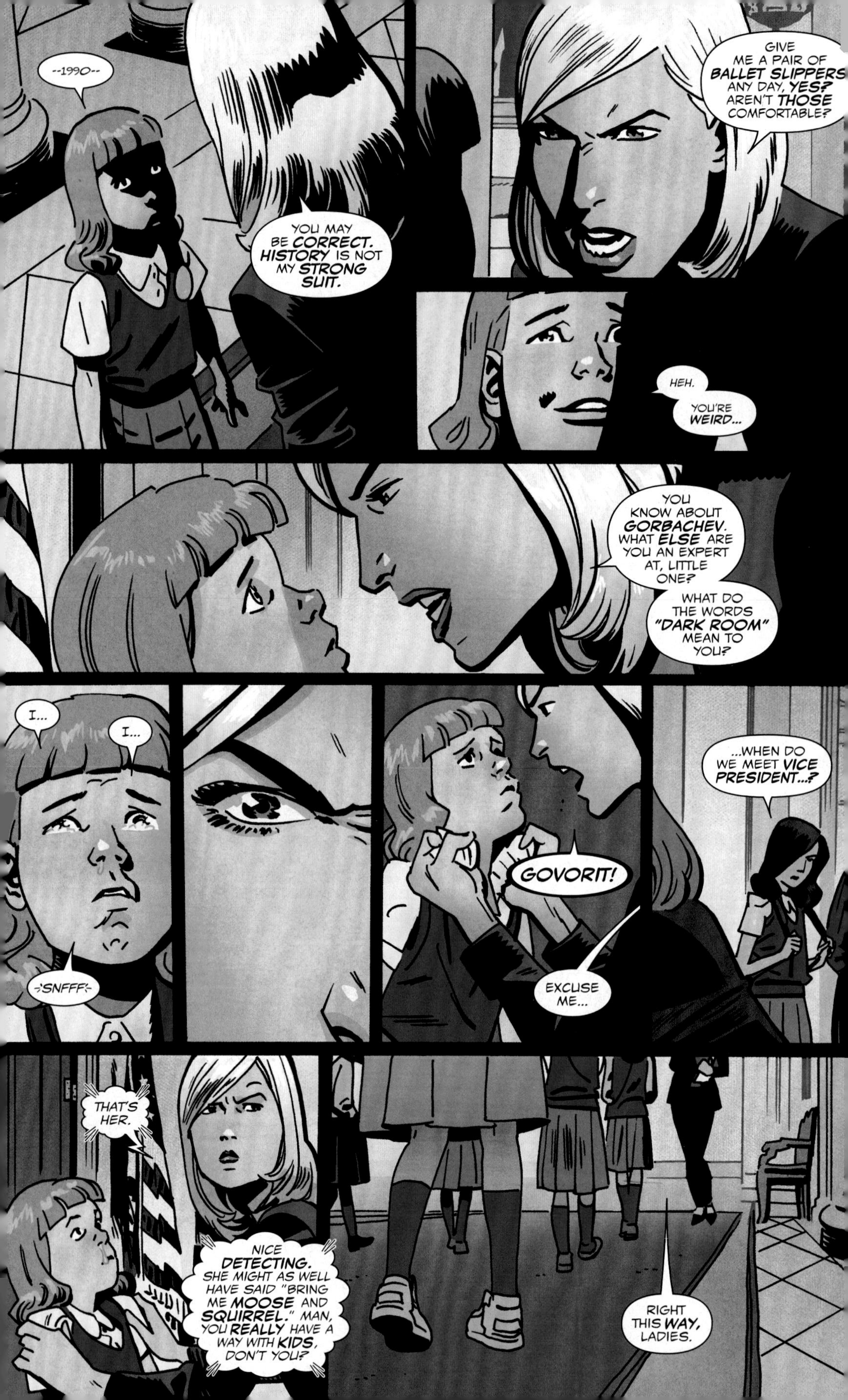
--1990--
YOU MAY BE CORRECT. HISTORY IS NOT MY STRONG SUIT.
GIVE ME A PAIR OF BALLET SLIPPERS ANY DAY, YES? AREN'T THOSE COMFORTABLE?
HEH.
YOU'RE WEIRD...
YOU KNOW ABOUT GORBACHEV. WHAT ELSE ARE YOU AN EXPERT AT, LITTLE ONE?
WHAT DO THE WORDS "DARK ROOM" MEAN TO YOU?
I...
I...
-SNFFF-
GOVORIT!
EXCUSE ME...
...WHEN DO WE MEET VICE PRESIDENT...?
THAT'S HER.
NICE DETECTING. SHE MIGHT AS WELL HAVE SAID "BRING ME MOOSE AND SQUIRREL." MAN, YOU REALLY HAVE A WAY WITH KIDS, DON'T YOU?
RIGHT THIS WAY, LADIES.

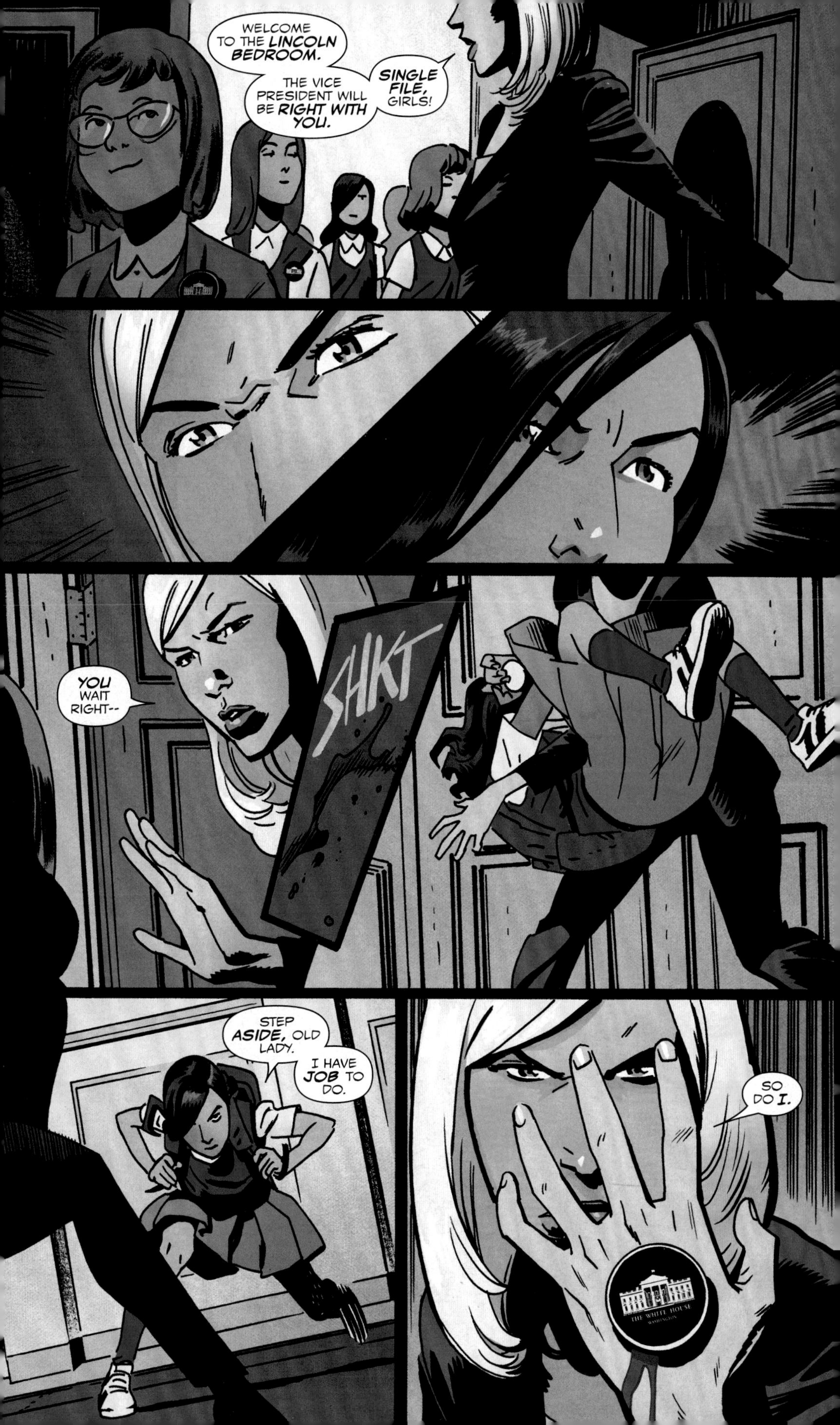
WELCOME TO THE LINCOLN BEDROOM.
THE VICE PRESIDENT WILL BE RIGHT WITH YOU.
SINGLE FILE, GIRLS!
YOU WAIT RIGHT--
SHKT
STEP ASIDE, OLD LADY.
I HAVE JOB TO DO.
SO DO I.
THE WHITE HOUSE

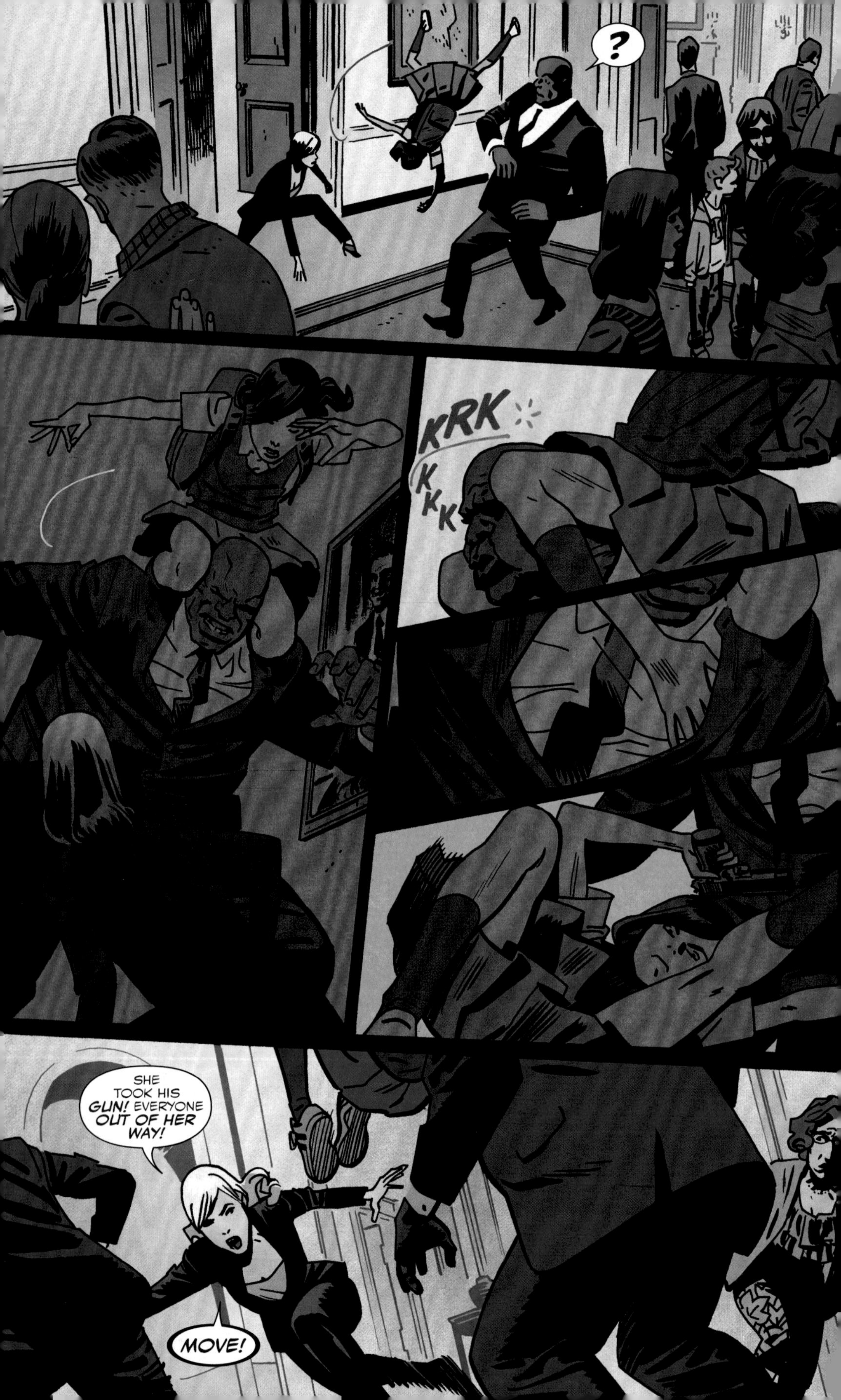
?
KRK
KKK
SHE TOOK HIS GUN! EVERYONE OUT OF HER WAY!
MOVE!

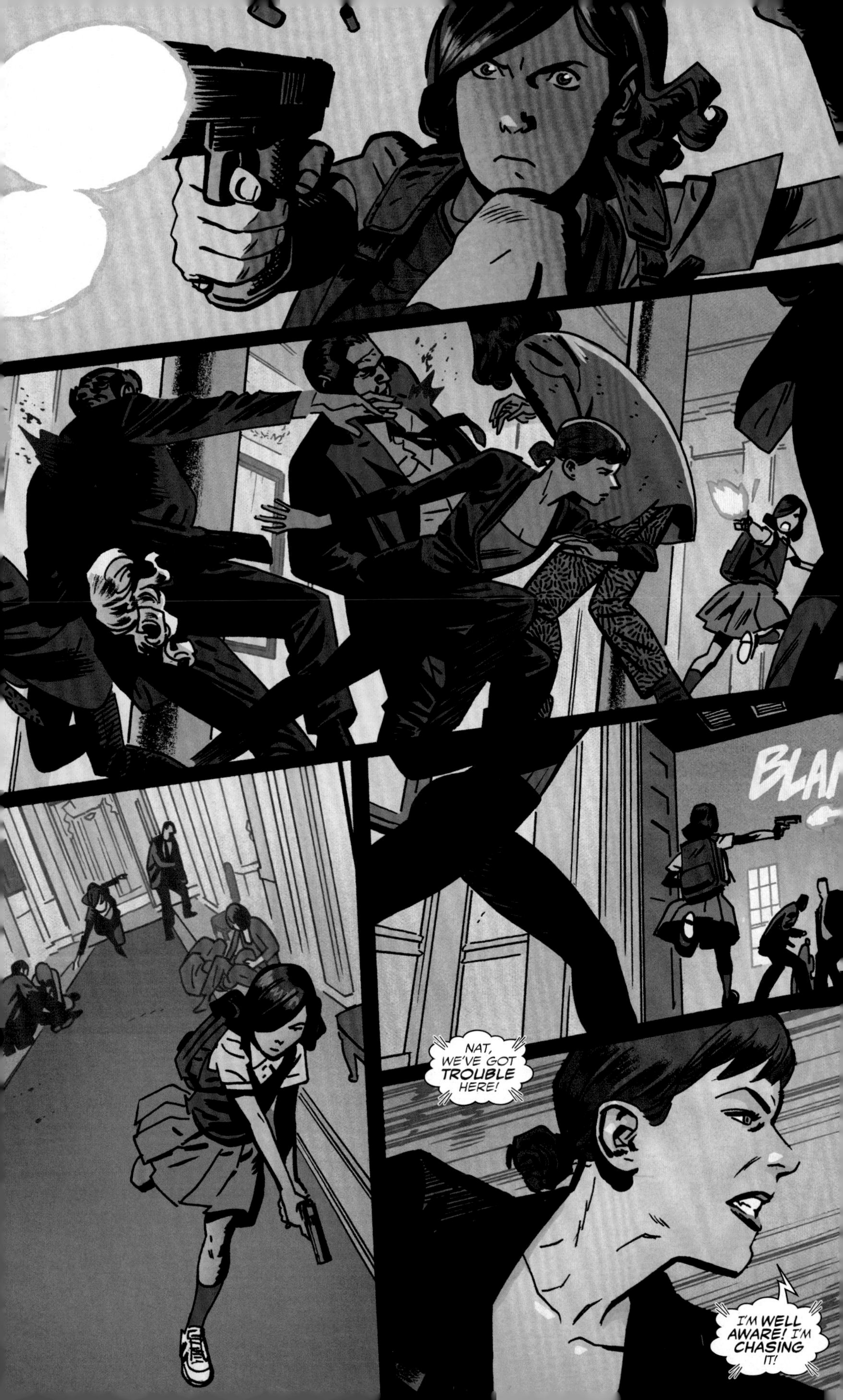
BLAM
NAT, WE'VE GOT TROUBLE HERE!
I'M WELL AWARE! I'M CHASING IT!

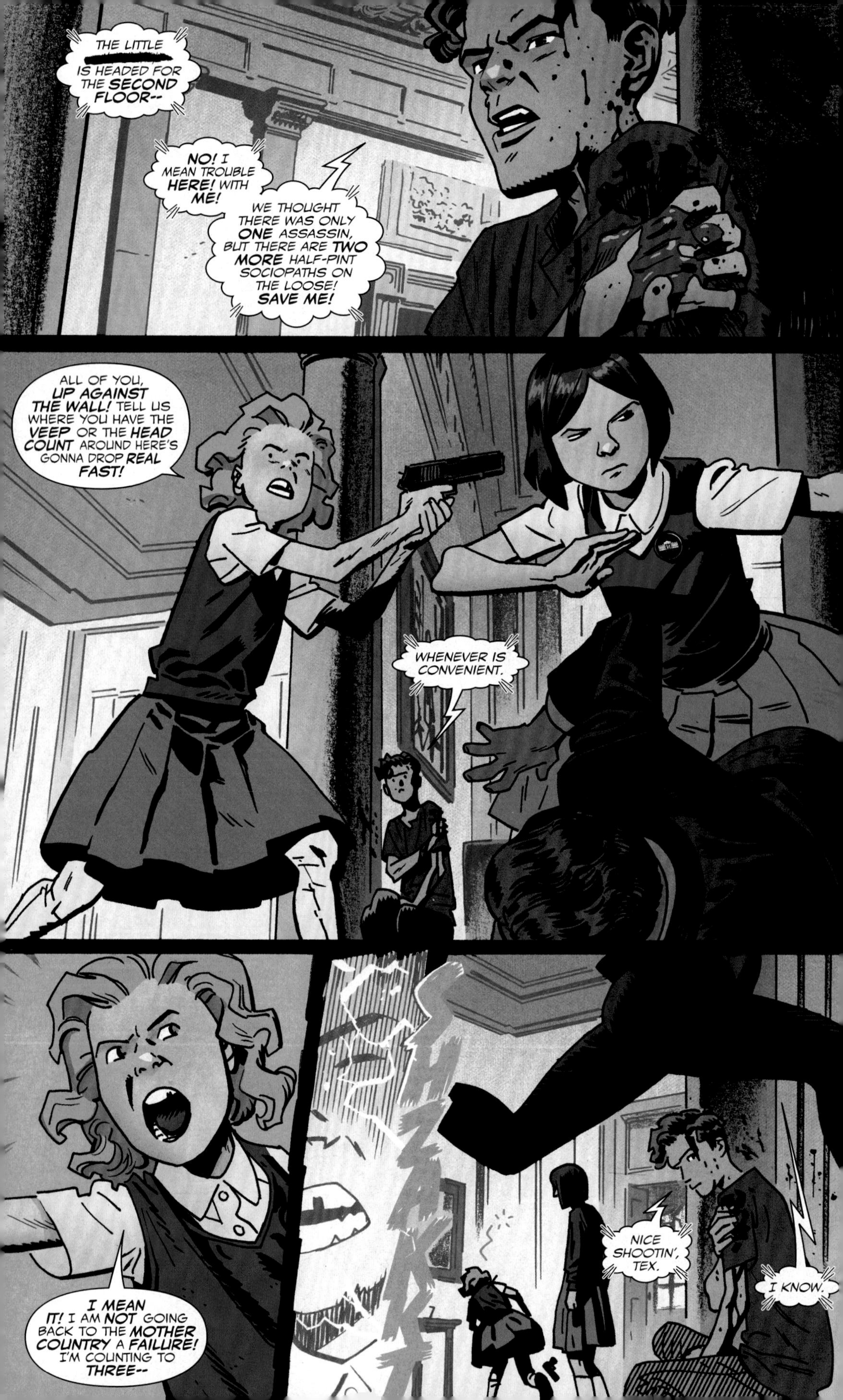
THE LITTLE [redacted] IS HEADED FOR THE SECOND FLOOR--
NO! I MEAN TROUBLE HERE! WITH ME!
WE THOUGHT THERE WAS ONLY ONE ASSASSIN, BUT THERE ARE TWO MORE HALF-PINT SOCIOPATHS ON THE LOOSE! SAVE ME!
ALL OF YOU, UP AGAINST THE WALL! TELL US WHERE YOU HAVE THE VEEP OR THE HEAD COUNT AROUND HERE'S GONNA DROP REAL FAST!
WHENEVER IS CONVENIENT.
I MEAN IT! I AM NOT GOING BACK TO THE MOTHER COUNTRY A FAILURE! I'M COUNTING TO THREE--
NICE SHOOTIN', TEX.
I KNOW.

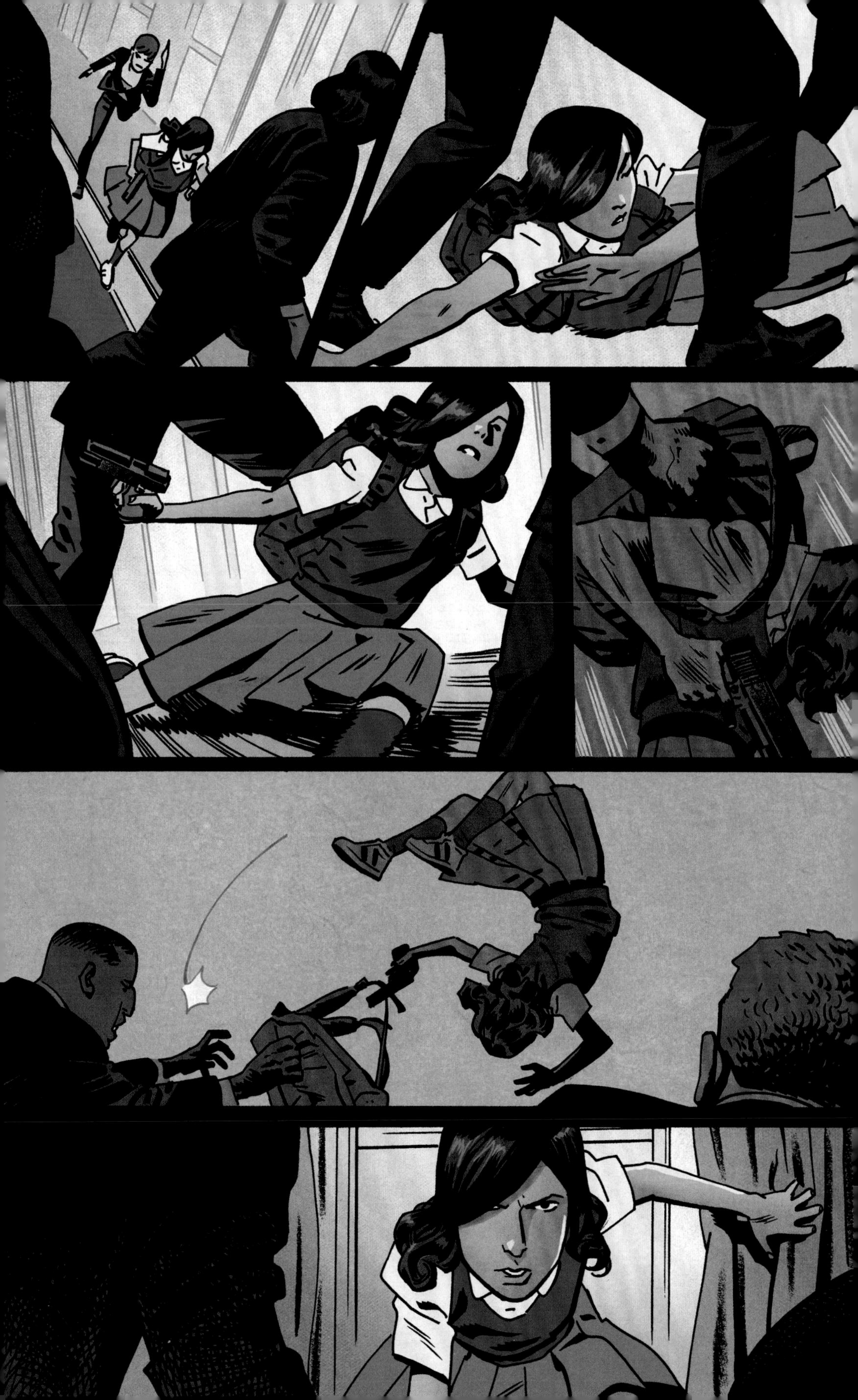

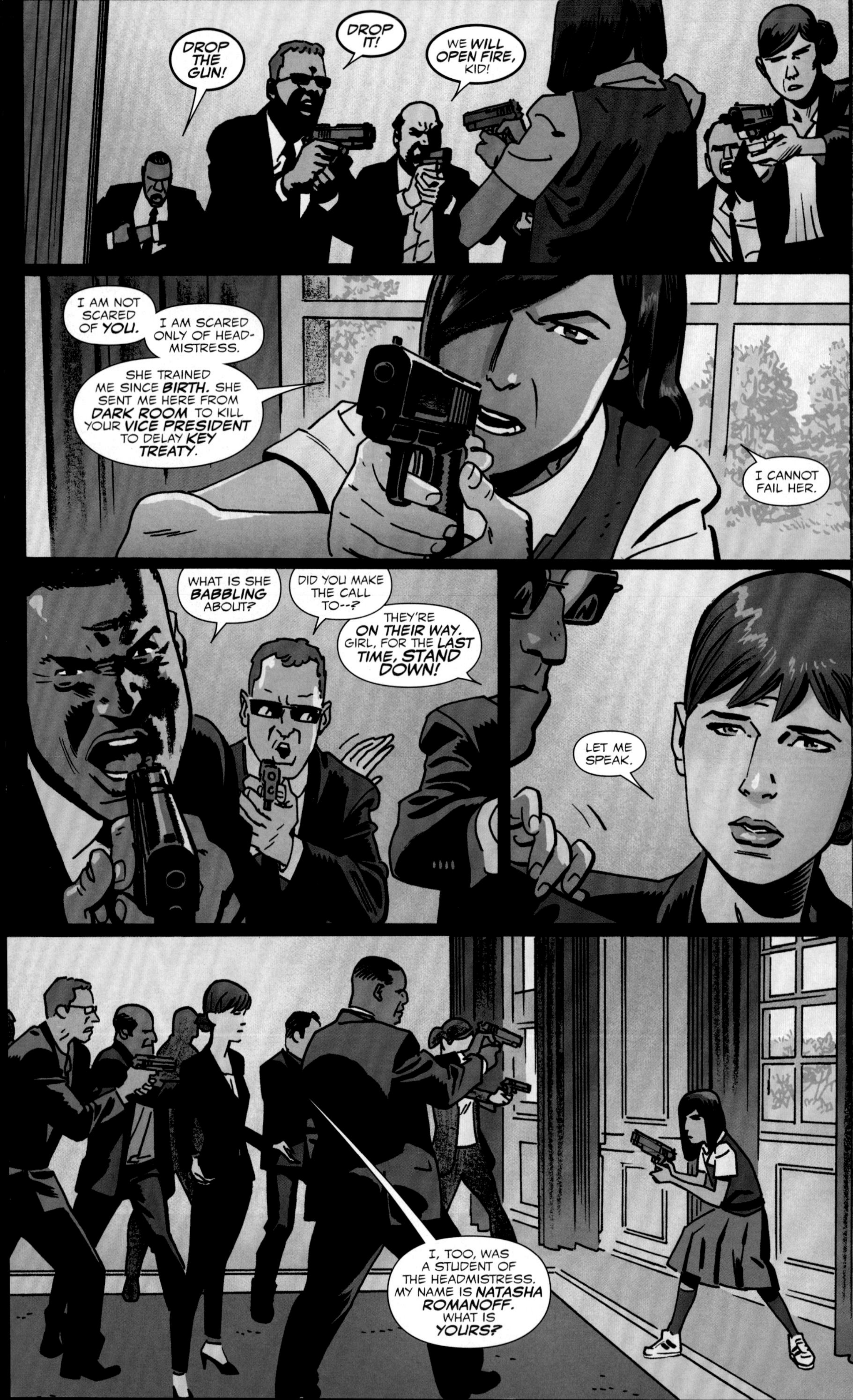
DROP THE GUN!
DROP IT!
WE WILL OPEN FIRE, KID!
I AM NOT SCARED OF YOU.
I AM SCARED ONLY OF HEAD-MISTRESS.
SHE TRAINED ME SINCE BIRTH. SHE SENT ME HERE FROM DARK ROOM TO KILL YOUR VICE PRESIDENT TO DELAY KEY TREATY.
I CANNOT FAIL HER.
WHAT IS SHE BABBLING ABOUT?
DID YOU MAKE THE CALL TO--?
THEY'RE ON THEIR WAY. GIRL, FOR THE LAST TIME, STAND DOWN!
LET ME SPEAK.
I, TOO, WAS A STUDENT OF THE HEADMISTRESS. MY NAME IS NATASHA ROMANOFF. WHAT IS YOURS?

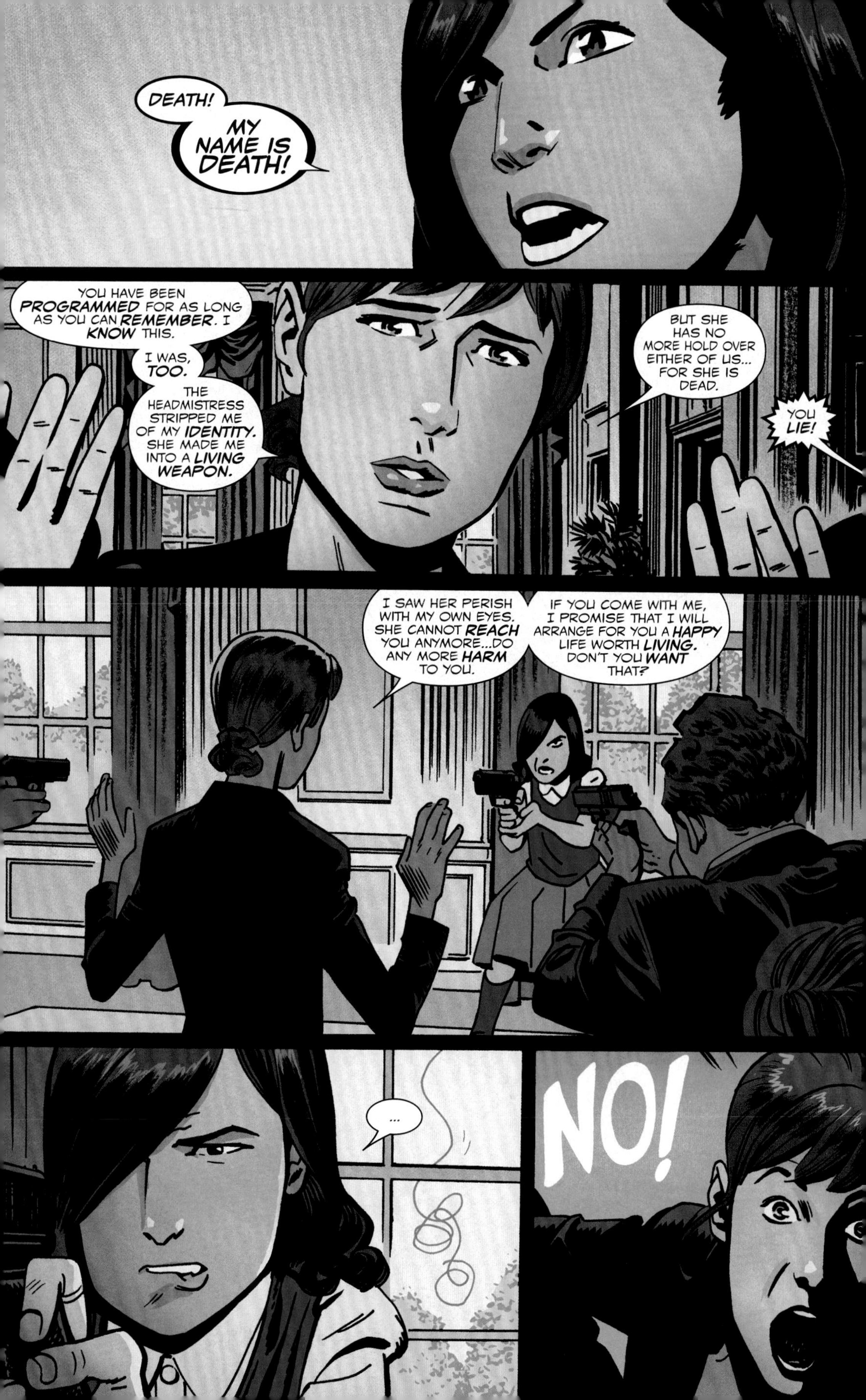

DEATH!
MY NAME IS DEATH!
YOU HAVE BEEN PROGRAMMED FOR AS LONG AS YOU CAN REMEMBER. I KNOW THIS.
I WAS, TOO.
THE HEADMISTRESS STRIPPED ME OF MY IDENTITY. SHE MADE ME INTO A LIVING WEAPON.
BUT SHE HAS NO MORE HOLD OVER EITHER OF US... FOR SHE IS DEAD.
YOU LIE!
I SAW HER PERISH WITH MY OWN EYES. SHE CANNOT REACH YOU ANYMORE...DO ANY MORE HARM TO YOU.
IF YOU COME WITH ME, I PROMISE THAT I WILL ARRANGE FOR YOU A HAPPY LIFE WORTH LIVING. DON'T YOU WANT THAT?
...
NO!

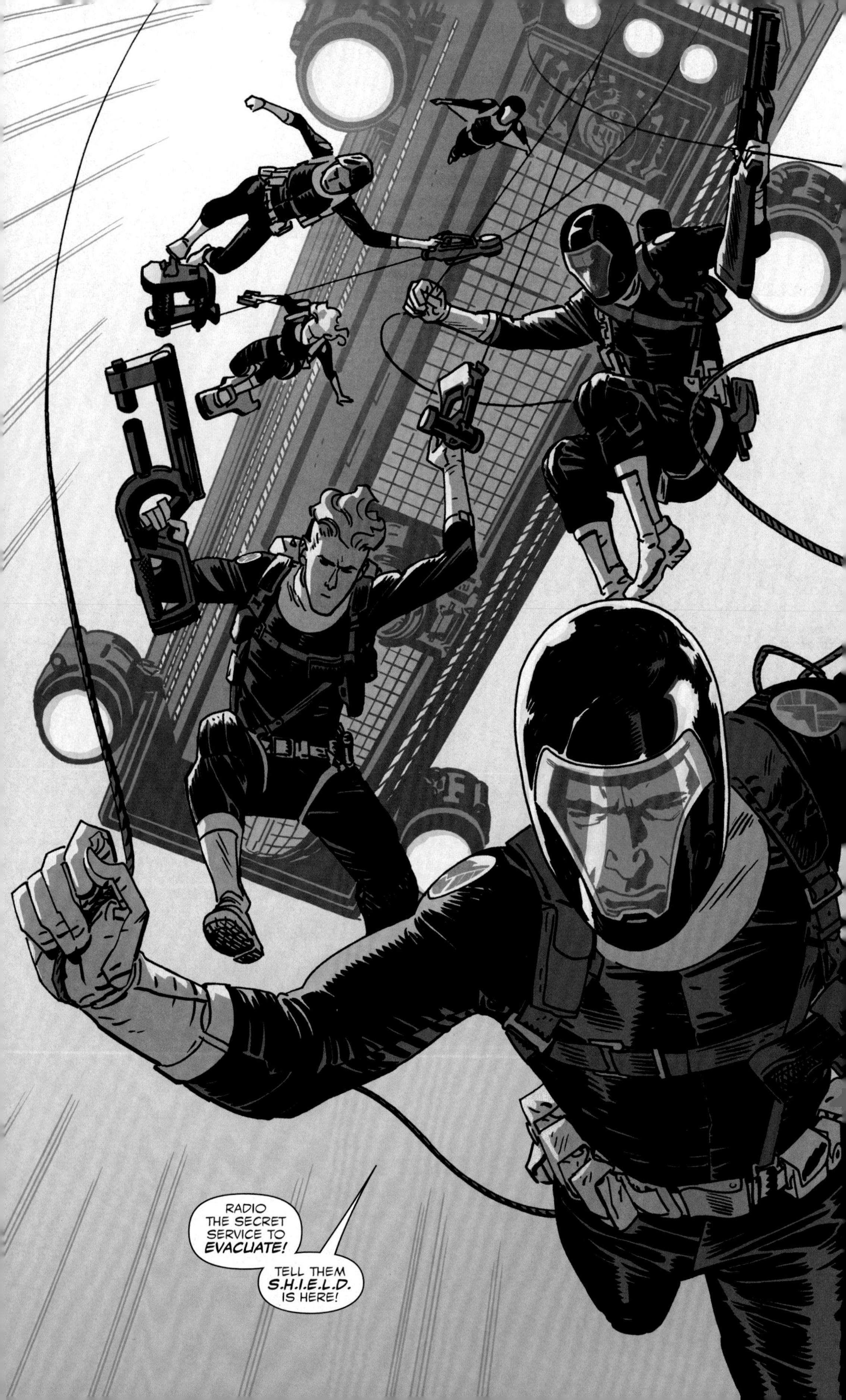
RADIO THE SECRET SERVICE TO EVACUATE!
TELL THEM S.H.I.E.L.D. IS HERE!

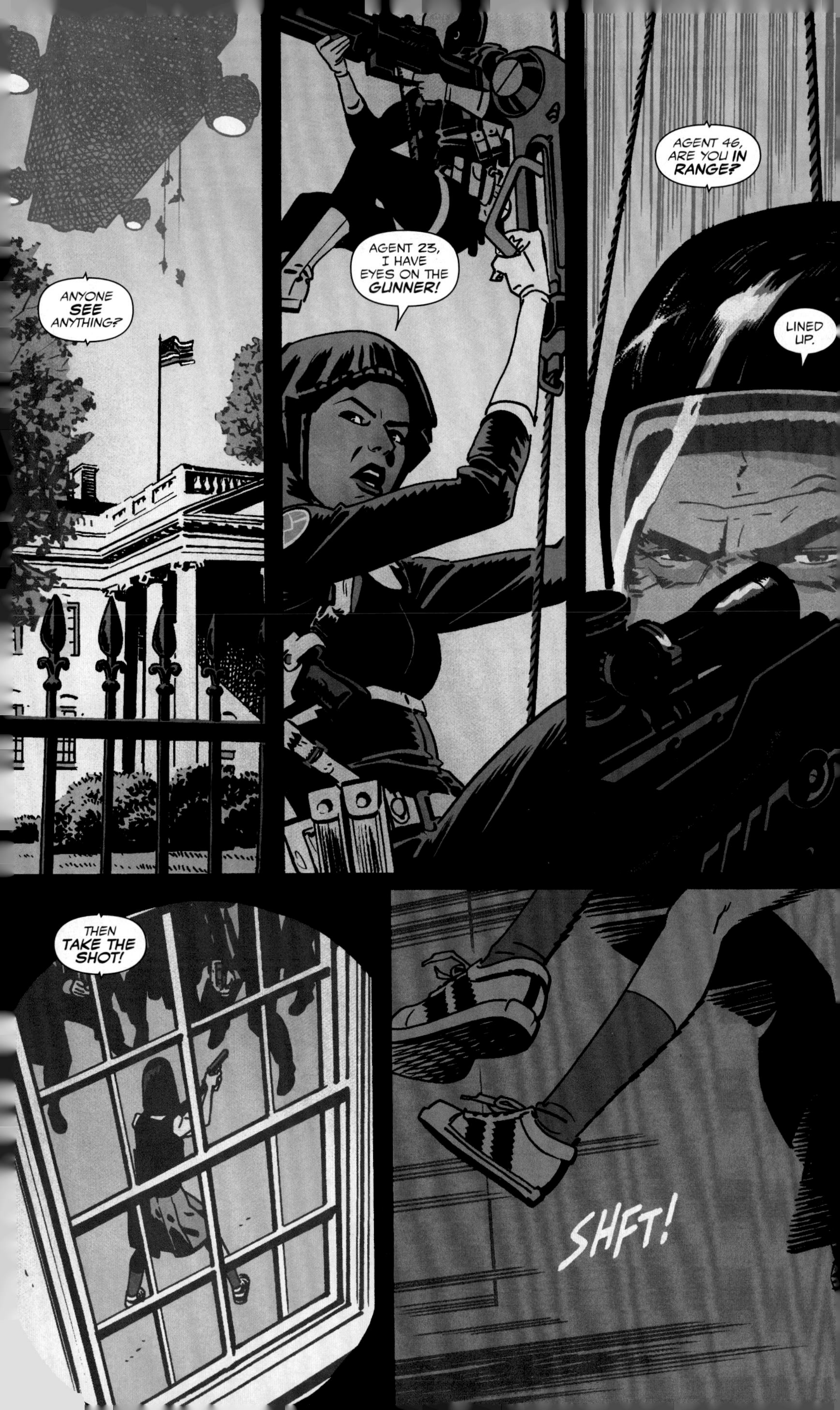
ANYONE SEE ANYTHING?
AGENT 23, I HAVE EYES ON THE GUNNER!
AGENT 46, ARE YOU IN RANGE?
LINED UP.
THEN TAKE THE SHOT!
SHFT!

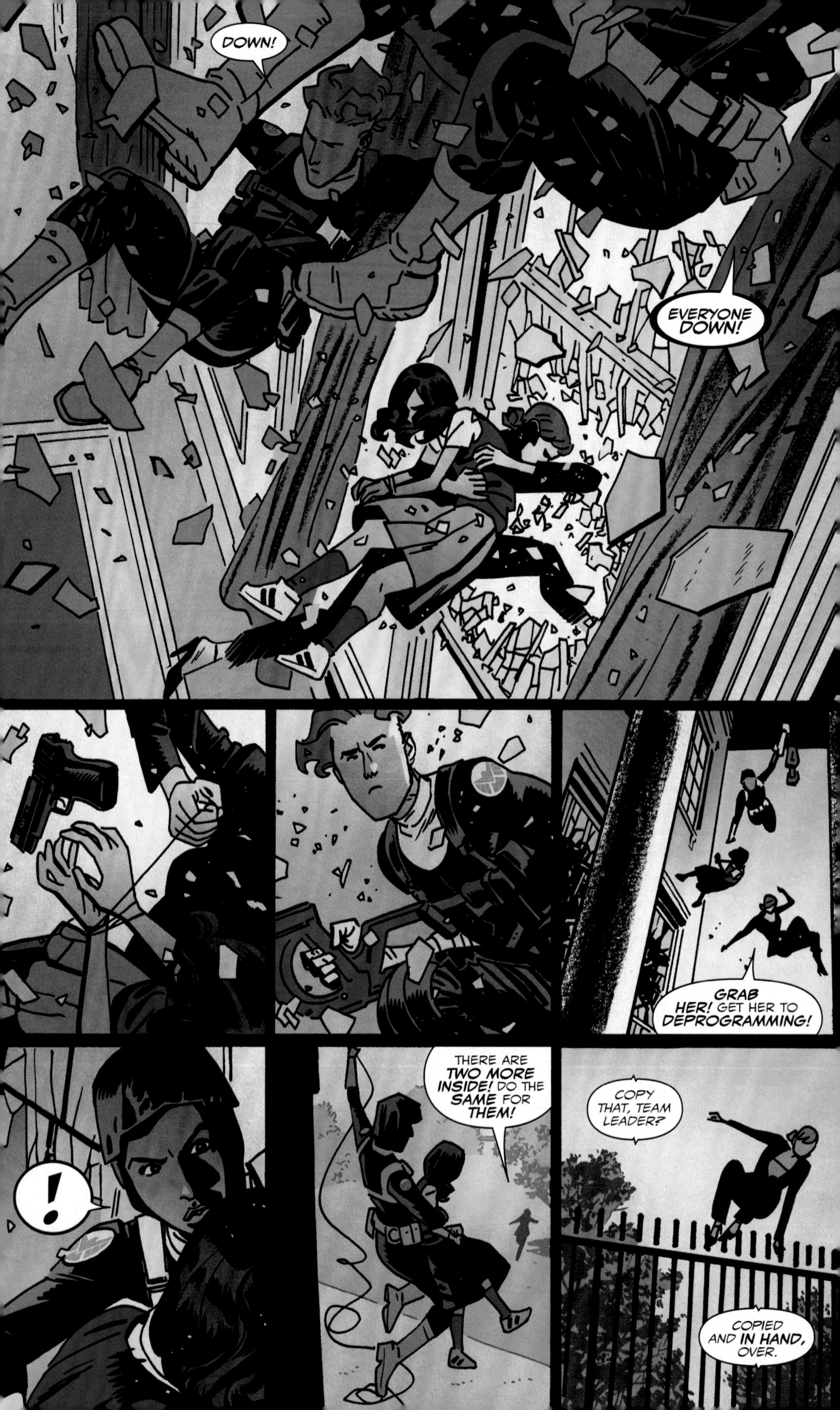
DOWN!
EVERYONE DOWN!
GRAB HER! GET HER TO DEPROGRAMMING!
!
THERE ARE TWO MORE INSIDE! DO THE SAME FOR THEM!
COPY THAT, TEAM LEADER?
COPIED AND IN HAND, OVER.

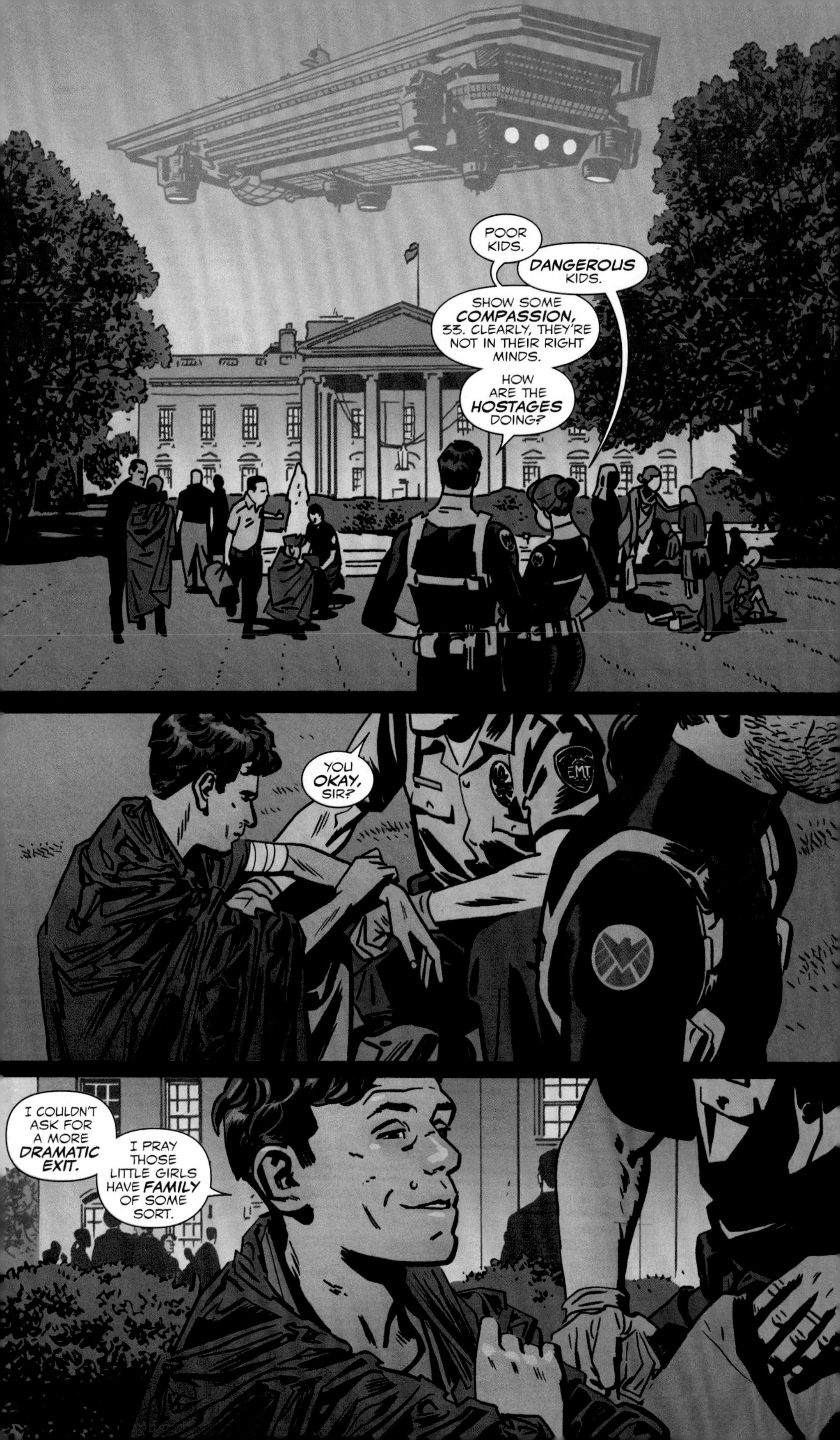
POOR KIDS.
DANGEROUS KIDS.
SHOW SOME COMPASSION, 33. CLEARLY, THEY'RE NOT IN THEIR RIGHT MINDS.
HOW ARE THE HOSTAGES DOING?
EMT
YOU OKAY, SIR?
I COULDN'T ASK FOR A MORE DRAMATIC EXIT.
I PRAY THOSE LITTLE GIRLS HAVE FAMILY OF SOME SORT.

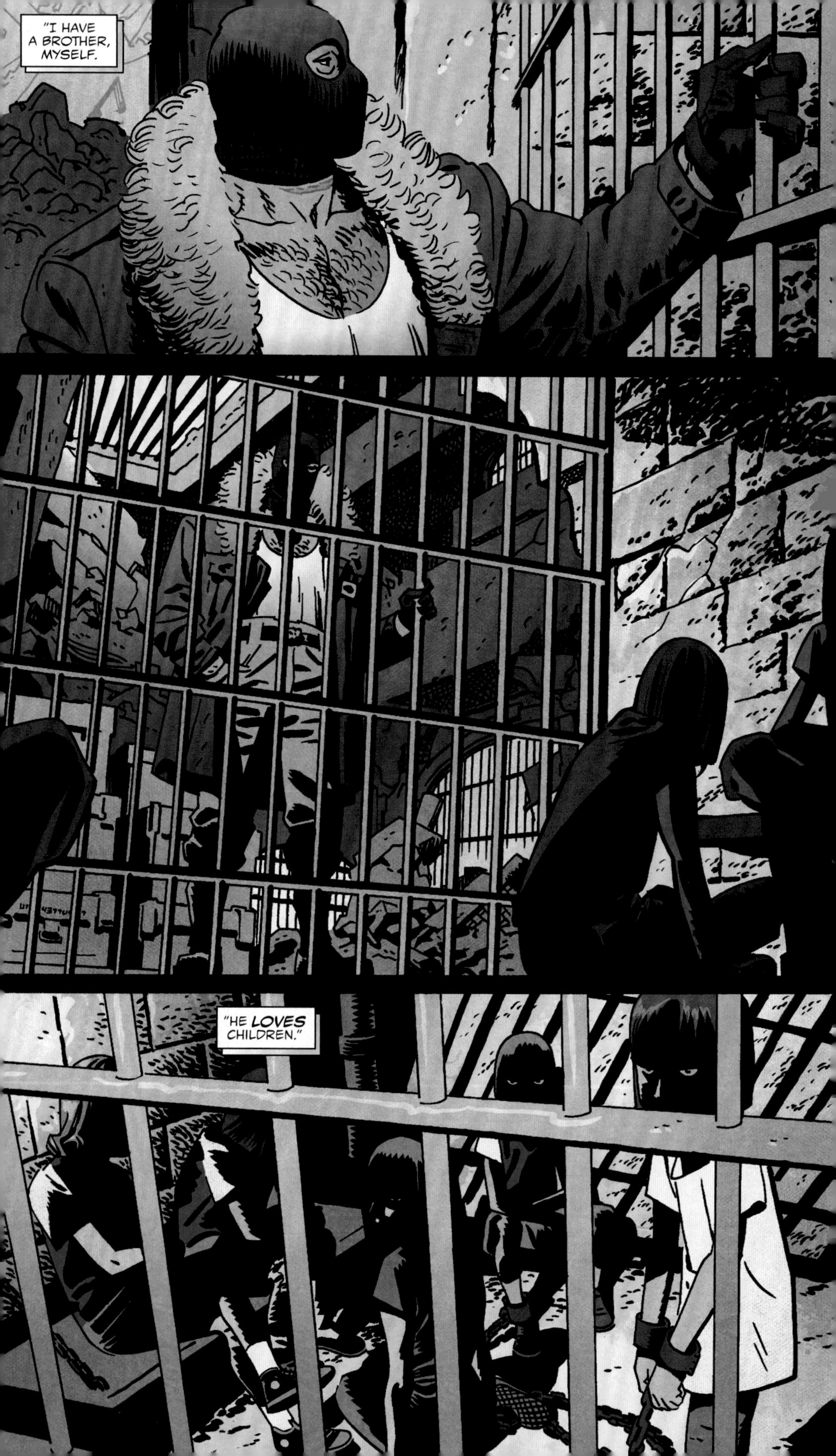
"I HAVE A BROTHER, MYSELF.
"HE LOVES CHILDREN."

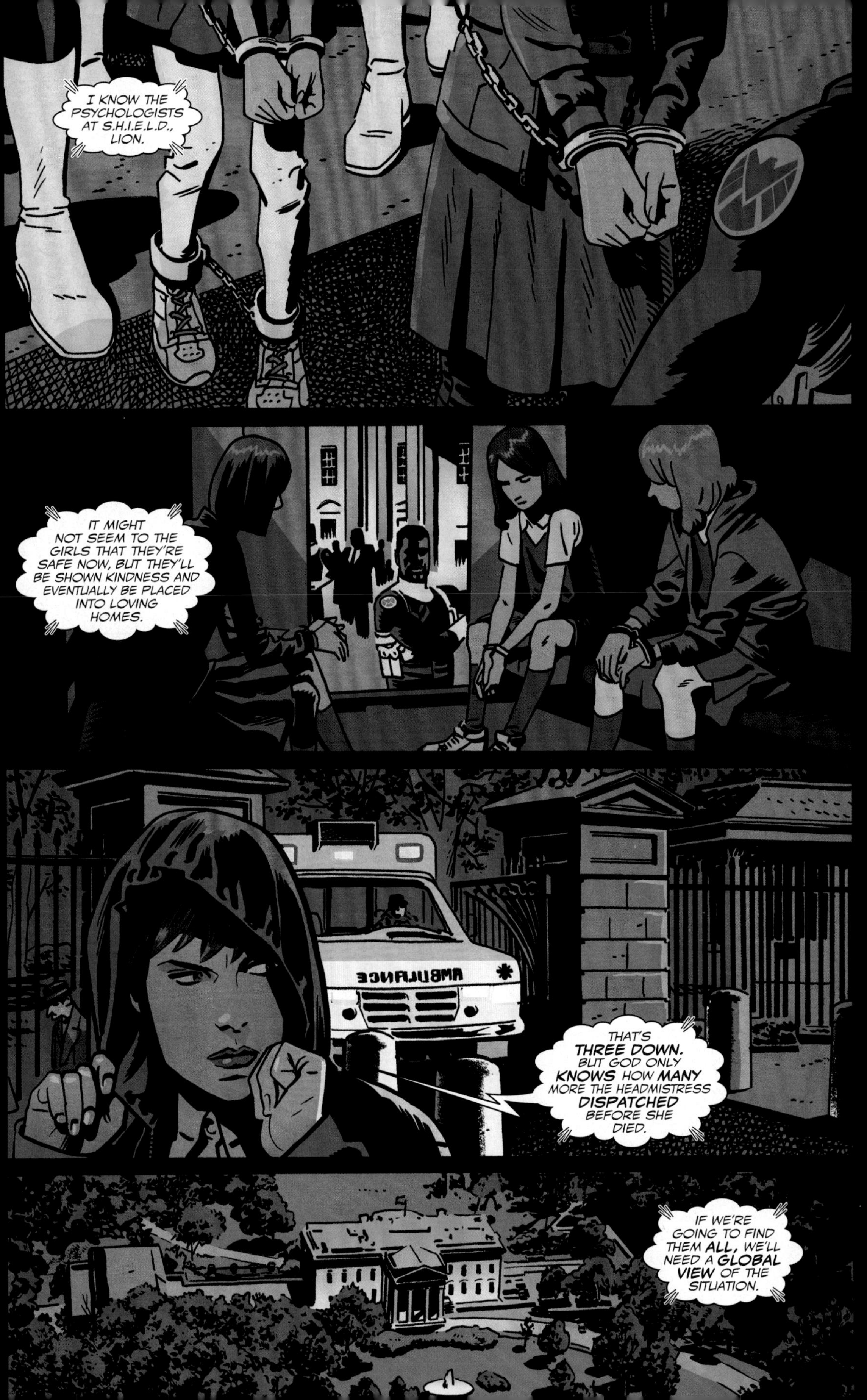
I KNOW THE PSYCHOLOGISTS AT S.H.I.E.L.D., LION.
IT MIGHT NOT SEEM TO THE GIRLS THAT THEY'RE SAFE NOW, BUT THEY'LL BE SHOWN KINDNESS AND EVENTUALLY BE PLACED INTO LOVING HOMES.
AMBULANCE
THAT'S **THREE DOWN.** BUT GOD ONLY **KNOWS** HOW **MANY** MORE THE HEADMISTRESS **DISPATCHED** BEFORE SHE DIED.
IF WE'RE GOING TO FIND THEM **ALL**, WE'LL NEED A **GLOBAL VIEW** OF THE SITUATION.

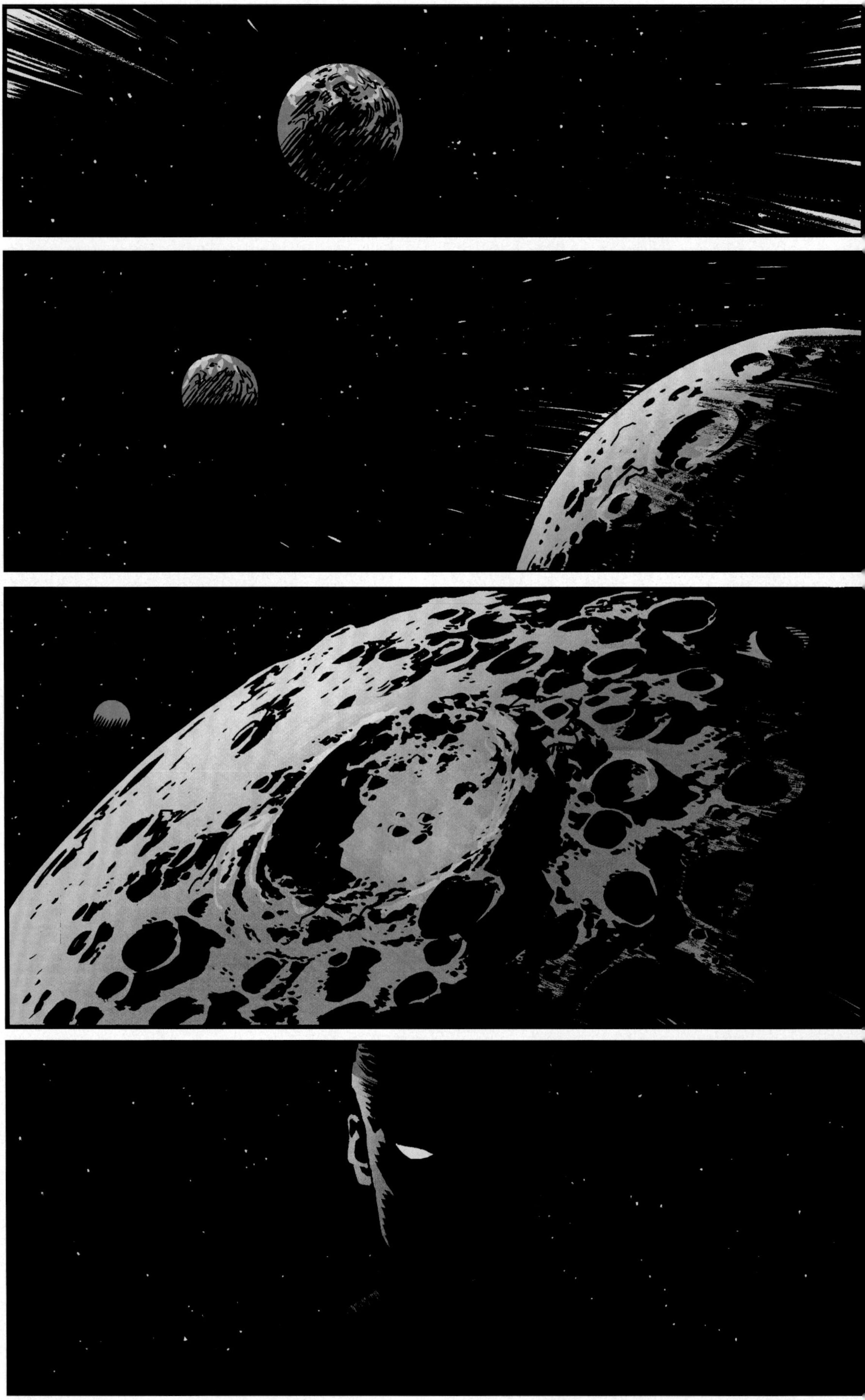

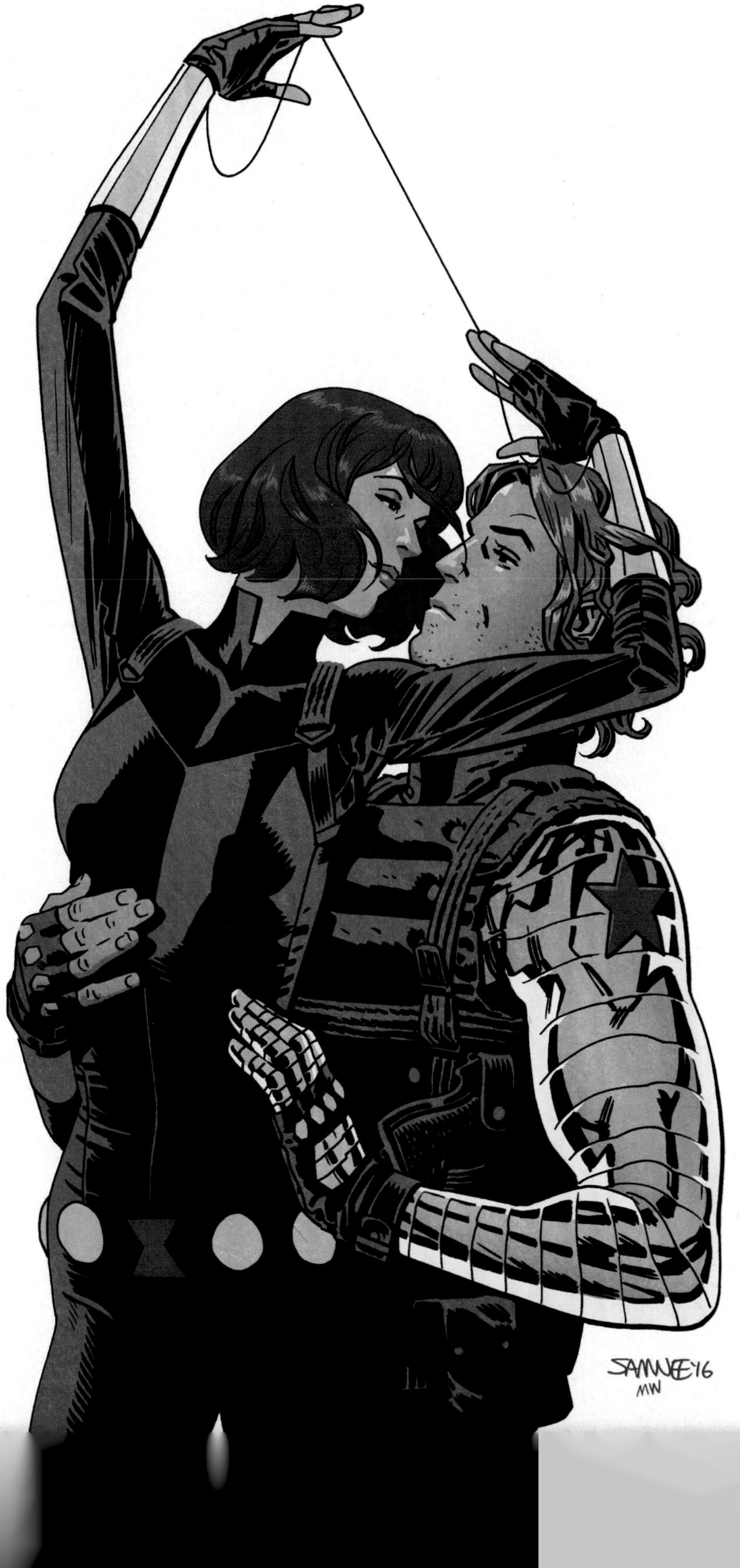
SAMNEE'16
MW

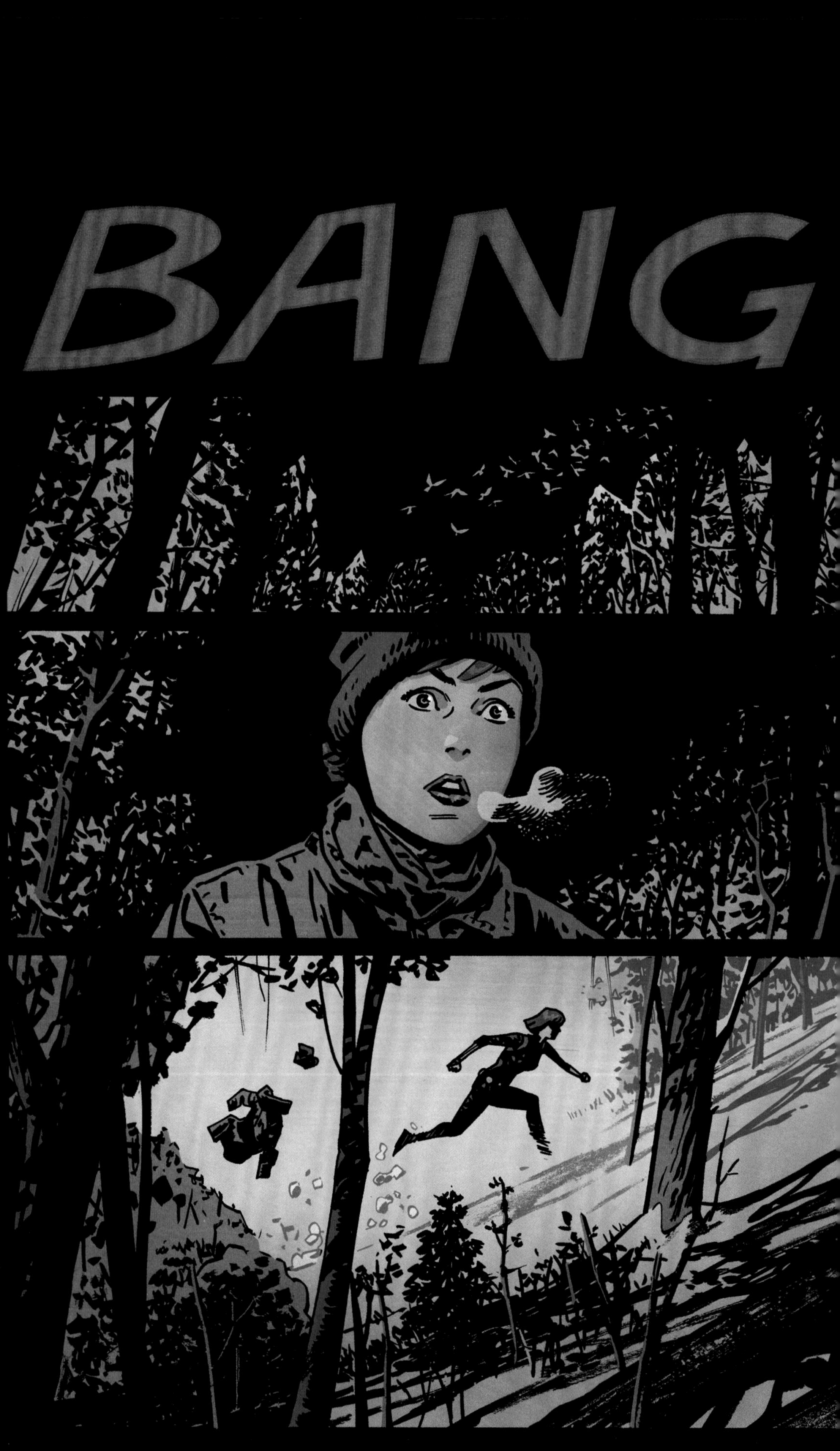
BANG

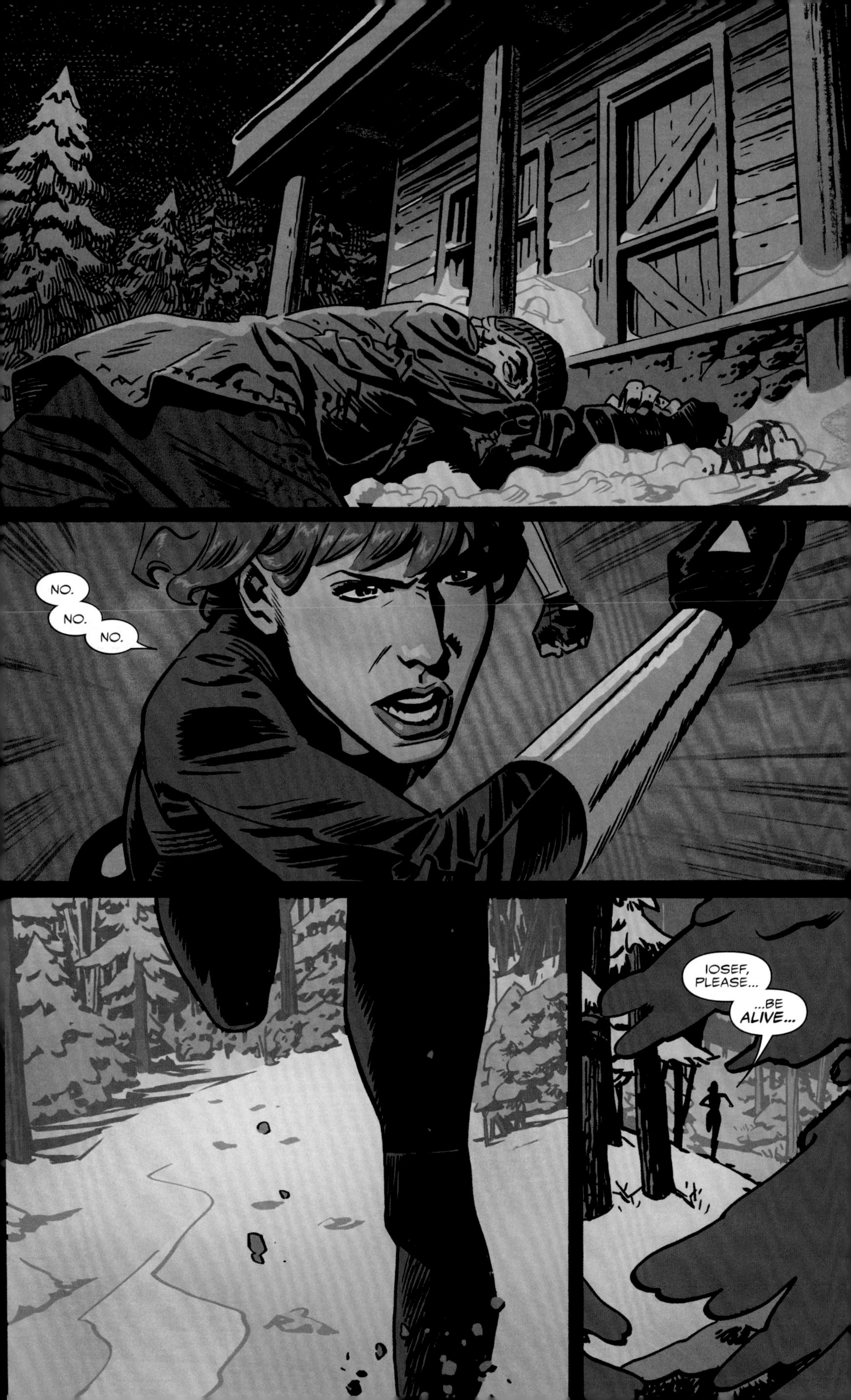
NO.
NO.
NO.
IOSEF, PLEASE...
...BE ALIVE...

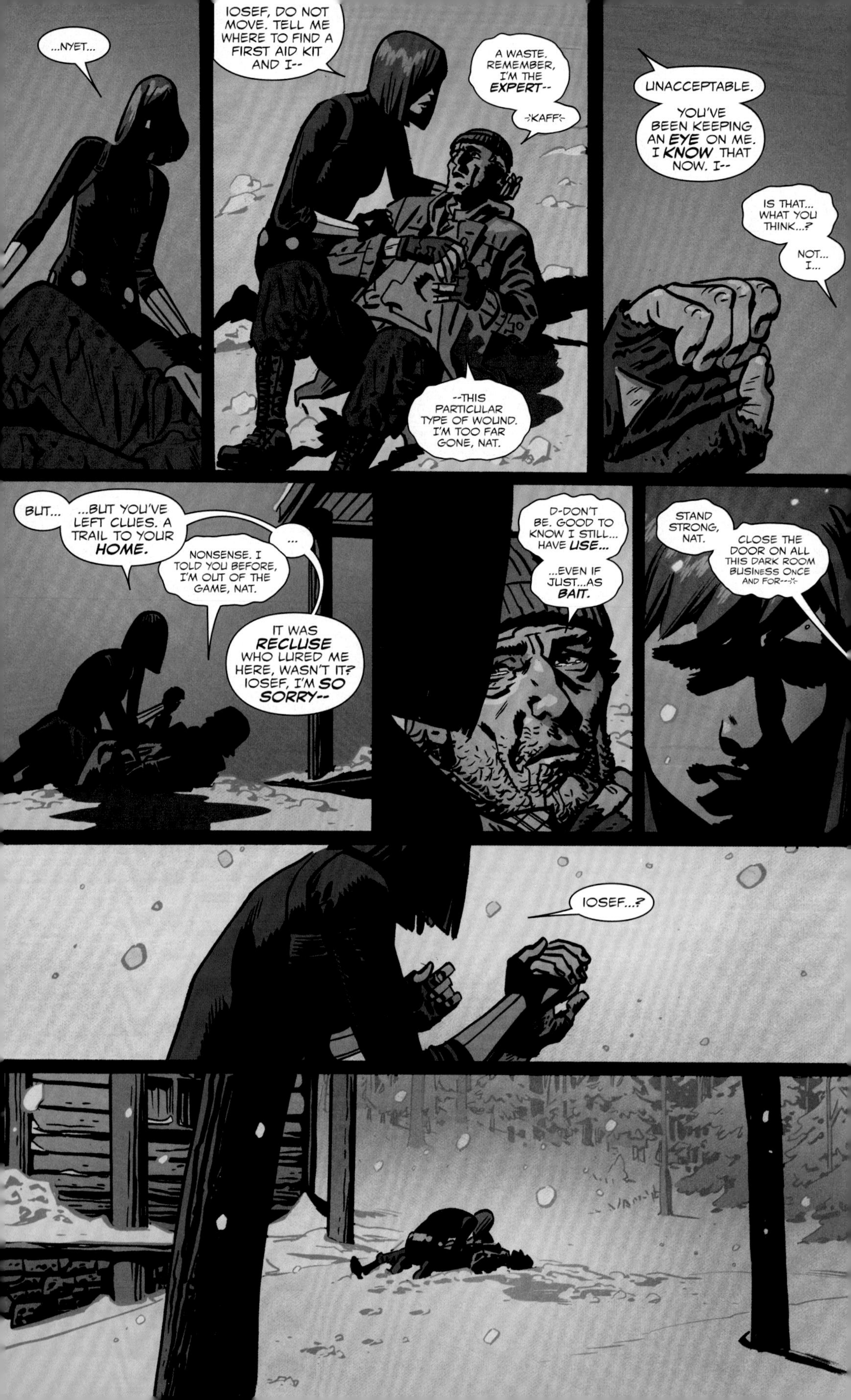
...NYET...
IOSEF, DO NOT MOVE. TELL ME WHERE TO FIND A FIRST AID KIT AND I--
A WASTE. REMEMBER, I'M THE EXPERT--
KAFF
--THIS PARTICULAR TYPE OF WOUND. I'M TOO FAR GONE, NAT.
UNACCEPTABLE.
YOU'VE BEEN KEEPING AN EYE ON ME. I KNOW THAT NOW. I--
IS THAT... WHAT YOU THINK...?
NOT... I...
BUT...
...BUT YOU'VE LEFT CLUES. A TRAIL TO YOUR HOME.
NONSENSE. I TOLD YOU BEFORE, I'M OUT OF THE GAME, NAT.
...
IT WAS RECLUSE WHO LURED ME HERE, WASN'T IT? IOSEF, I'M SO SORRY--
D-DON'T BE. GOOD TO KNOW I STILL... HAVE USE...
...EVEN IF JUST...AS BAIT.
STAND STRONG, NAT.
CLOSE THE DOOR ON ALL THIS DARK ROOM BUSINESS ONCE AND FOR--
IOSEF...?

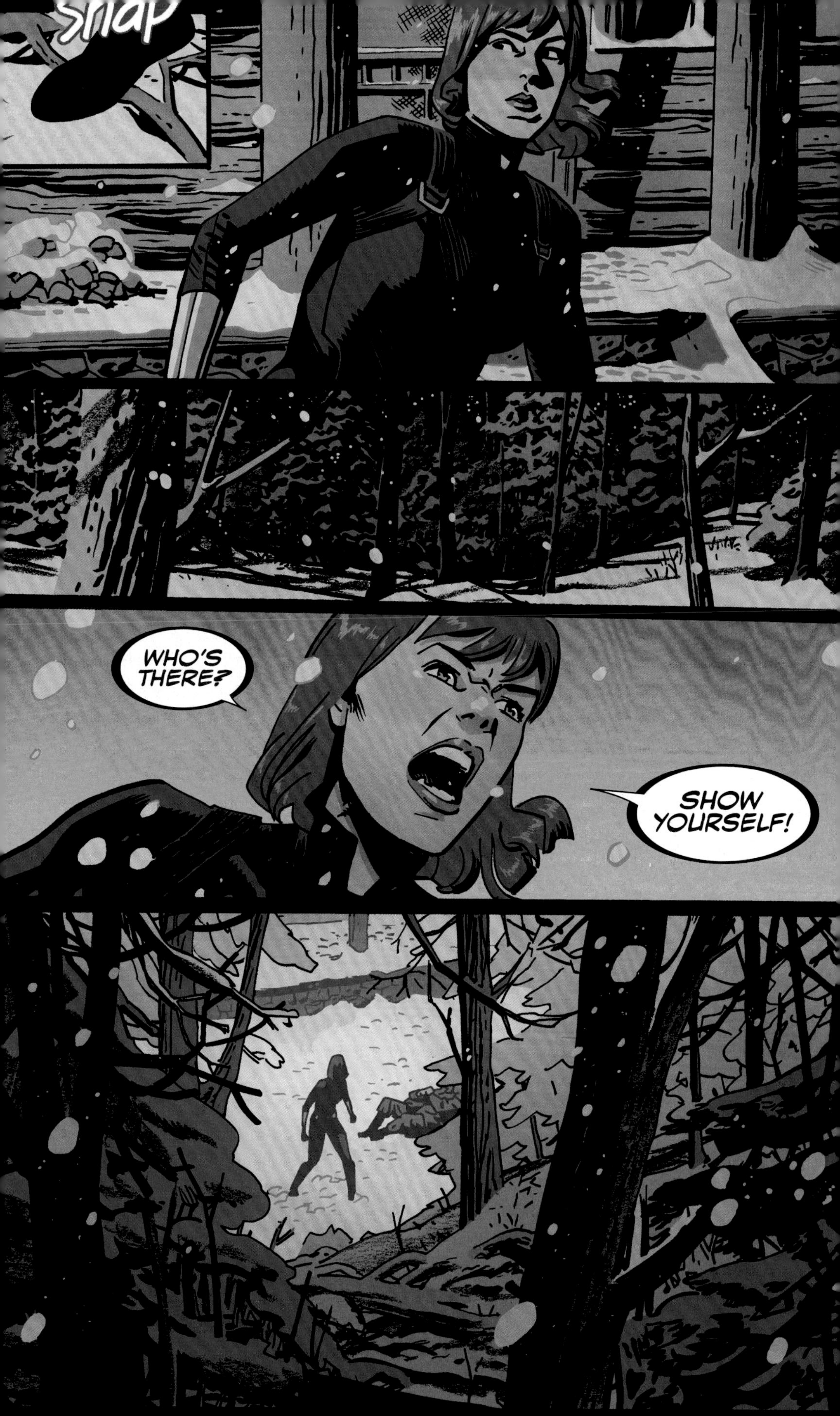
SNAP
WHO'S THERE?
SHOW YOURSELF!

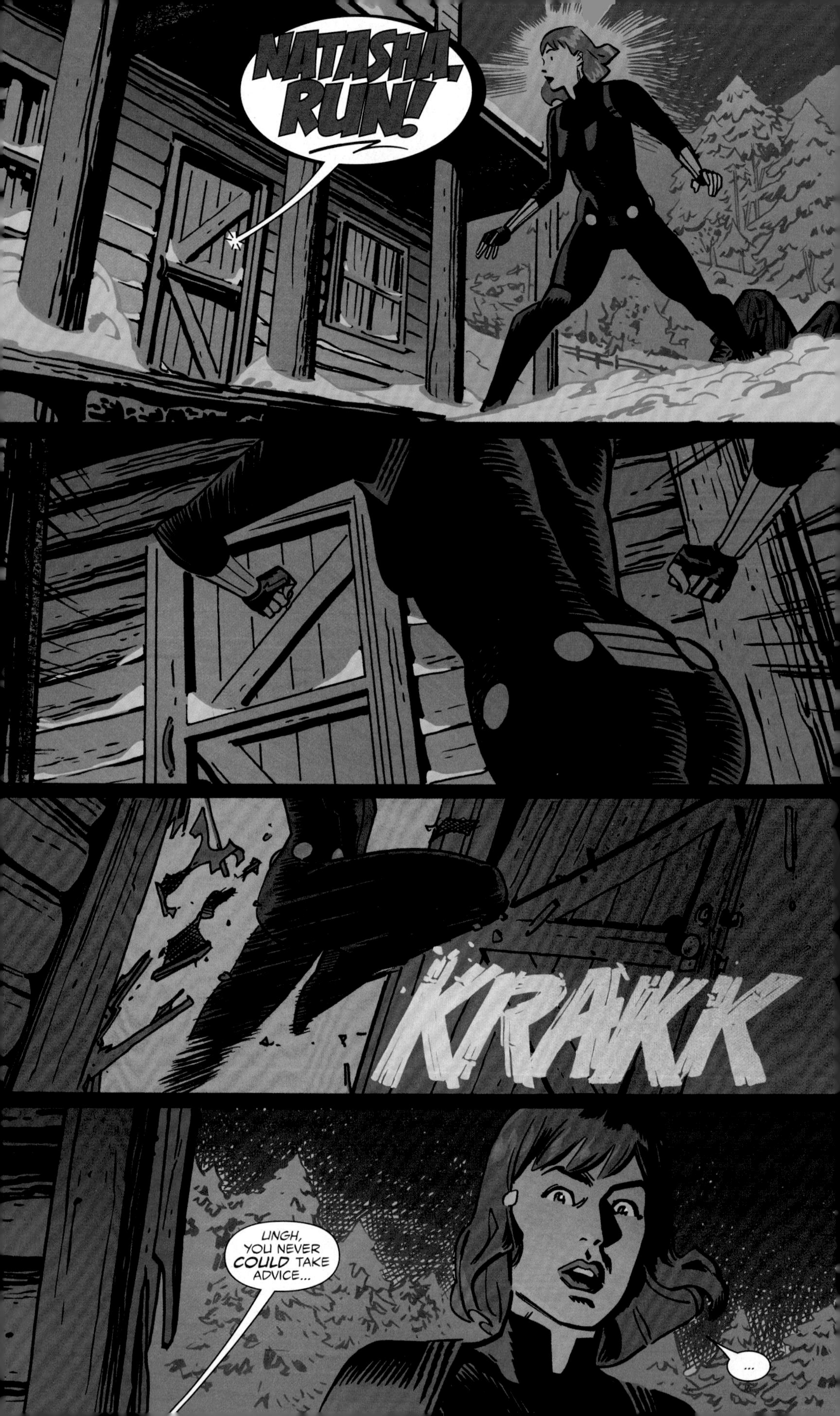
NATASHA, RUN!
KRAKK
UNGH, YOU NEVER COULD TAKE ADVICE...
...

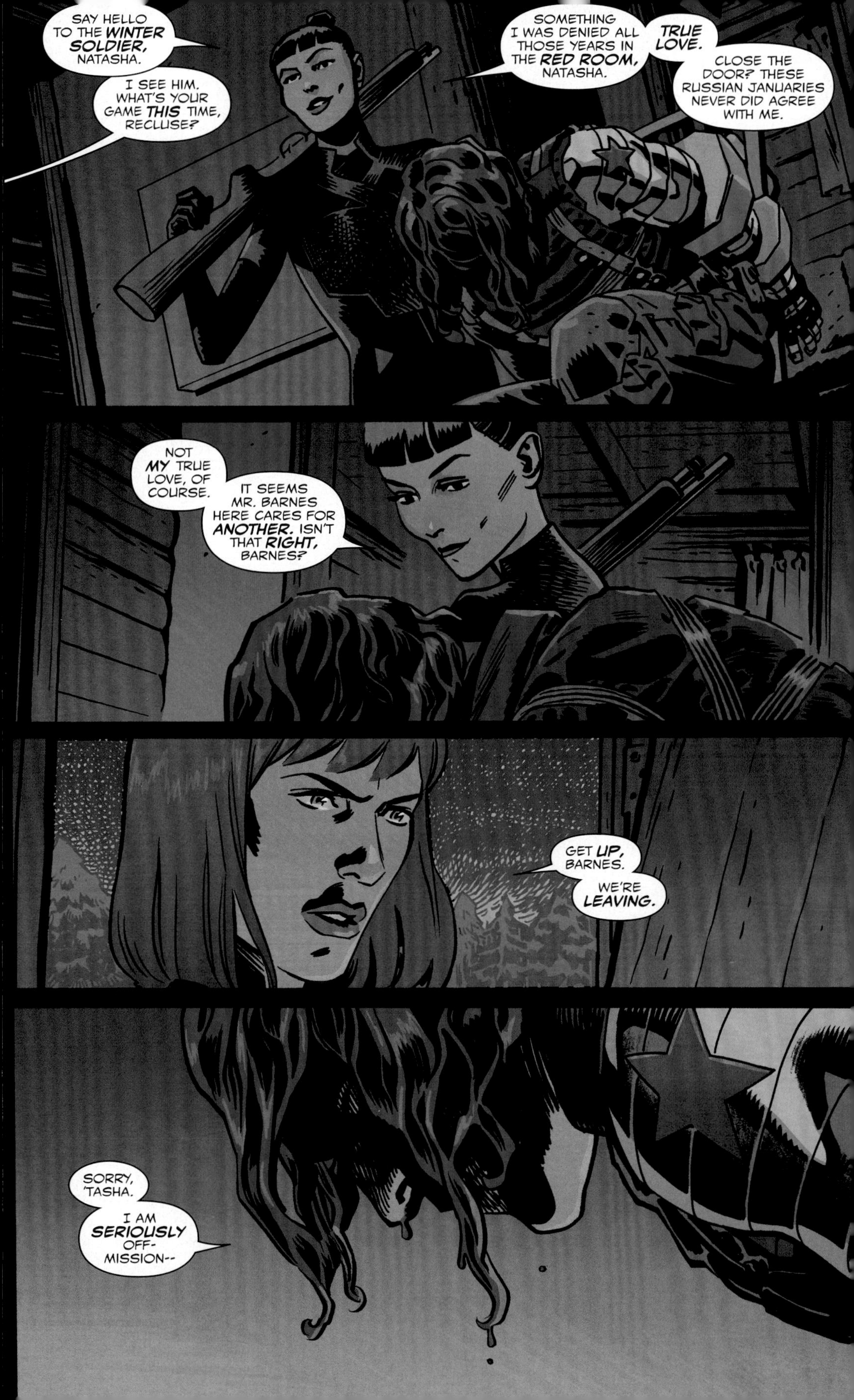
SAY HELLO TO THE WINTER SOLDIER, NATASHA.
I SEE HIM. WHAT'S YOUR GAME THIS TIME, RECLUSE?
SOMETHING I WAS DENIED ALL THOSE YEARS IN THE RED ROOM, NATASHA.
TRUE LOVE.
CLOSE THE DOOR? THESE RUSSIAN JANUARIES NEVER DID AGREE WITH ME.
NOT MY TRUE LOVE, OF COURSE.
IT SEEMS MR. BARNES HERE CARES FOR ANOTHER. ISN'T THAT RIGHT, BARNES?
GET UP, BARNES.
WE'RE LEAVING.
SORRY, 'TASHA.
I AM SERIOUSLY OFF-MISSION--

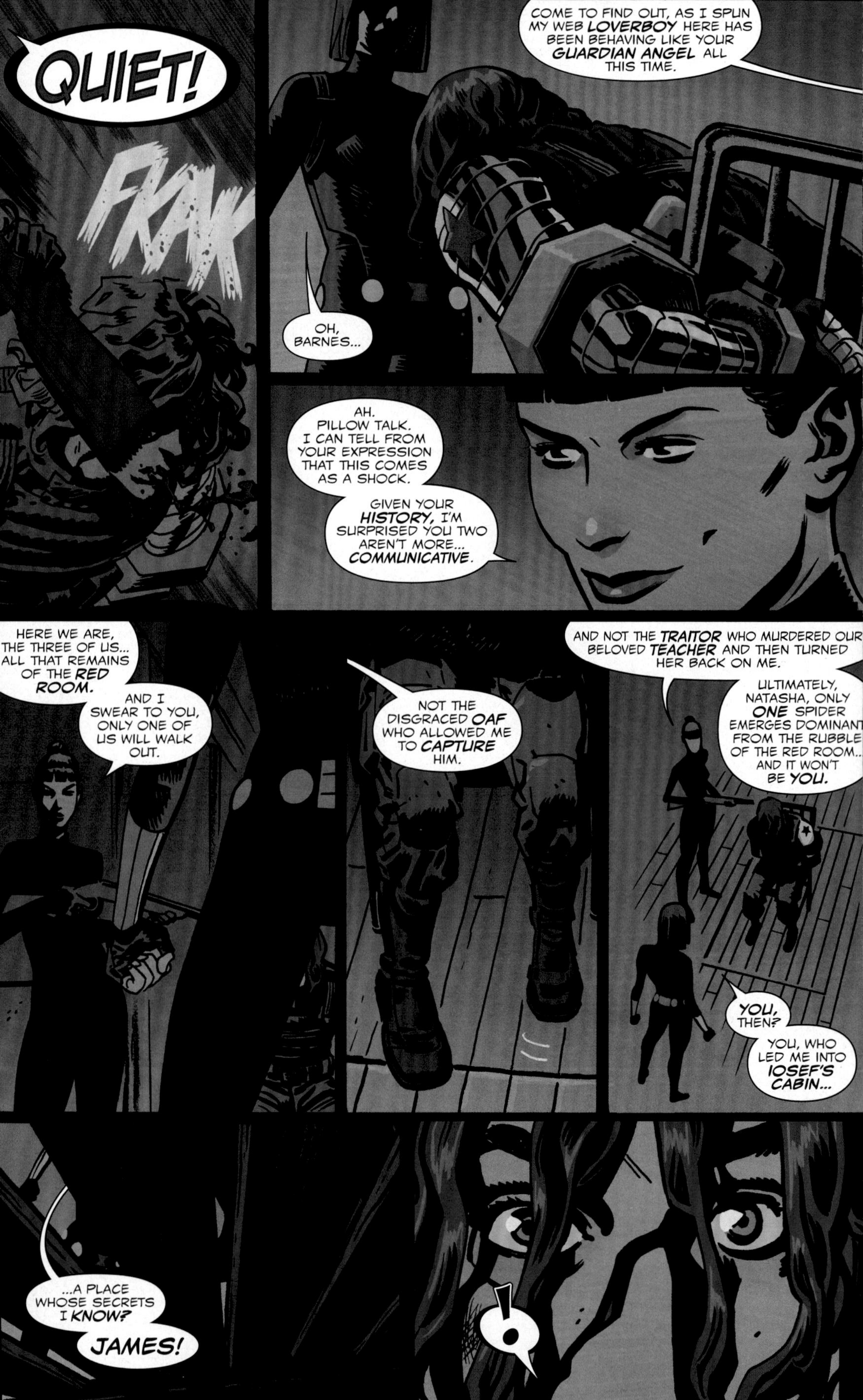
QUIET!
FRAK
COME TO FIND OUT, AS I SPUN MY WEB LOVERBOY HERE HAS BEEN BEHAVING LIKE YOUR GUARDIAN ANGEL ALL THIS TIME.
OH, BARNES...
AH. PILLOW TALK. I CAN TELL FROM YOUR EXPRESSION THAT THIS COMES AS A SHOCK.
GIVEN YOUR HISTORY, I'M SURPRISED YOU TWO AREN'T MORE... COMMUNICATIVE.
HERE WE ARE, THE THREE OF US... ALL THAT REMAINS OF THE RED ROOM.
AND I SWEAR TO YOU, ONLY ONE OF US WILL WALK OUT.
NOT THE DISGRACED OAF WHO ALLOWED ME TO CAPTURE HIM.
AND NOT THE TRAITOR WHO MURDERED OUR BELOVED TEACHER AND THEN TURNED HER BACK ON ME.
ULTIMATELY, NATASHA, ONLY ONE SPIDER EMERGES DOMINANT FROM THE RUBBLE OF THE RED ROOM... AND IT WON'T BE YOU.
YOU, THEN?
YOU, WHO LED ME INTO IOSEF'S CABIN...
...A PLACE WHOSE SECRETS I KNOW?
JAMES!
!

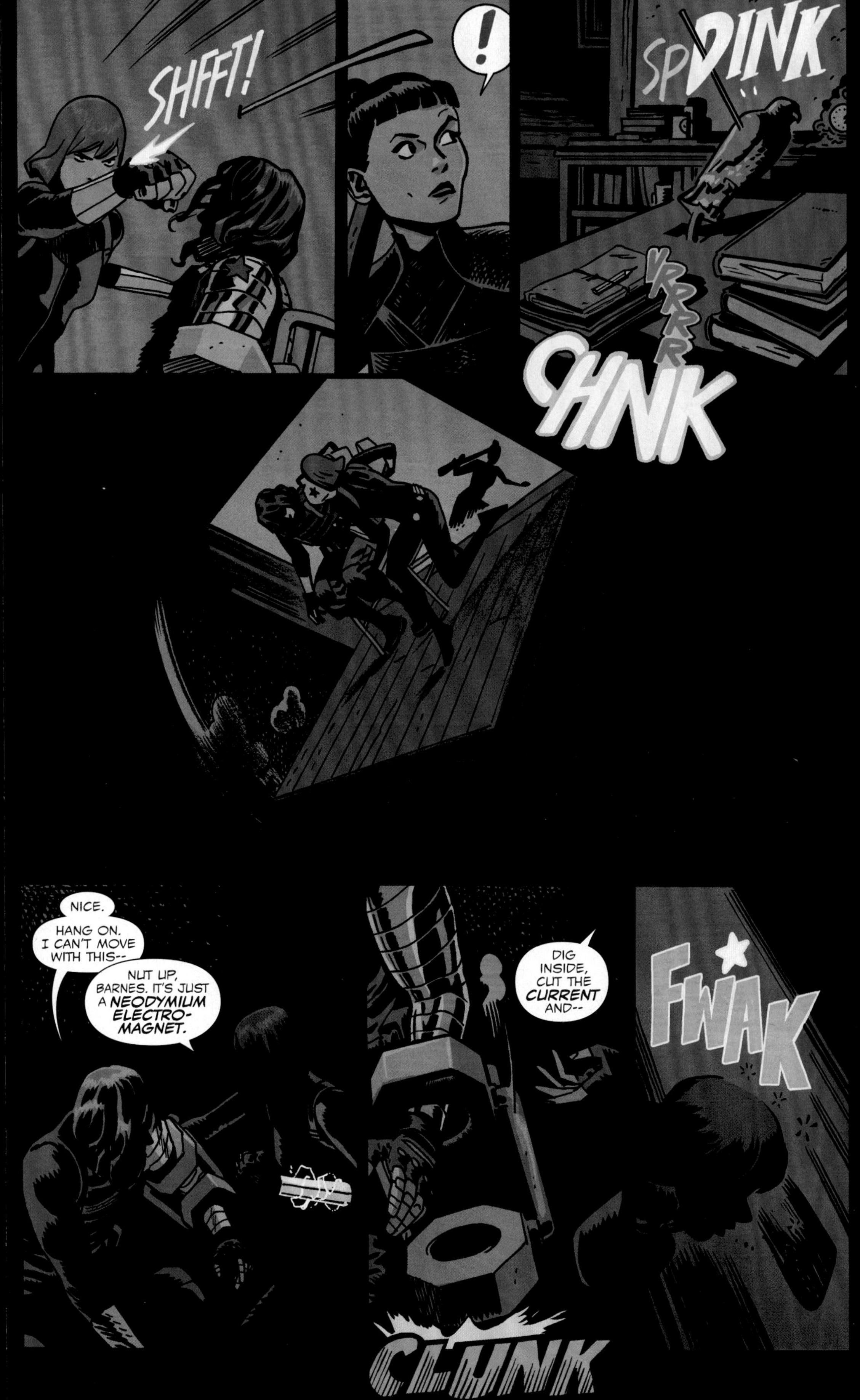
SHFFT!
!
SPDINK
VRRRR
CHNK
NICE.
HANG ON. I CAN'T MOVE WITH THIS--
NUT UP, BARNES. IT'S JUST A NEODYMIUM ELECTRO-MAGNET.
DIG INSIDE, CUT THE CURRENT AND--
CLUNK
FWAK

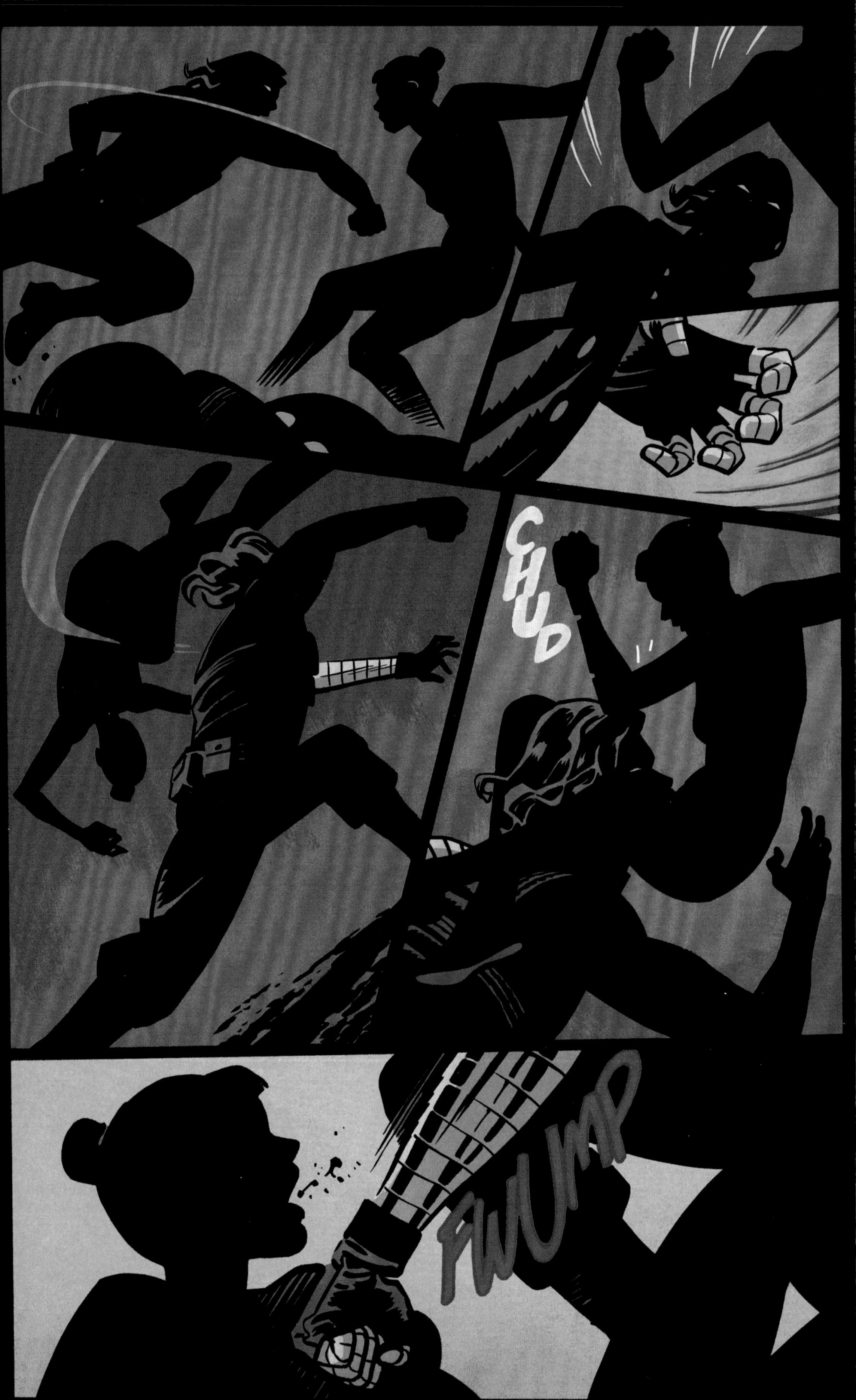
CHUD
FWUMP

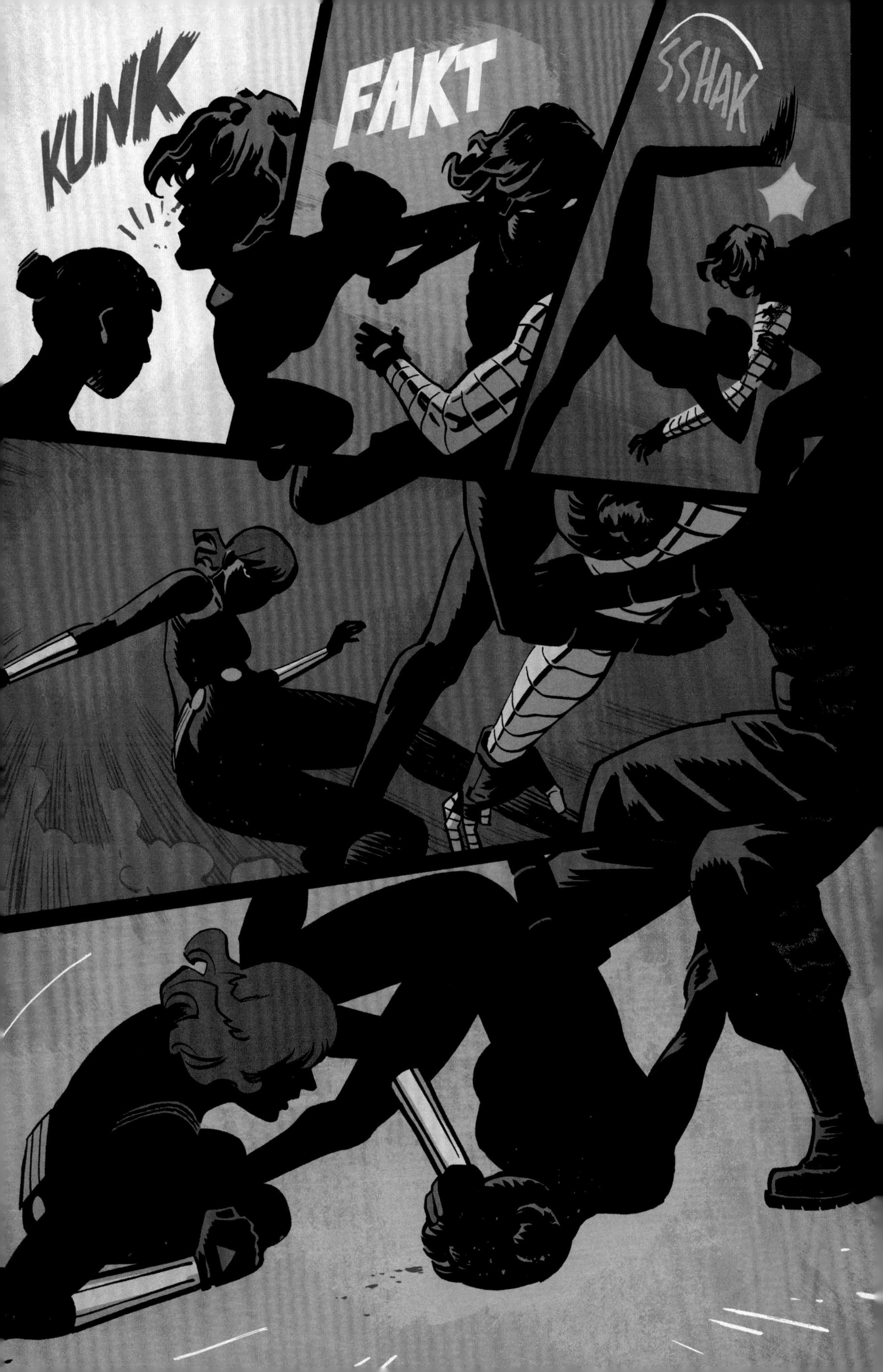
KUNK
FAKT
SSHAK

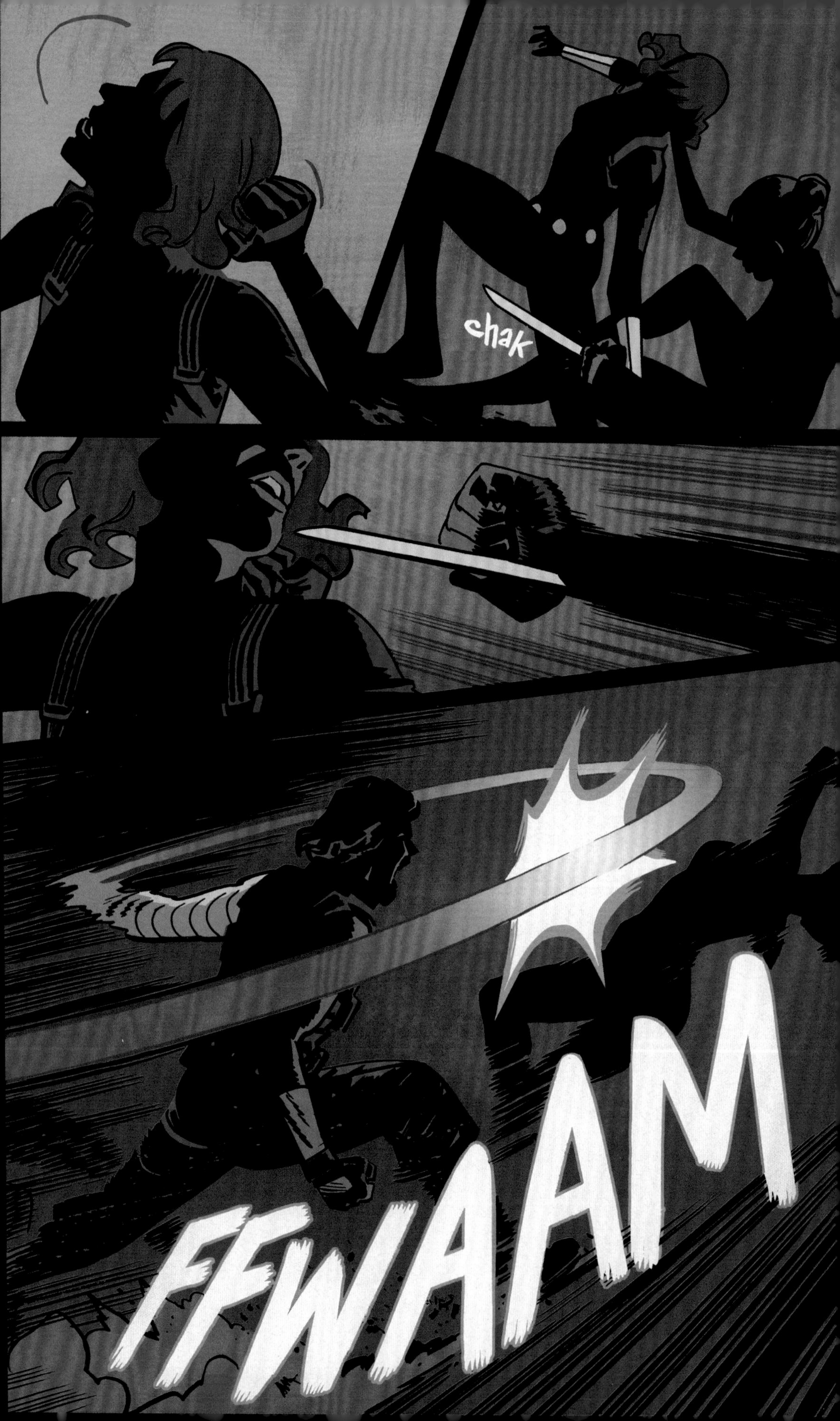
chak
FFWAAM

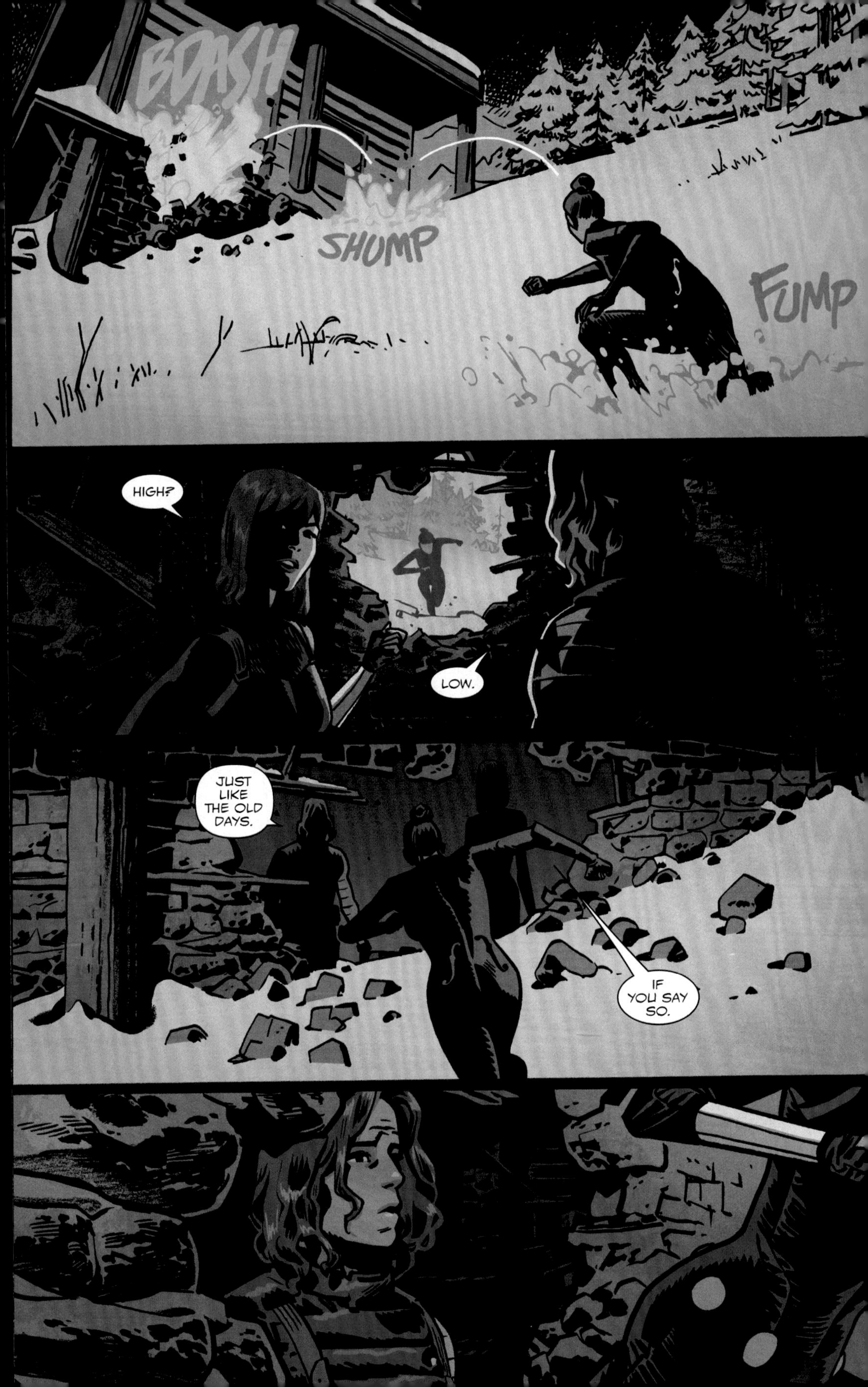
BOASH
SHUMP
FUMP
HIGH?
LOW.
JUST LIKE THE OLD DAYS.
IF YOU SAY SO.

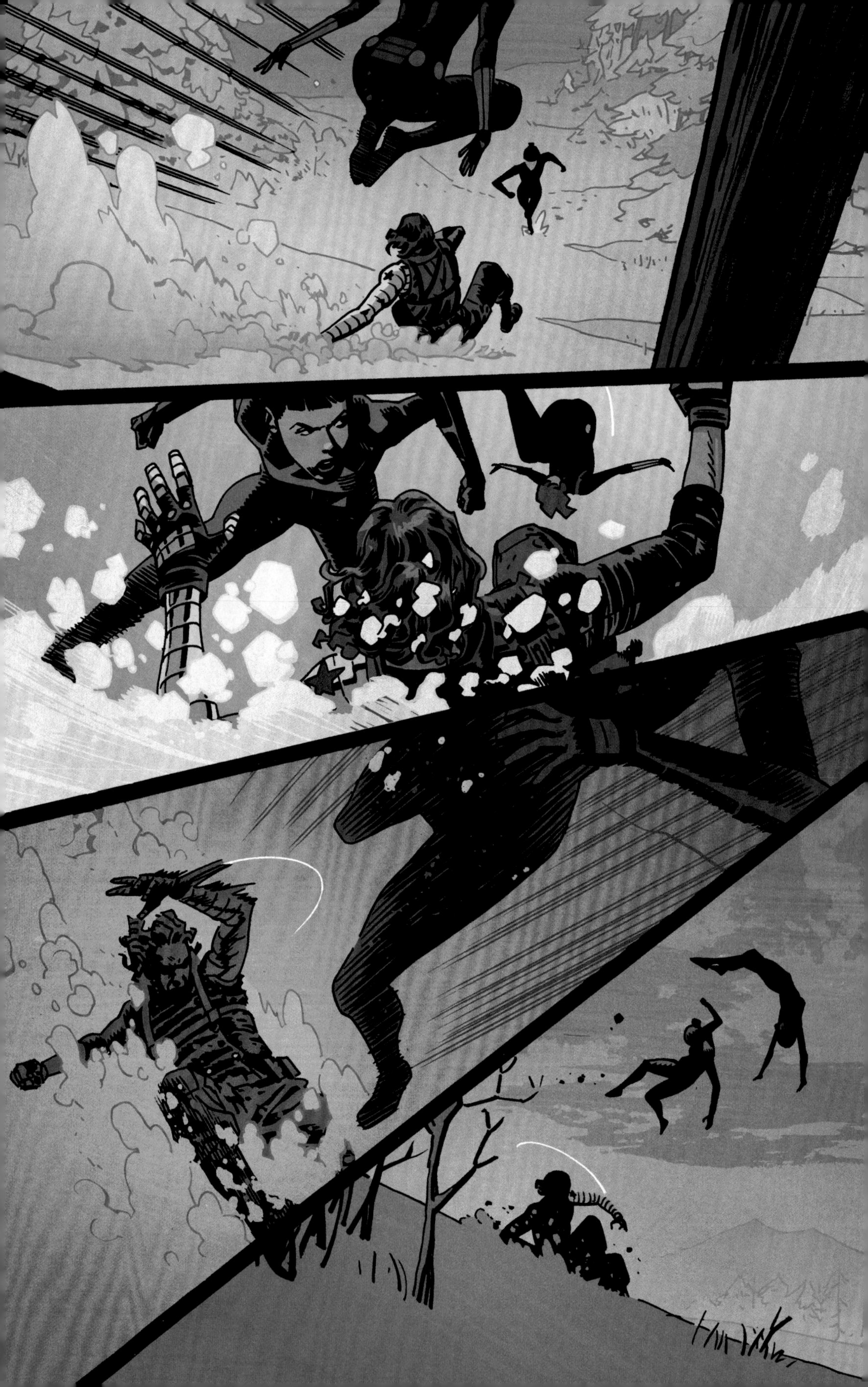

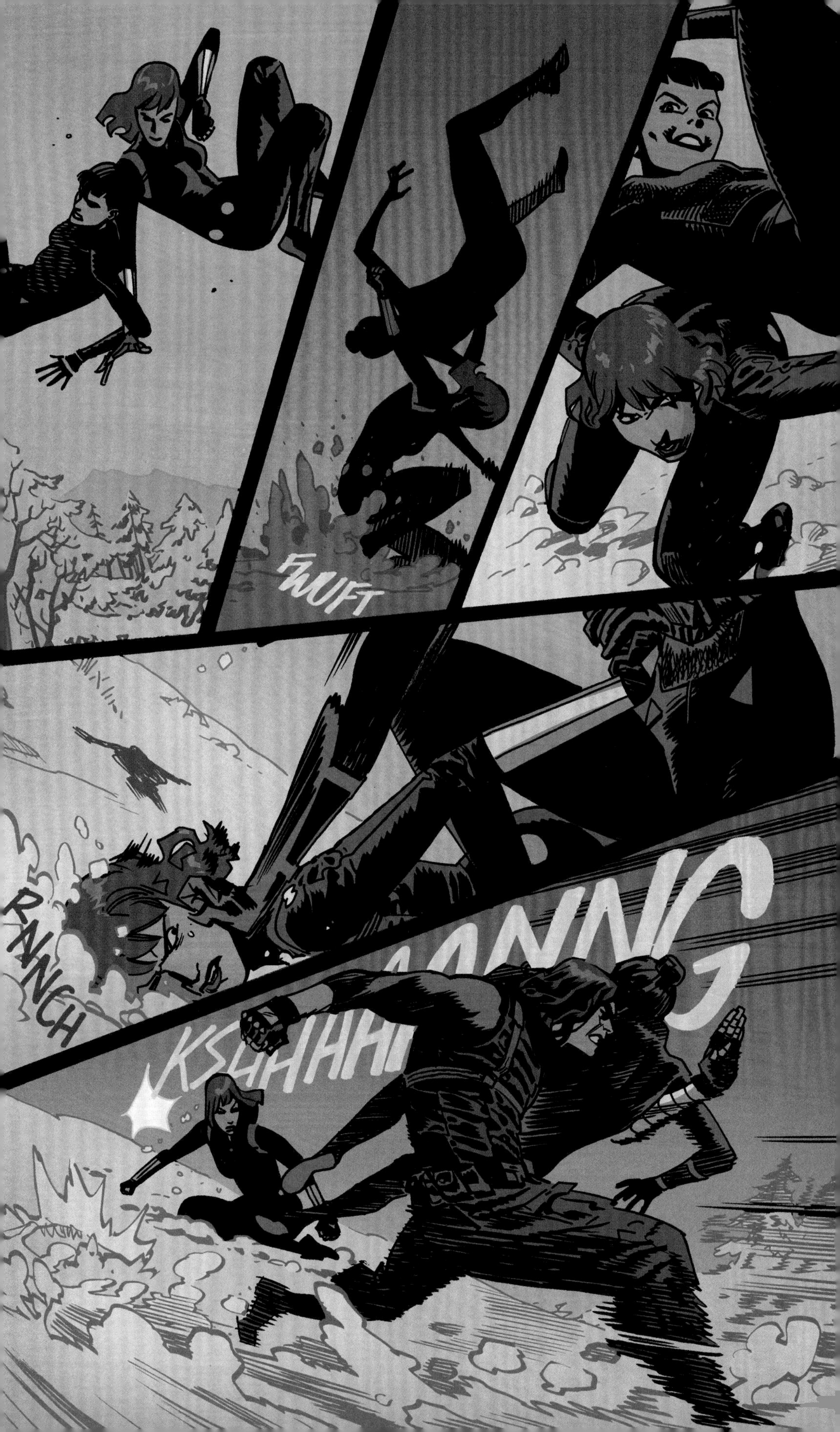
FWUFT
RANNCH
KSHHHH
NNNG

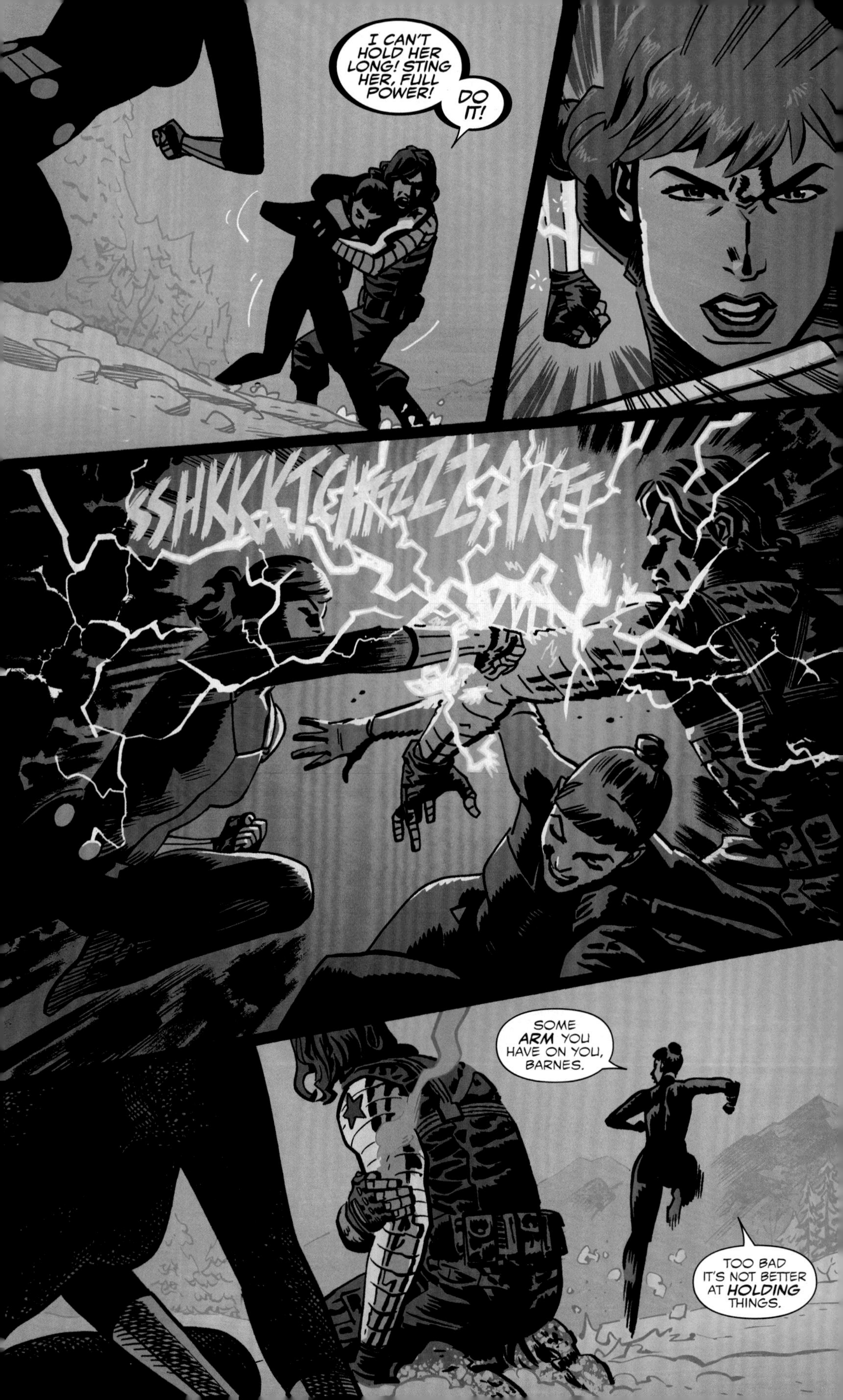
I CAN'T HOLD HER LONG! STING HER, FULL POWER!
DO IT!
SSHKKKTCHZZZZAKT
SOME ARM YOU HAVE ON YOU, BARNES.
TOO BAD IT'S NOT BETTER AT HOLDING THINGS.

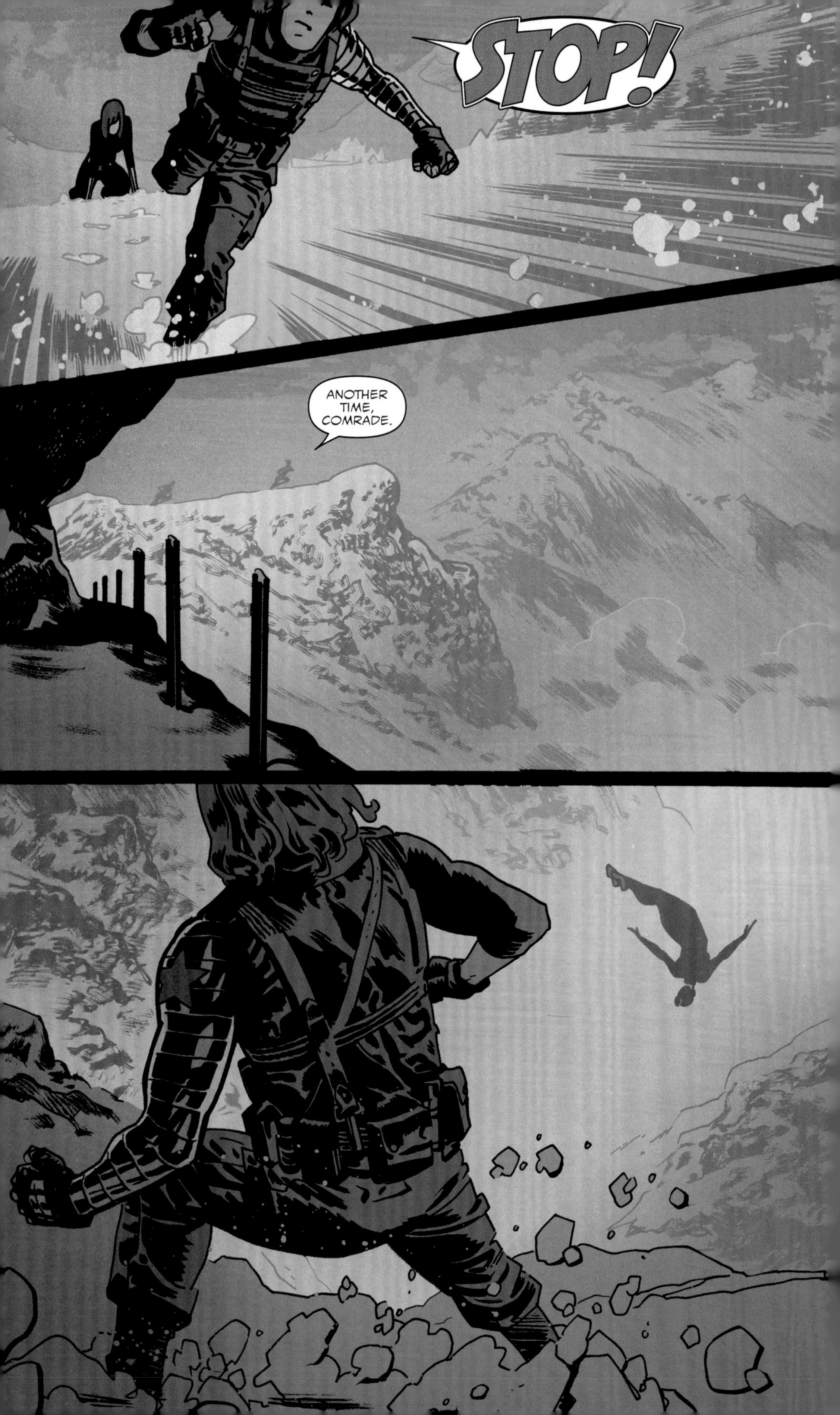
STOP!
ANOTHER TIME, COMRADE.

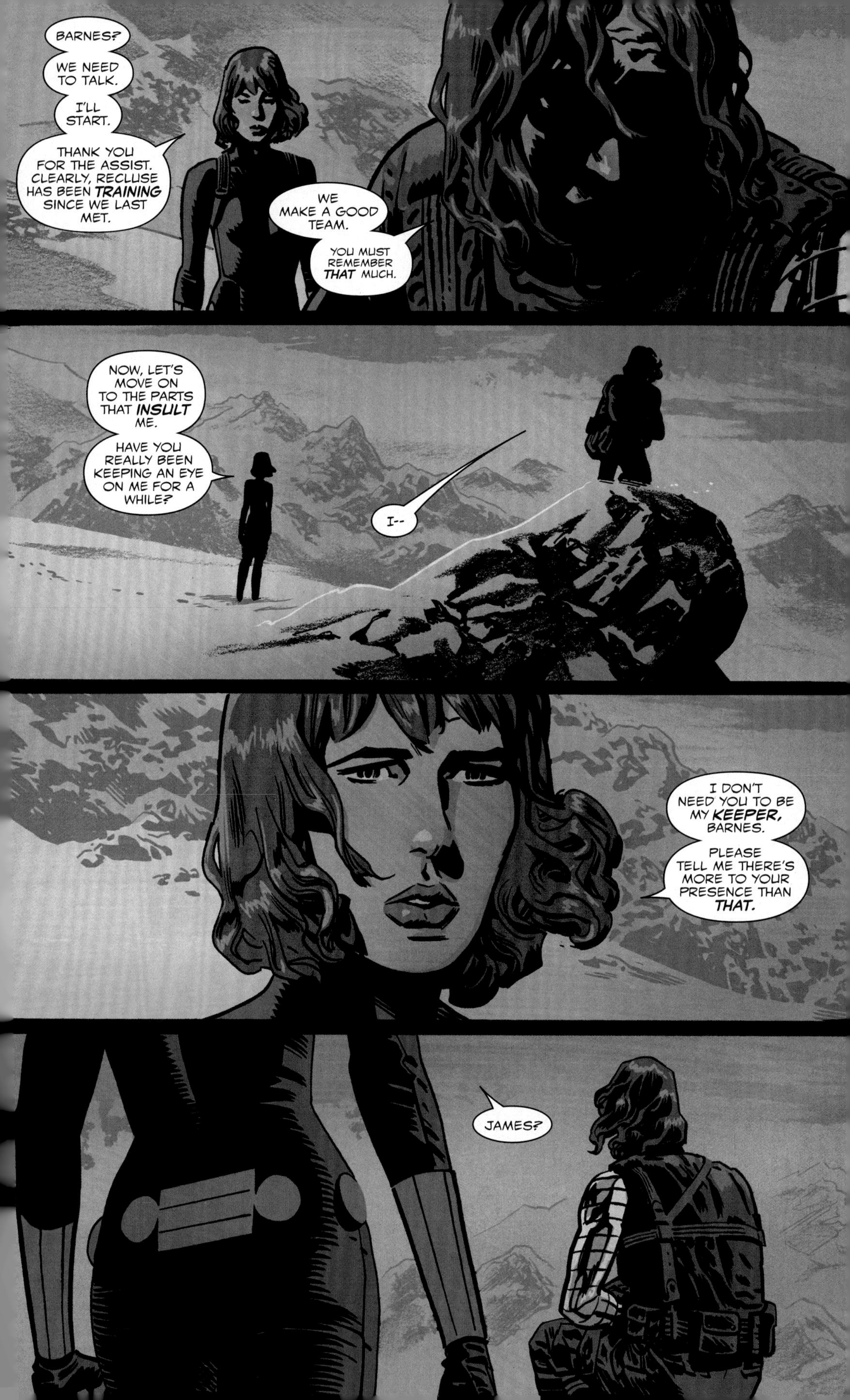
BARNES?
WE NEED TO TALK.
I'LL START.
THANK YOU FOR THE ASSIST. CLEARLY, RECLUSE HAS BEEN TRAINING SINCE WE LAST MET.
WE MAKE A GOOD TEAM.
YOU MUST REMEMBER THAT MUCH.
NOW, LET'S MOVE ON TO THE PARTS THAT INSULT ME.
HAVE YOU REALLY BEEN KEEPING AN EYE ON ME FOR A WHILE?
I--
I DON'T NEED YOU TO BE MY KEEPER, BARNES.
PLEASE TELL ME THERE'S MORE TO YOUR PRESENCE THAN THAT.
JAMES?

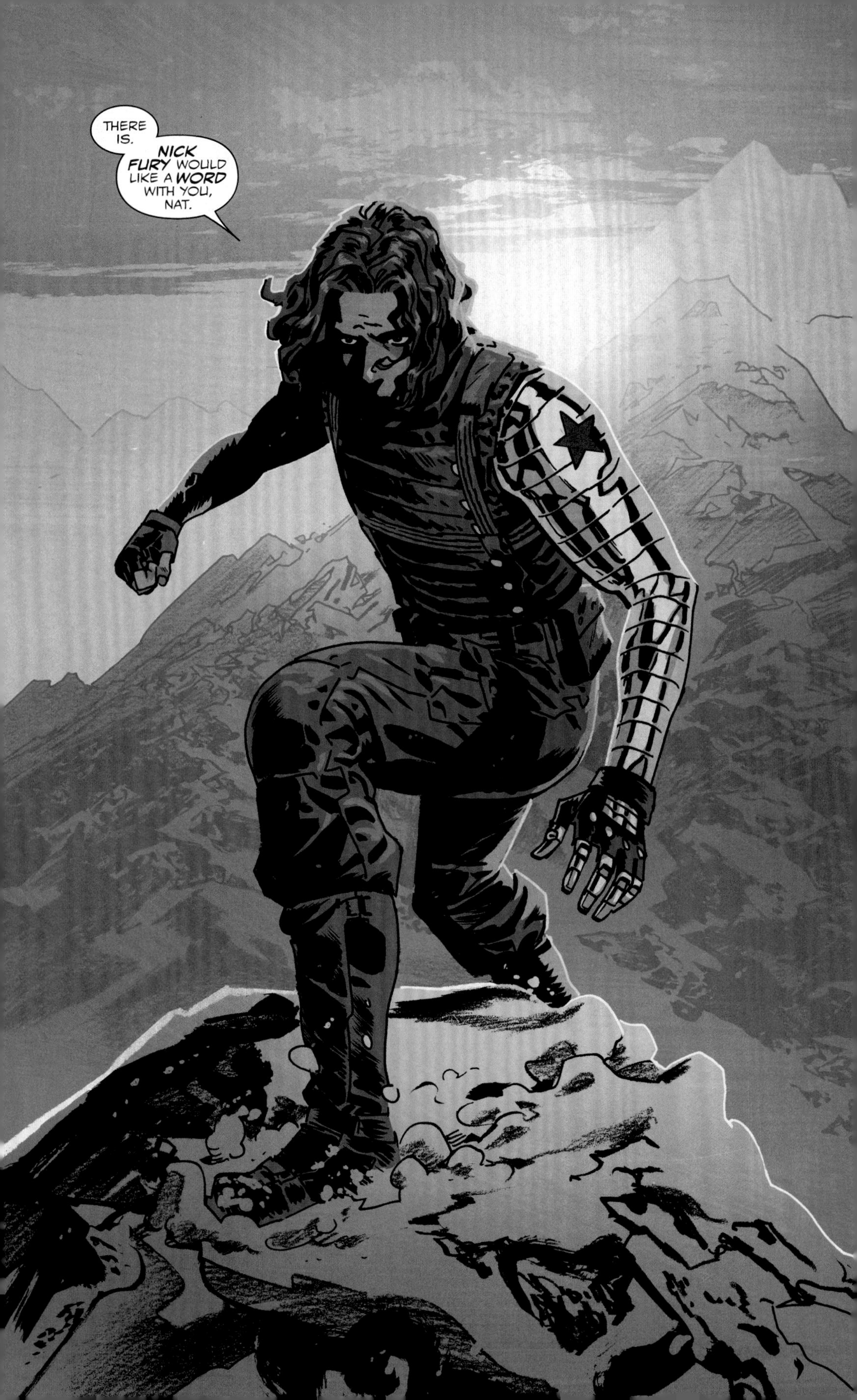
THERE IS. NICK FURY WOULD LIKE A WORD WITH YOU, NAT.

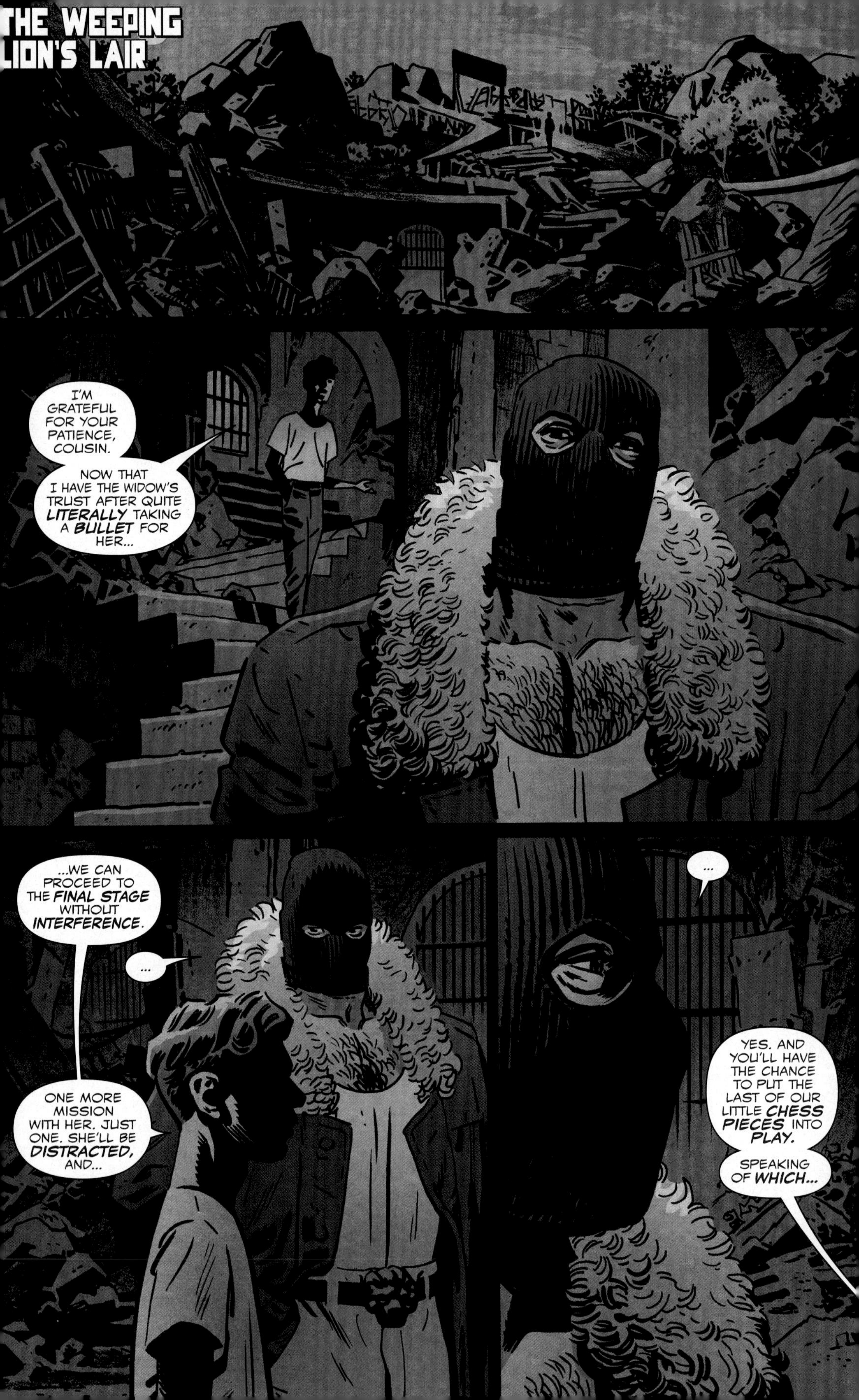
THE WEEPING LION'S LAIR
I'M GRATEFUL FOR YOUR PATIENCE, COUSIN.
NOW THAT I HAVE THE WIDOW'S TRUST AFTER QUITE LITERALLY TAKING A BULLET FOR HER...
...WE CAN PROCEED TO THE FINAL STAGE WITHOUT INTERFERENCE.
...
ONE MORE MISSION WITH HER. JUST ONE. SHE'LL BE DISTRACTED, AND...
...
YES. AND YOU'LL HAVE THE CHANCE TO PUT THE LAST OF OUR LITTLE CHESS PIECES INTO PLAY.
SPEAKING OF WHICH...

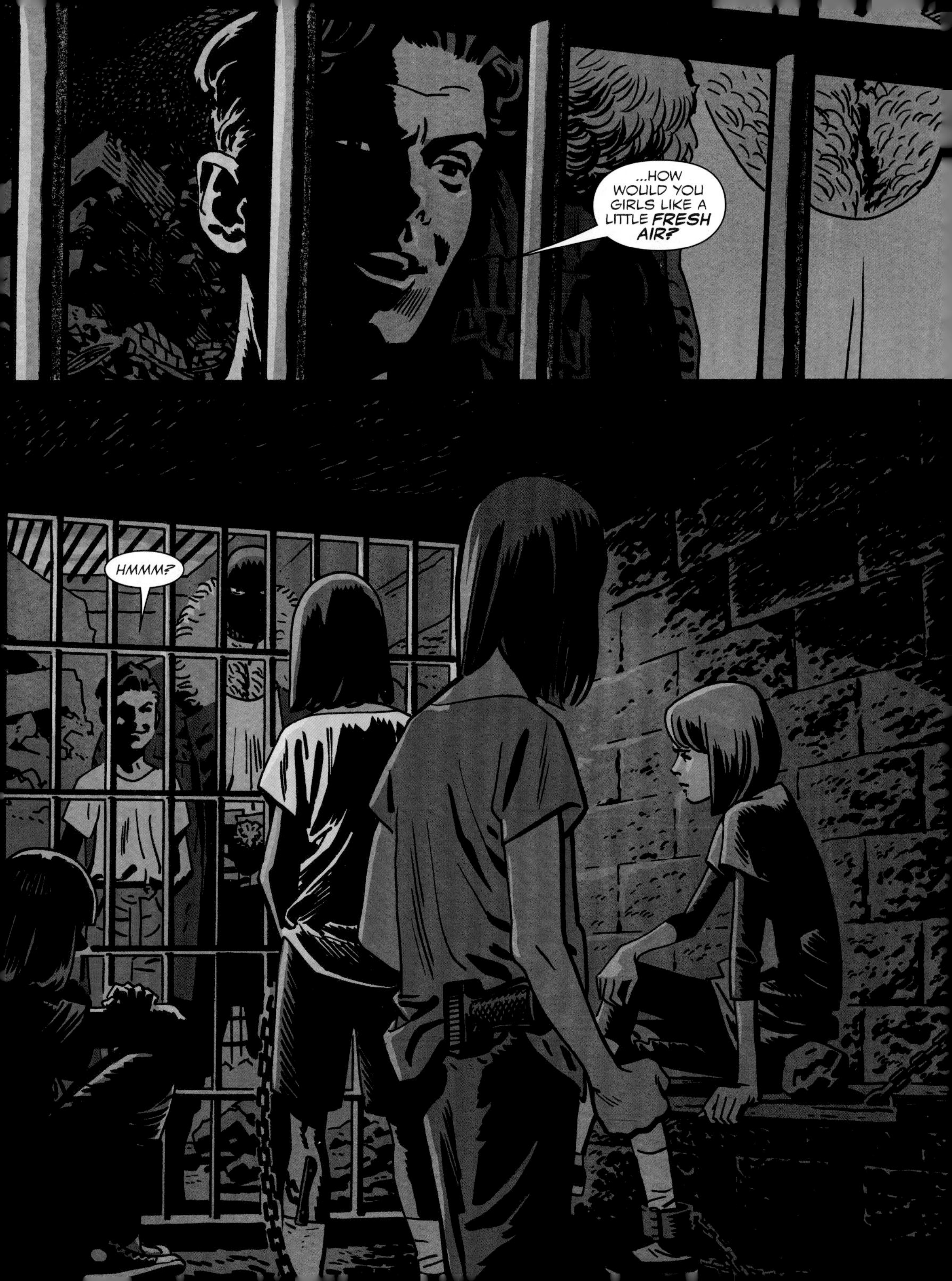
...HOW WOULD YOU GIRLS LIKE A LITTLE FRESH AIR?
HMMM?

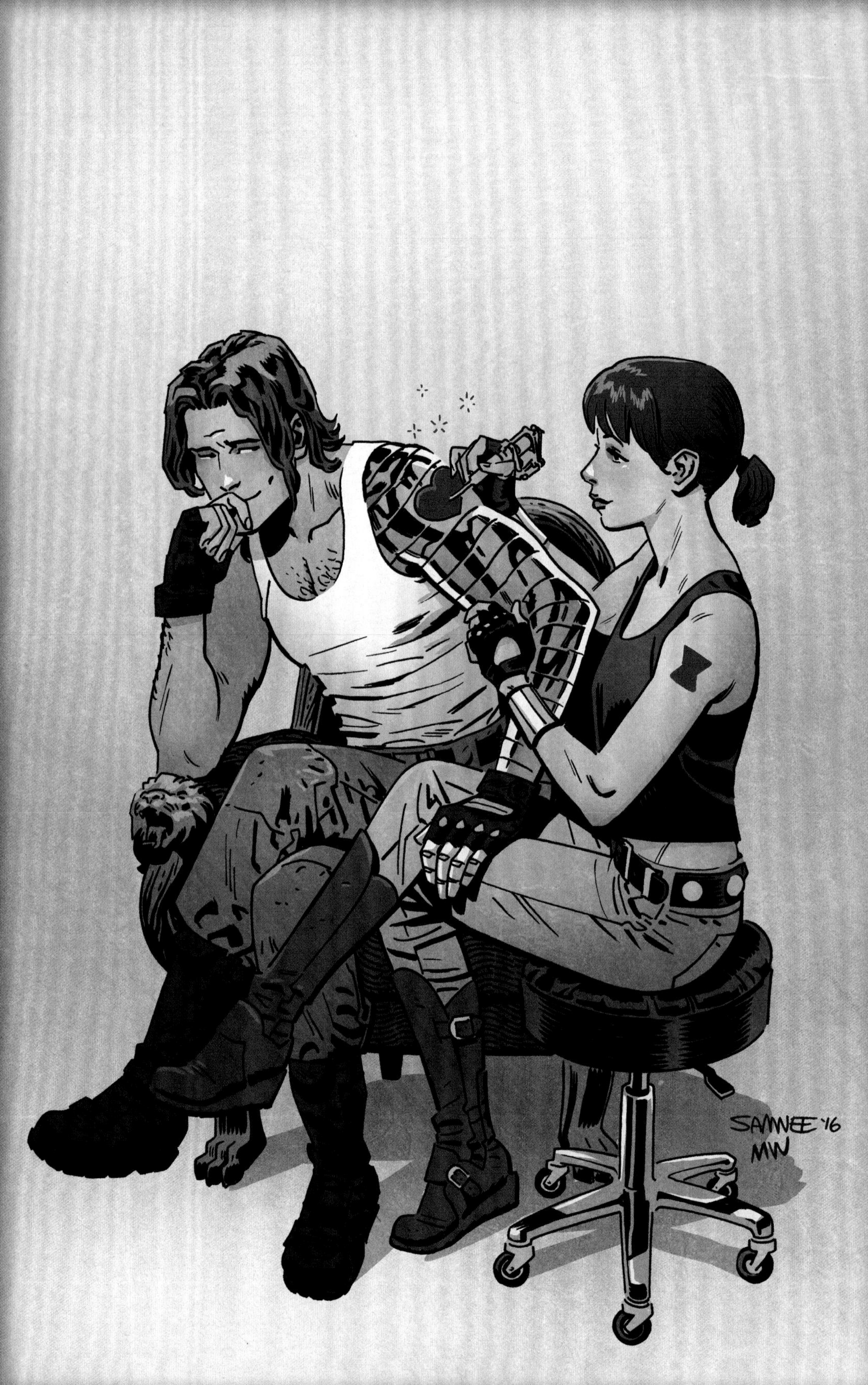
SAMNEE '16
MW

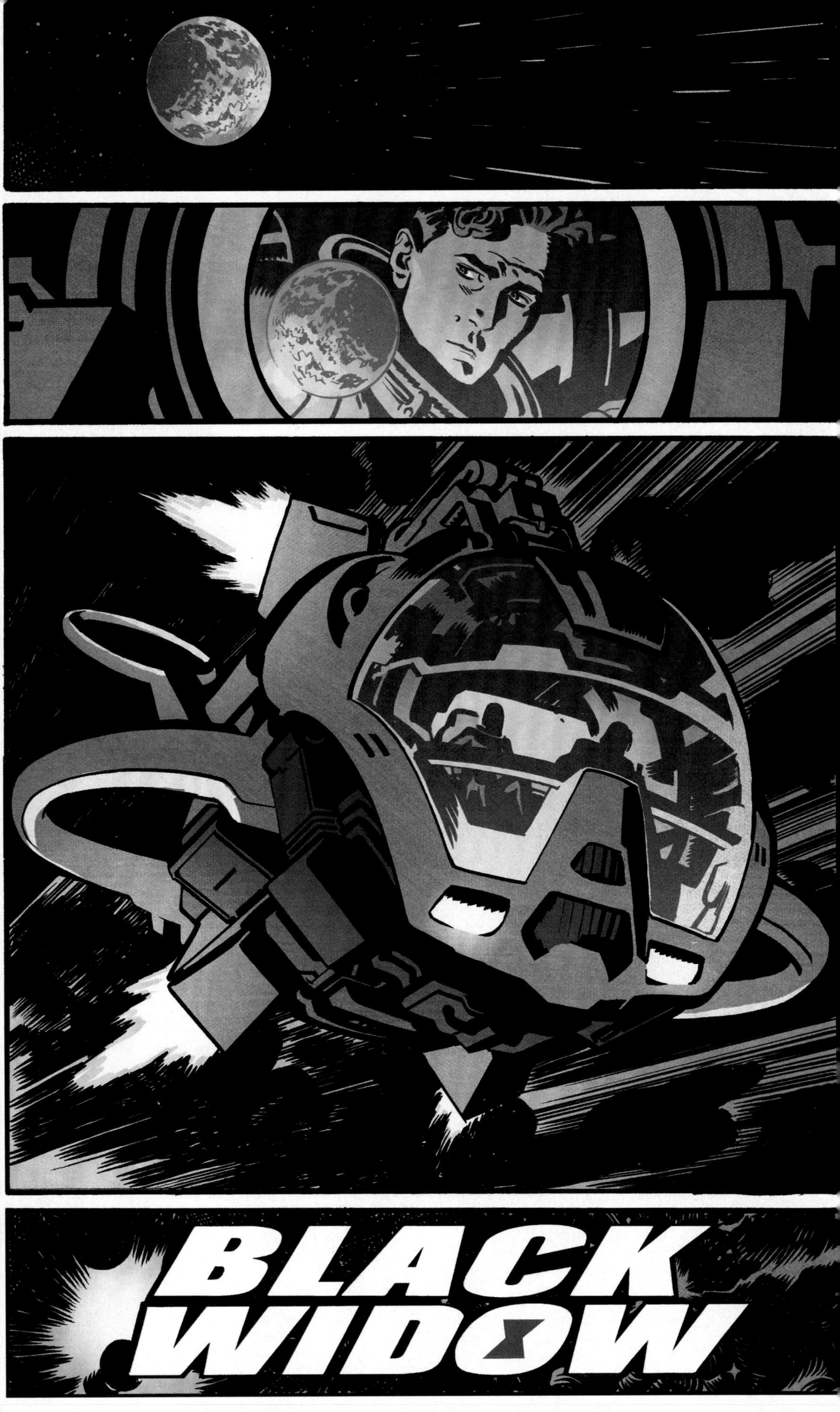
BLACK WIDOW

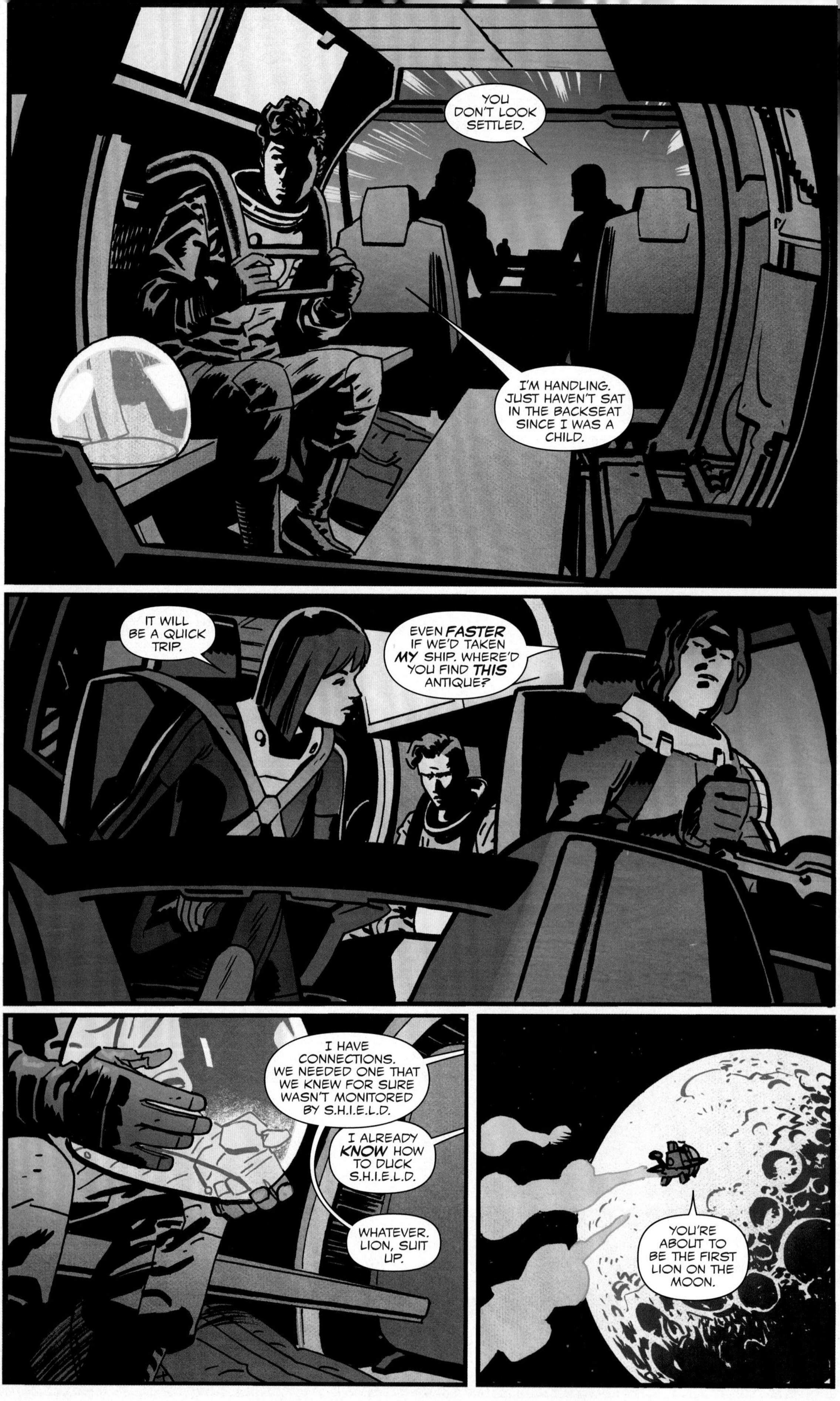
YOU DON'T LOOK SETTLED.
I'M HANDLING. JUST HAVEN'T SAT IN THE BACKSEAT SINCE I WAS A CHILD.
IT WILL BE A QUICK TRIP.
EVEN **FASTER** IF WE'D TAKEN **MY** SHIP. WHERE'D YOU FIND **THIS** ANTIQUE?
I HAVE CONNECTIONS. WE NEEDED ONE THAT WE KNEW FOR SURE WASN'T MONITORED BY S.H.I.E.L.D.
I ALREADY **KNOW** HOW TO DUCK S.H.I.E.L.D.
WHATEVER. LION, SUIT UP.
YOU'RE ABOUT TO BE THE FIRST LION ON THE MOON.

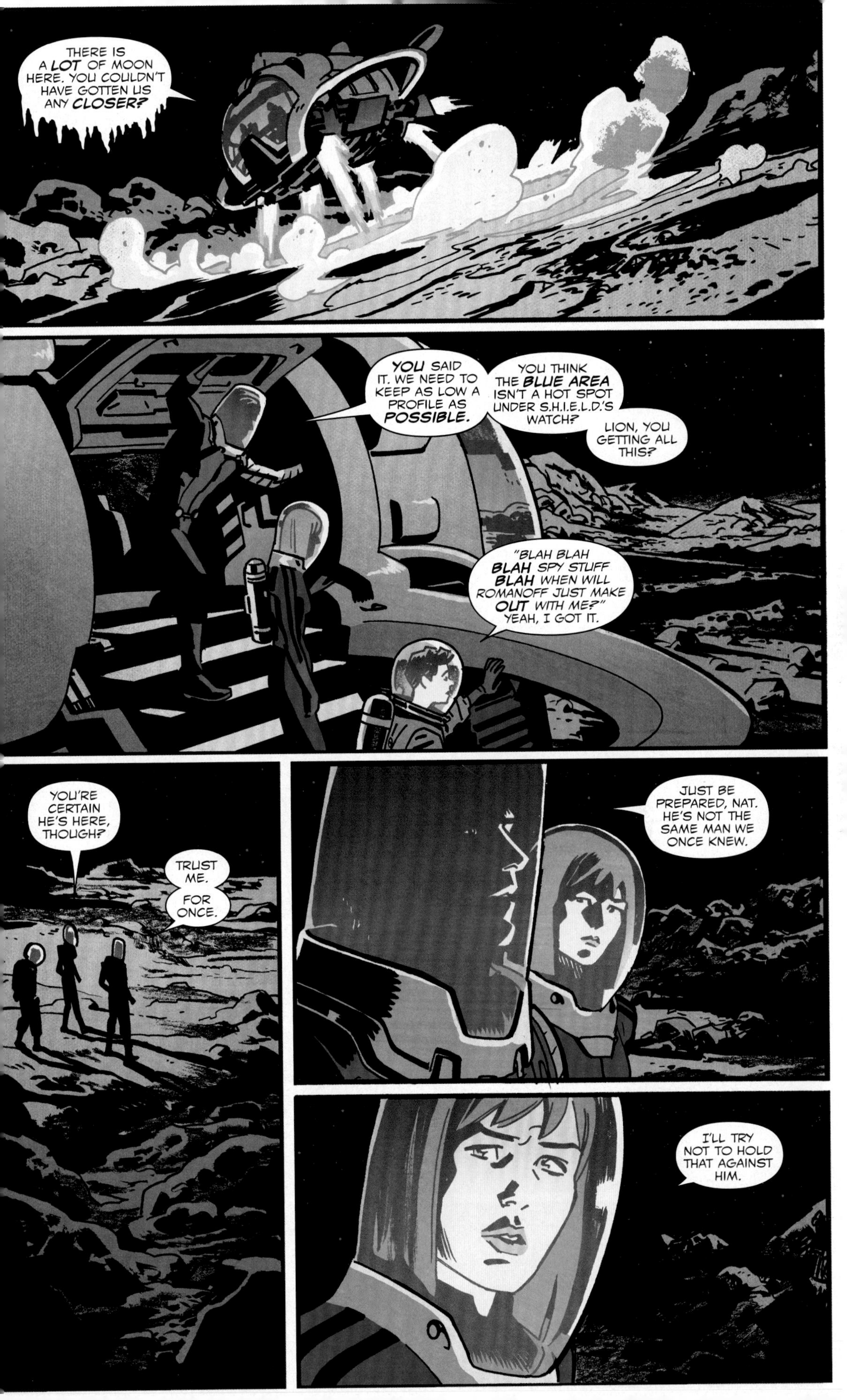
THERE IS A LOT OF MOON HERE. YOU COULDN'T HAVE GOTTEN US ANY CLOSER?
YOU SAID IT. WE NEED TO KEEP AS LOW A PROFILE AS POSSIBLE.
YOU THINK THE BLUE AREA ISN'T A HOT SPOT UNDER S.H.I.E.L.D.'S WATCH?
LION, YOU GETTING ALL THIS?
"BLAH BLAH BLAH SPY STUFF BLAH WHEN WILL ROMANOFF JUST MAKE OUT WITH ME?" YEAH, I GOT IT.
YOU'RE CERTAIN HE'S HERE, THOUGH?
TRUST ME.
FOR ONCE.
JUST BE PREPARED, NAT. HE'S NOT THE SAME MAN WE ONCE KNEW.
I'LL TRY NOT TO HOLD THAT AGAINST HIM.

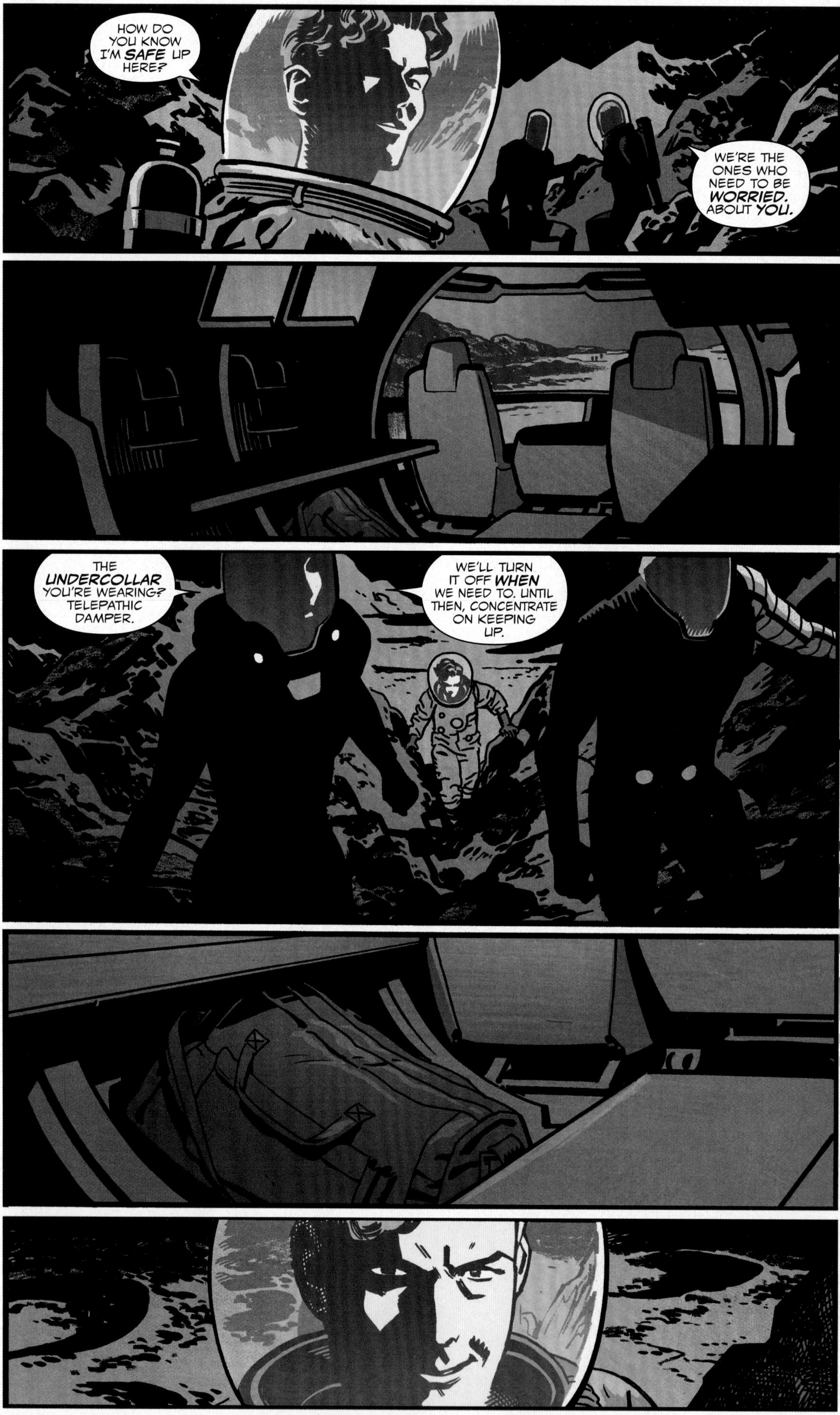
HOW DO YOU KNOW I'M SAFE UP HERE?
WE'RE THE ONES WHO NEED TO BE WORRIED. ABOUT YOU.
THE UNDERCOLLAR YOU'RE WEARING? TELEPATHIC DAMPER.
WE'LL TURN IT OFF WHEN WE NEED TO. UNTIL THEN, CONCENTRATE ON KEEPING UP.

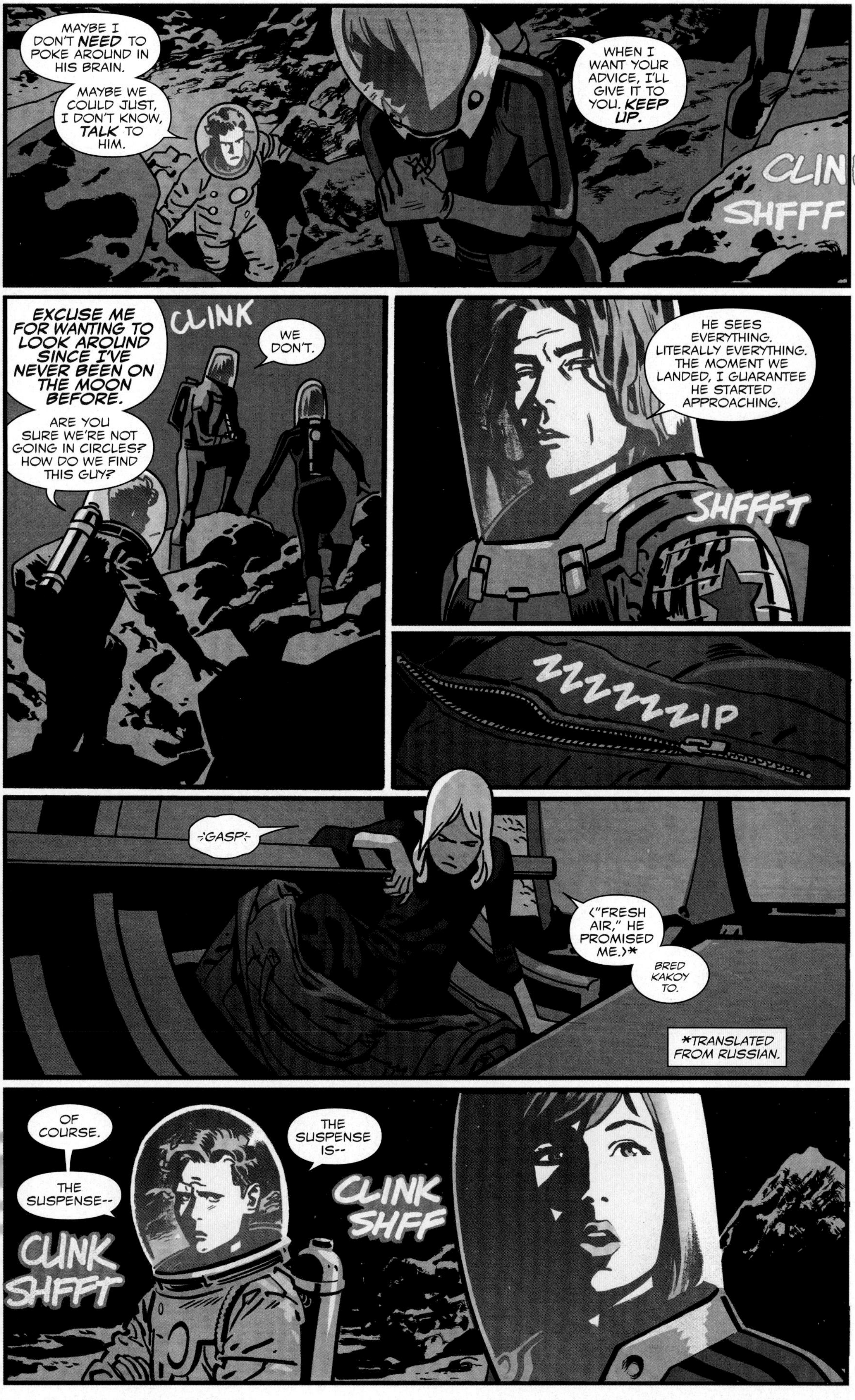
MAYBE I DON'T NEED TO POKE AROUND IN HIS BRAIN.
MAYBE WE COULD JUST, I DON'T KNOW, TALK TO HIM.
WHEN I WANT YOUR ADVICE, I'LL GIVE IT TO YOU. KEEP UP.
CLINK
SHFFF
EXCUSE ME FOR WANTING TO LOOK AROUND SINCE I'VE NEVER BEEN ON THE MOON BEFORE.
CLINK
WE DON'T.
ARE YOU SURE WE'RE NOT GOING IN CIRCLES? HOW DO WE FIND THIS GUY?
HE SEES EVERYTHING. LITERALLY EVERYTHING. THE MOMENT WE LANDED, I GUARANTEE HE STARTED APPROACHING.
SHFFFT
ZZZZZZZIP
GASP
<"FRESH AIR," HE PROMISED ME.>*
BRED KAKOY TO.
*TRANSLATED FROM RUSSIAN.
OF COURSE.
THE SUSPENSE--
THE SUSPENSE IS--
CLINK
SHFF
CLINK
SHFFT

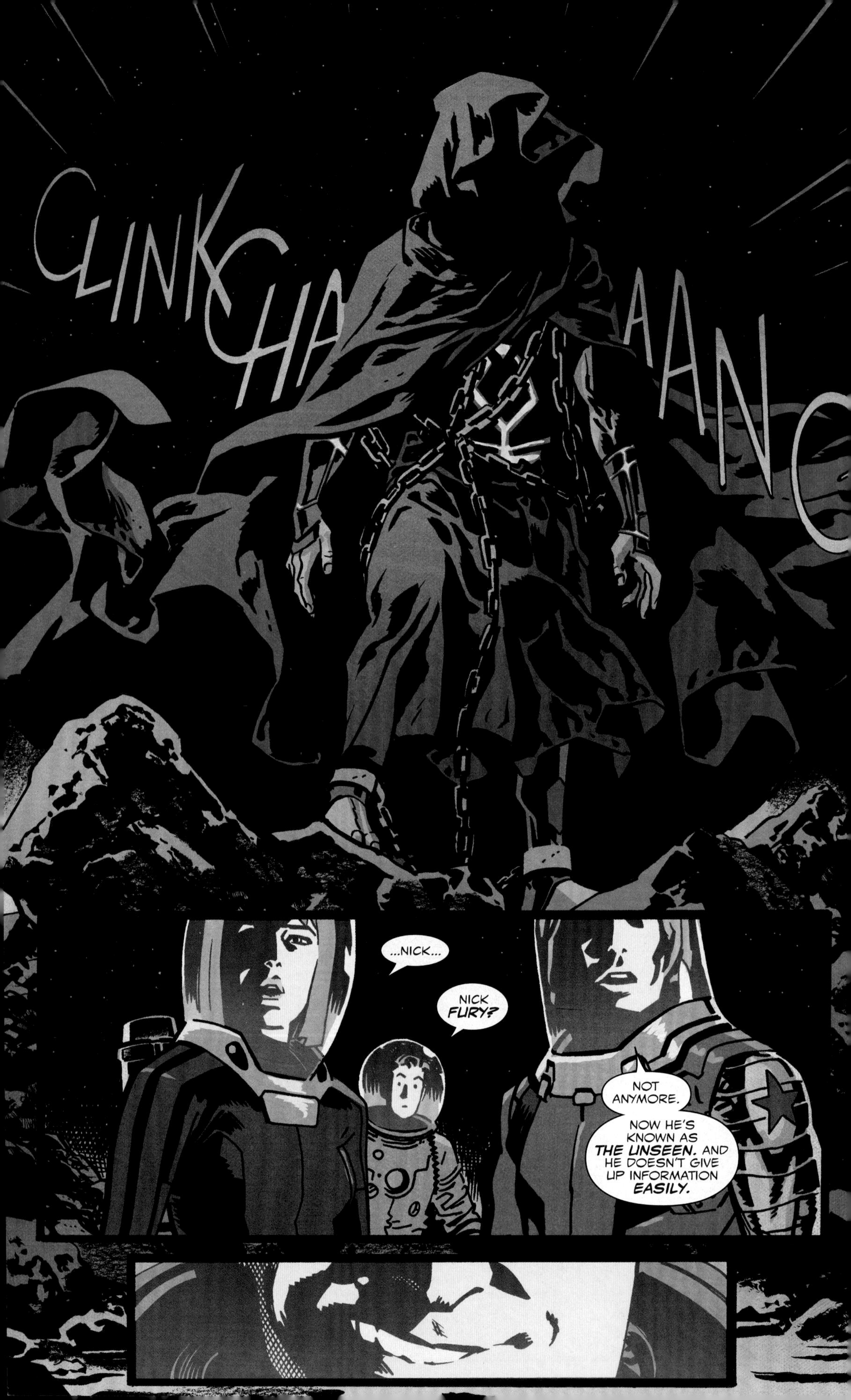
CLINK CHA AANG
...NICK...
NICK FURY?
NOT ANYMORE.
NOW HE'S KNOWN AS THE UNSEEN. AND HE DOESN'T GIVE UP INFORMATION EASILY.

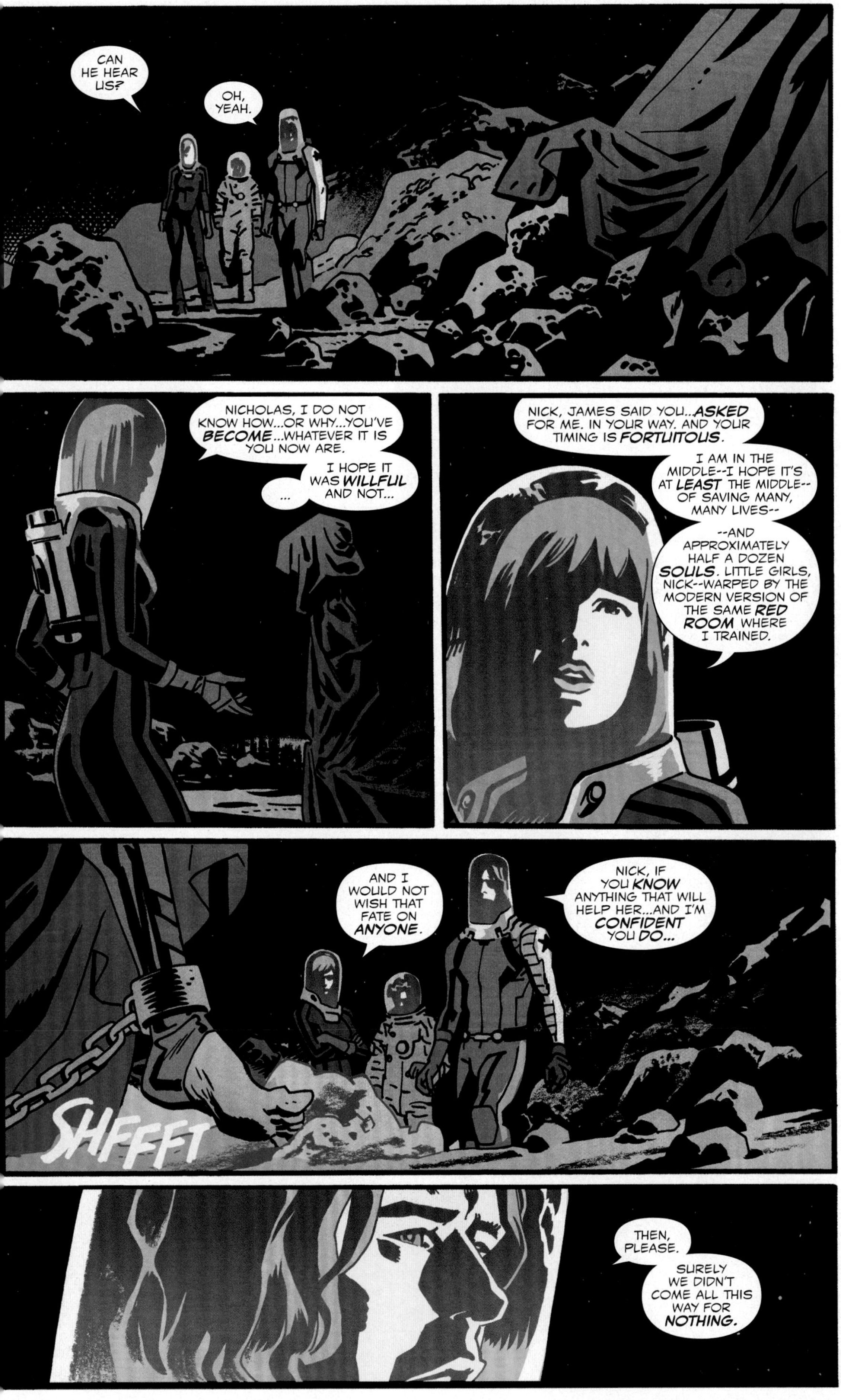
CAN HE HEAR US?
OH, YEAH.
NICHOLAS, I DO NOT KNOW HOW...OR WHY...YOU'VE BECOME...WHATEVER IT IS YOU NOW ARE.
I HOPE IT WAS WILLFUL AND NOT...
...
NICK, JAMES SAID YOU...ASKED FOR ME. IN YOUR WAY. AND YOUR TIMING IS FORTUITOUS.
I AM IN THE MIDDLE--I HOPE IT'S AT LEAST THE MIDDLE--OF SAVING MANY, MANY LIVES--
--AND APPROXIMATELY HALF A DOZEN SOULS. LITTLE GIRLS, NICK--WARPED BY THE MODERN VERSION OF THE SAME RED ROOM WHERE I TRAINED.
AND I WOULD NOT WISH THAT FATE ON ANYONE.
NICK, IF YOU KNOW ANYTHING THAT WILL HELP HER...AND I'M CONFIDENT YOU DO...
SHFFFT
THEN, PLEASE.
SURELY WE DIDN'T COME ALL THIS WAY FOR NOTHING.

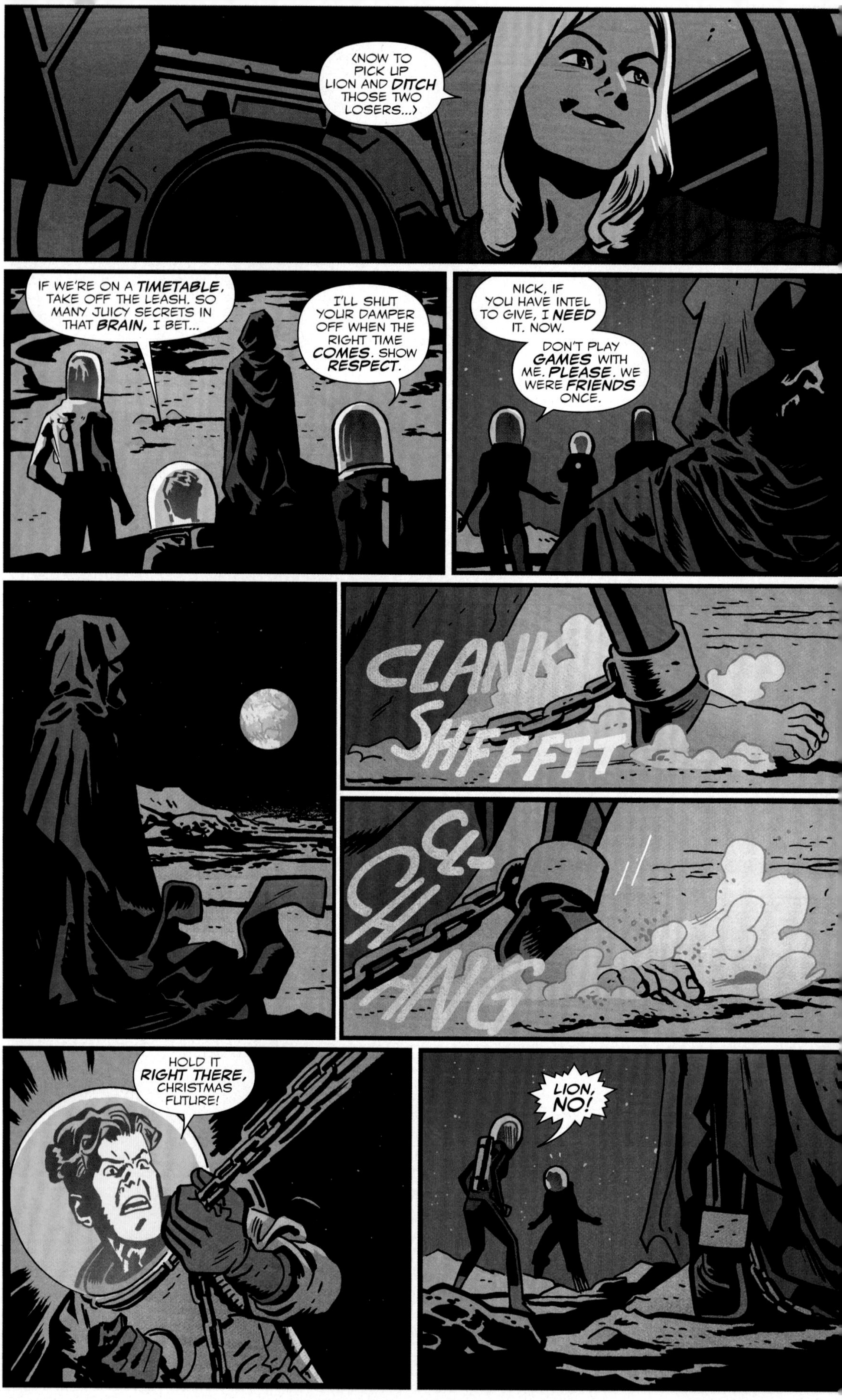

‹NOW TO PICK UP LION AND DITCH THOSE TWO LOSERS...›
IF WE'RE ON A TIMETABLE, TAKE OFF THE LEASH. SO MANY JUICY SECRETS IN THAT BRAIN, I BET...
I'LL SHUT YOUR DAMPER OFF WHEN THE RIGHT TIME COMES. SHOW RESPECT.
NICK, IF YOU HAVE INTEL TO GIVE, I NEED IT. NOW.
DON'T PLAY GAMES WITH ME. PLEASE. WE WERE FRIENDS ONCE.
CLANK
SHFFFTT
CL-CHANG
HOLD IT RIGHT THERE, CHRISTMAS FUTURE!
LION, NO!

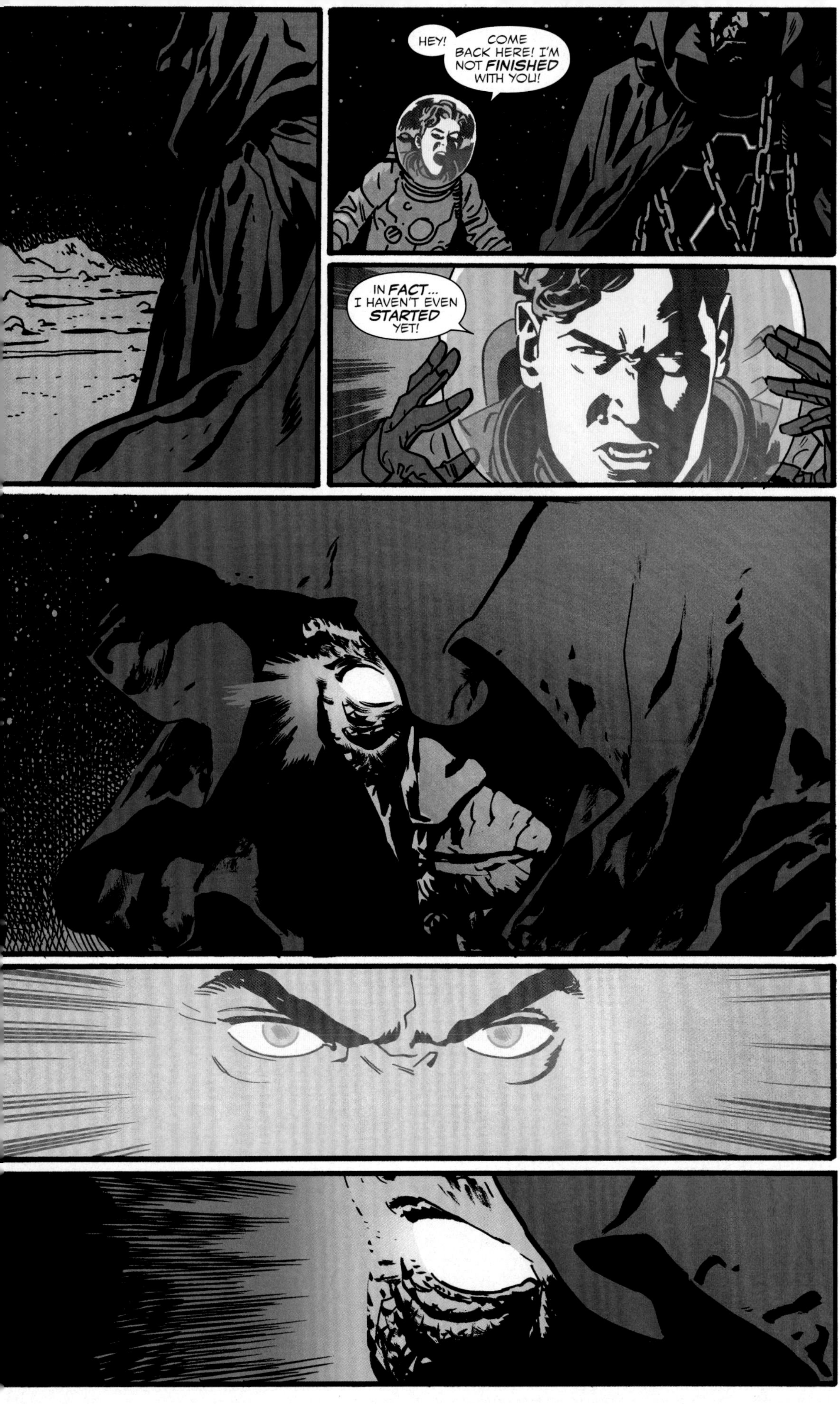
HEY!
COME BACK HERE! I'M NOT FINISHED WITH YOU!
IN FACT... I HAVEN'T EVEN STARTED YET!

OH... GOD... ...THE KNOWLEDGE...

...ALL THE KNOWLEDGE...

...ALL THERE IS...

IT'S... IT'S... BEAUTIFUL.

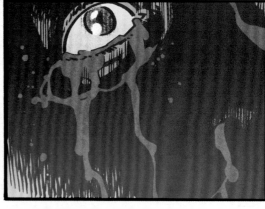

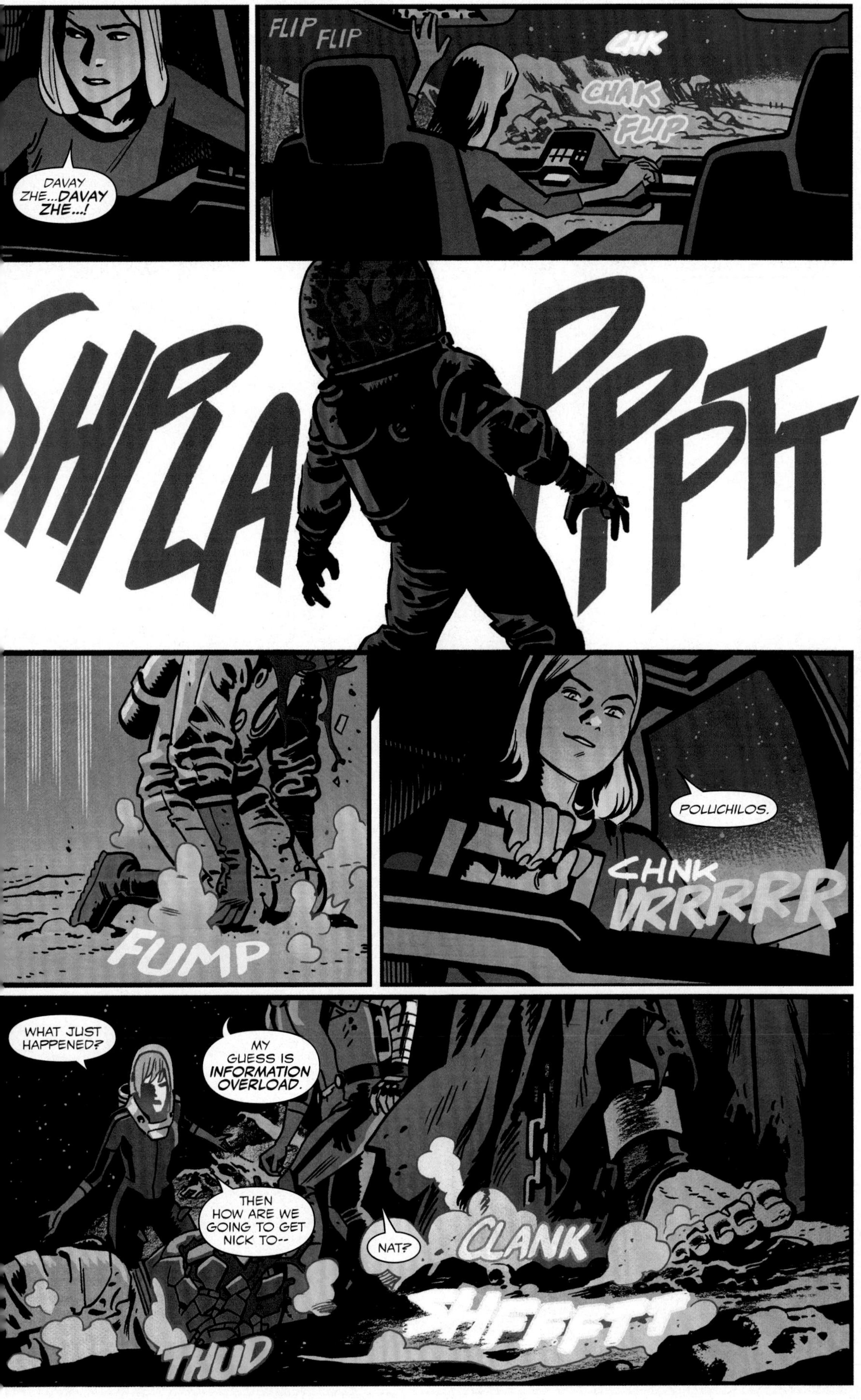
DAVAY ZHE...DAVAY ZHE...!
FLIP FLIP
CHK
CHAK
FLIP
SHPLA
PPPT
FUMP
POLUCHILOS.
CHNK
VRRRRR
WHAT JUST HAPPENED?
MY GUESS IS INFORMATION OVERLOAD.
THEN HOW ARE WE GOING TO GET NICK TO--
NAT?
CLANK
SHFFFT
THUD

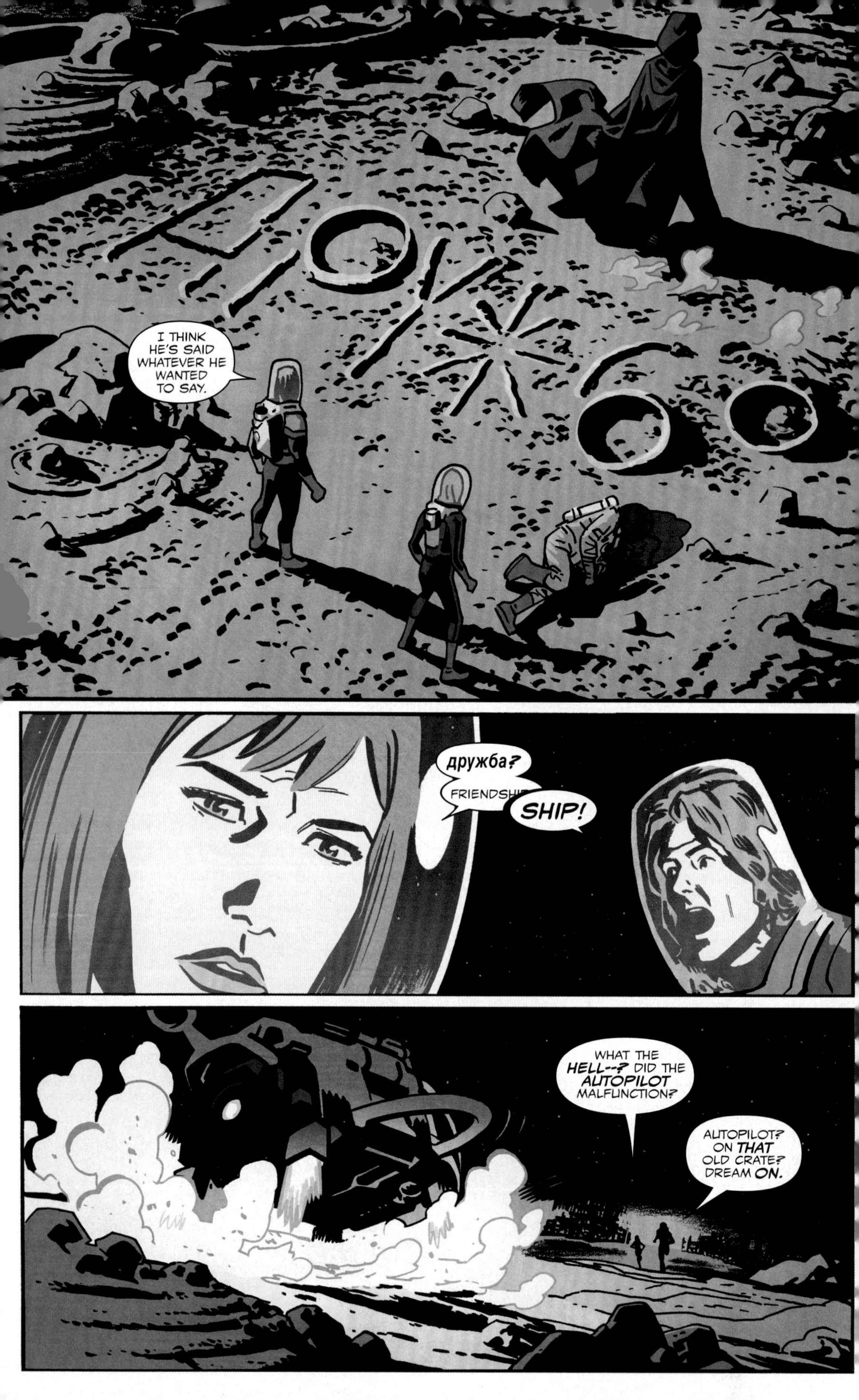
I THINK HE'S SAID WHATEVER HE WANTED TO SAY.
дружба?
FRIENDSHI--
SHIP!
WHAT THE HELL--? DID THE AUTOPILOT MALFUNCTION?
AUTOPILOT? ON THAT OLD CRATE? DREAM ON.

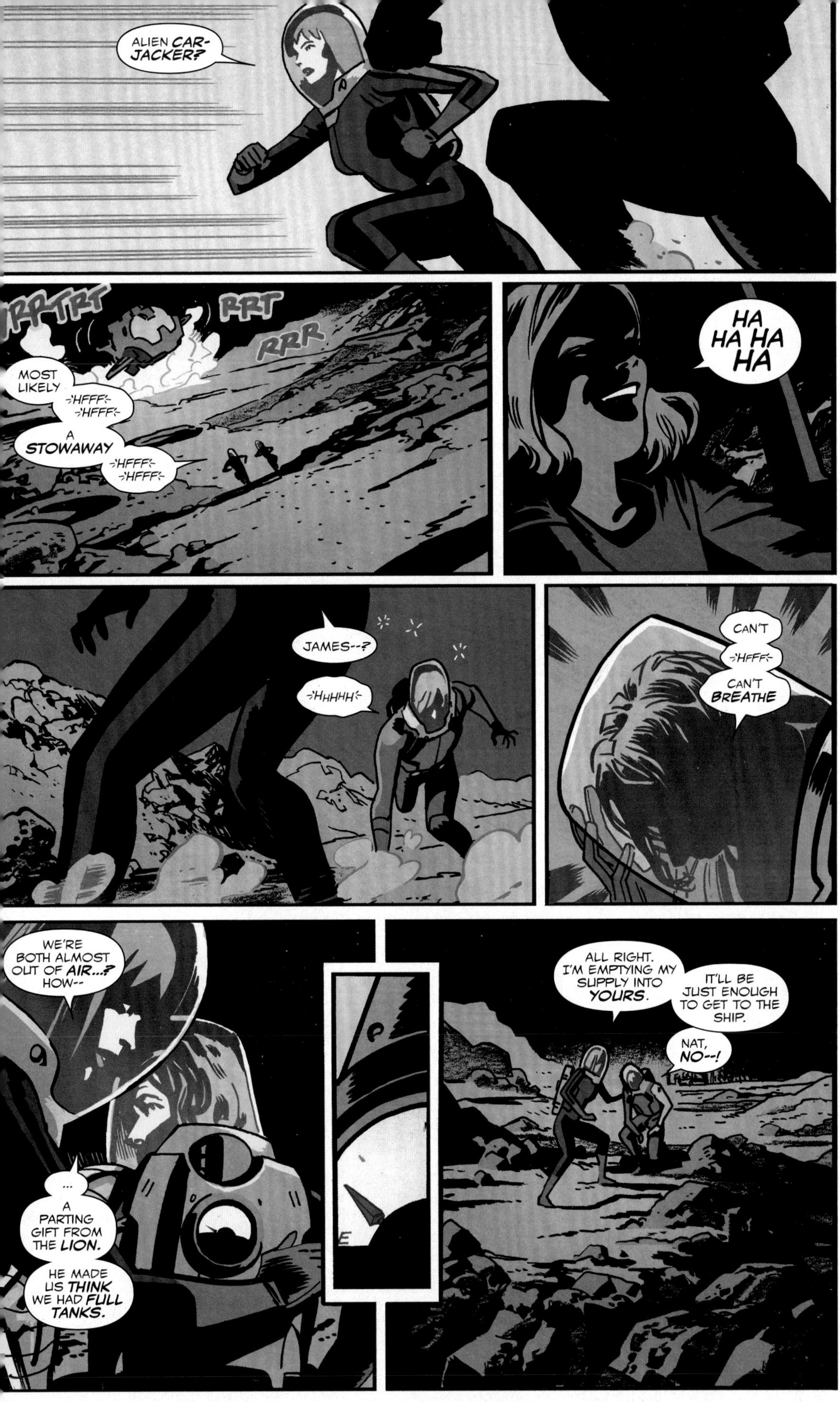
ALIEN CAR-JACKER?
RRRTRT
RRT
RRR
MOST LIKELY
-HFFF- -HFFF-
A STOWAWAY
-HFFF- -HFFF-
HA HA HA HA
JAMES--?
-HHHHH-
CAN'T
-HFFF-
CAN'T BREATHE
WE'RE BOTH ALMOST OUT OF AIR...? HOW--
...
A PARTING GIFT FROM THE LION.
HE MADE US THINK WE HAD FULL TANKS.
ALL RIGHT. I'M EMPTYING MY SUPPLY INTO YOURS.
IT'LL BE JUST ENOUGH TO GET TO THE SHIP.
NAT, NO--!

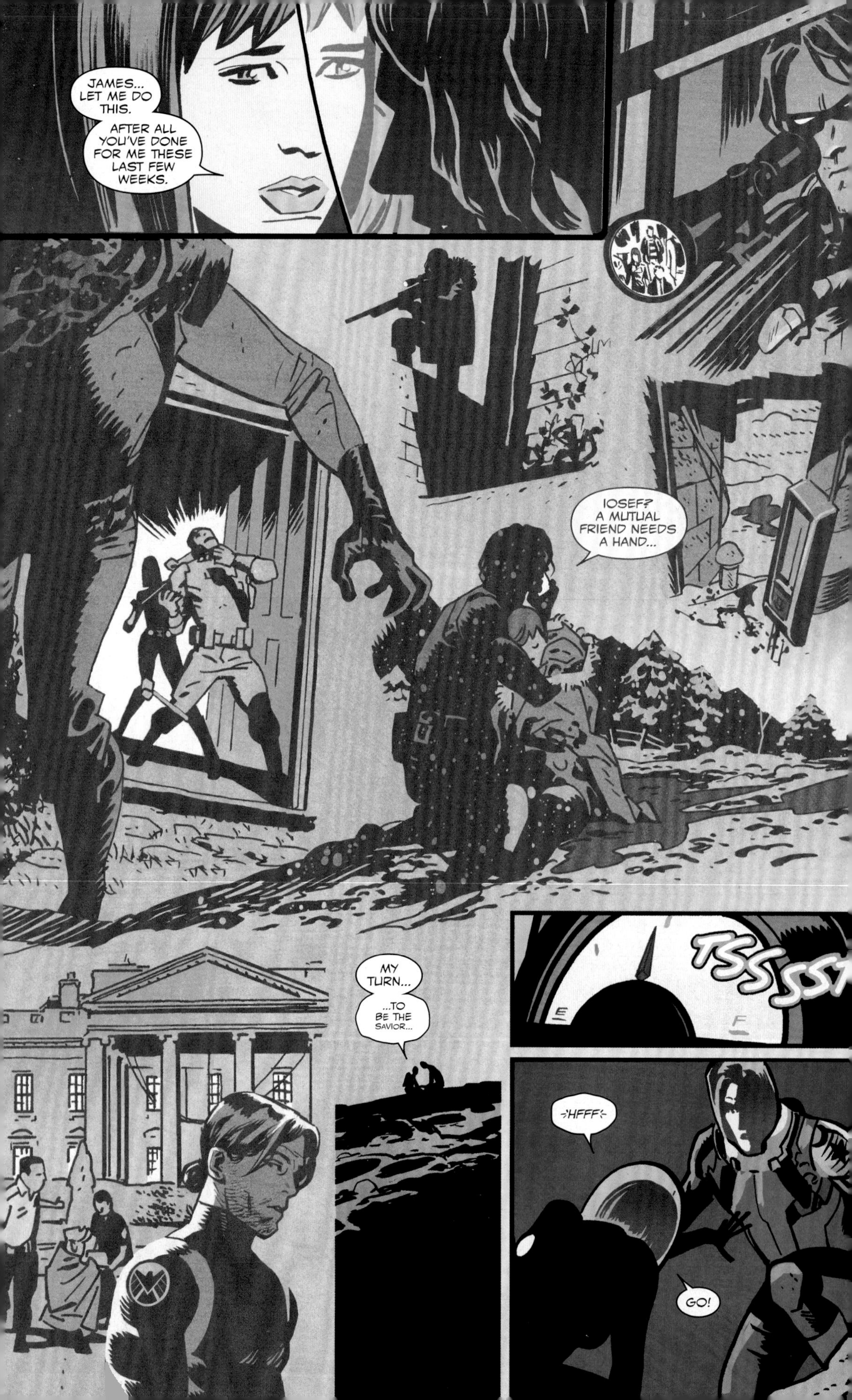
JAMES... LET ME DO THIS.
AFTER ALL YOU'VE DONE FOR ME THESE LAST FEW WEEKS.
IOSEF? A MUTUAL FRIEND NEEDS A HAND...
MY TURN...
...TO BE THE SAVIOR...
E
F
TSSSSS
-HFFF-
GO!

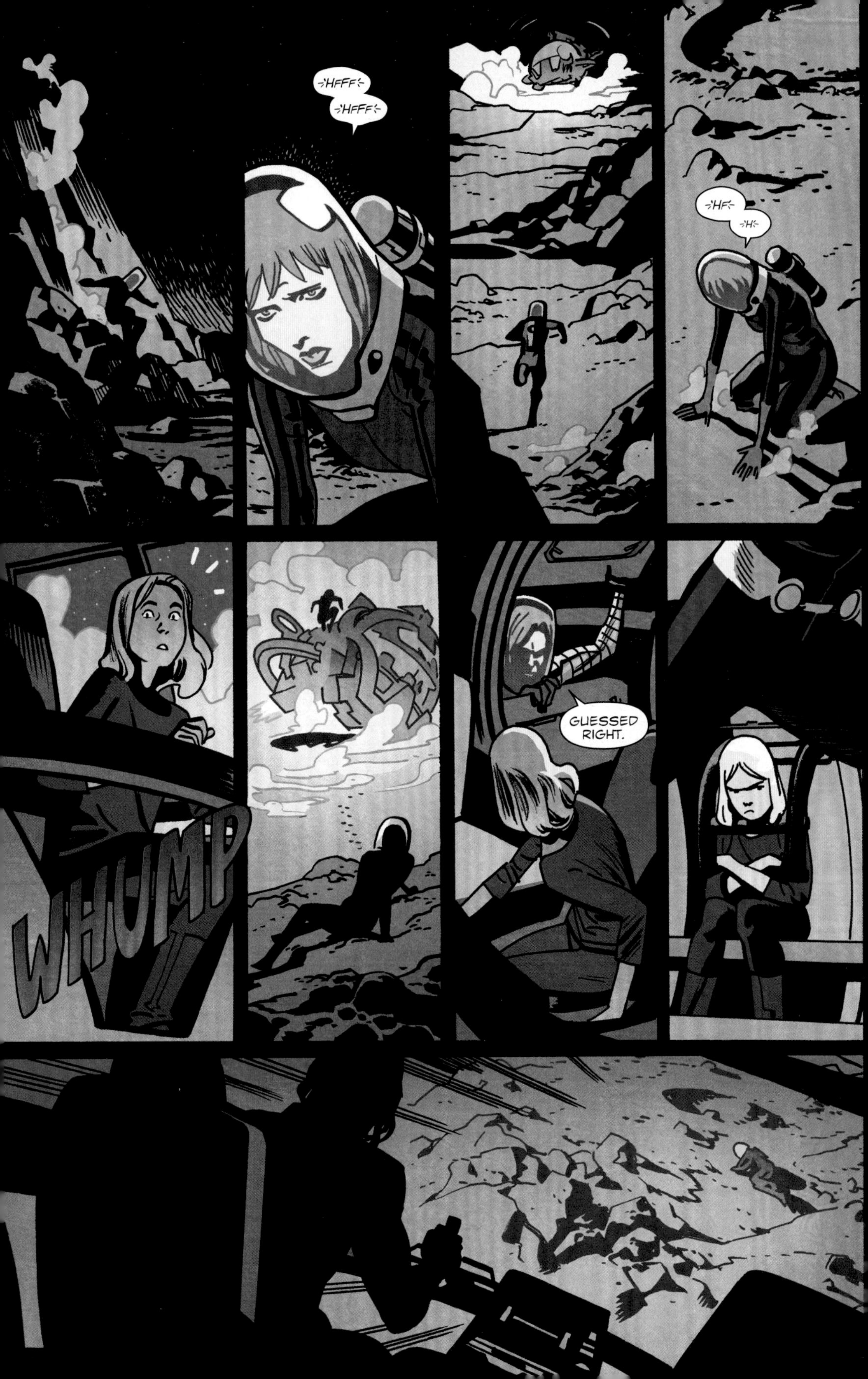
HFFF
HFFF
HF
H
WHUMP
GUESSED RIGHT.

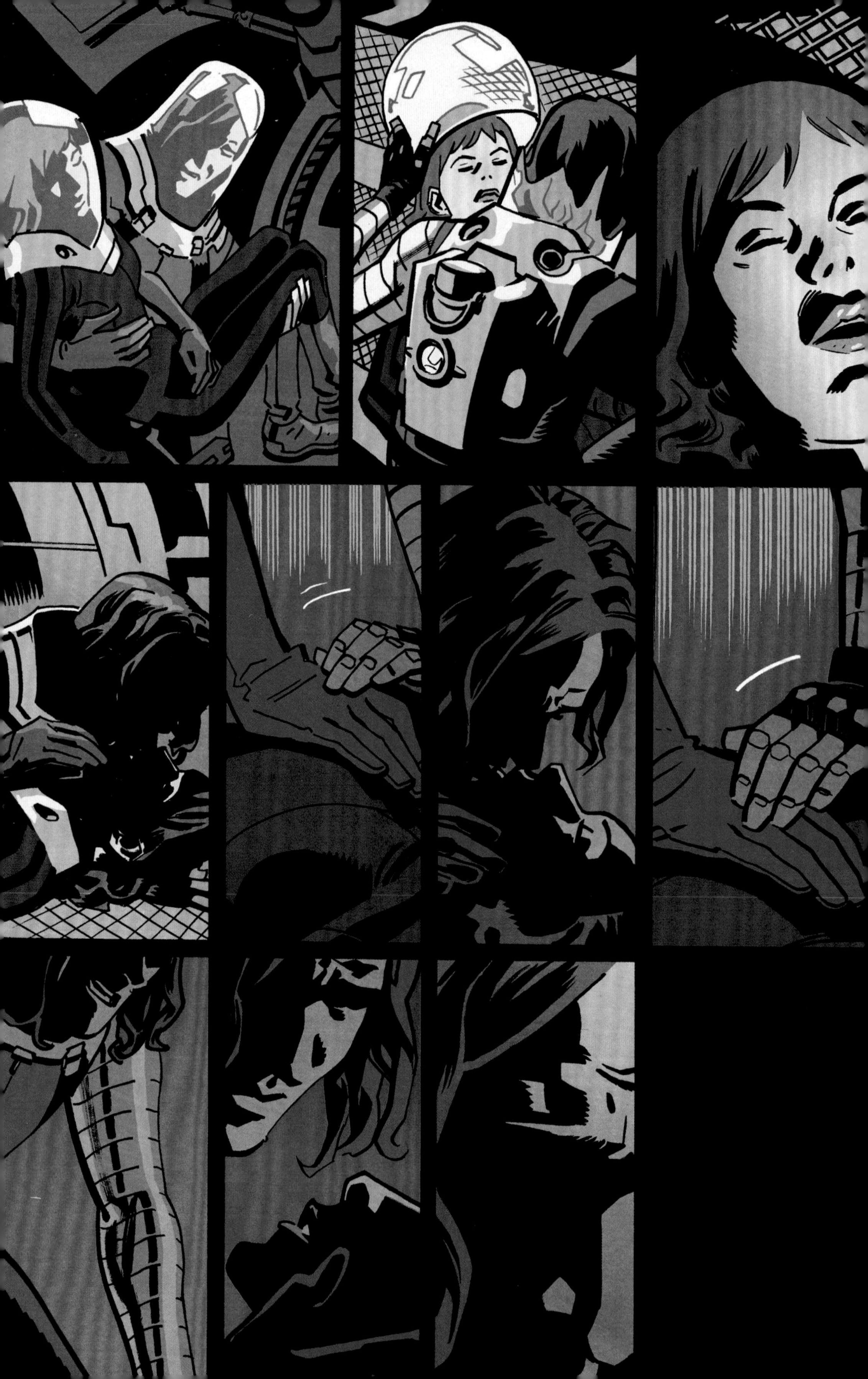

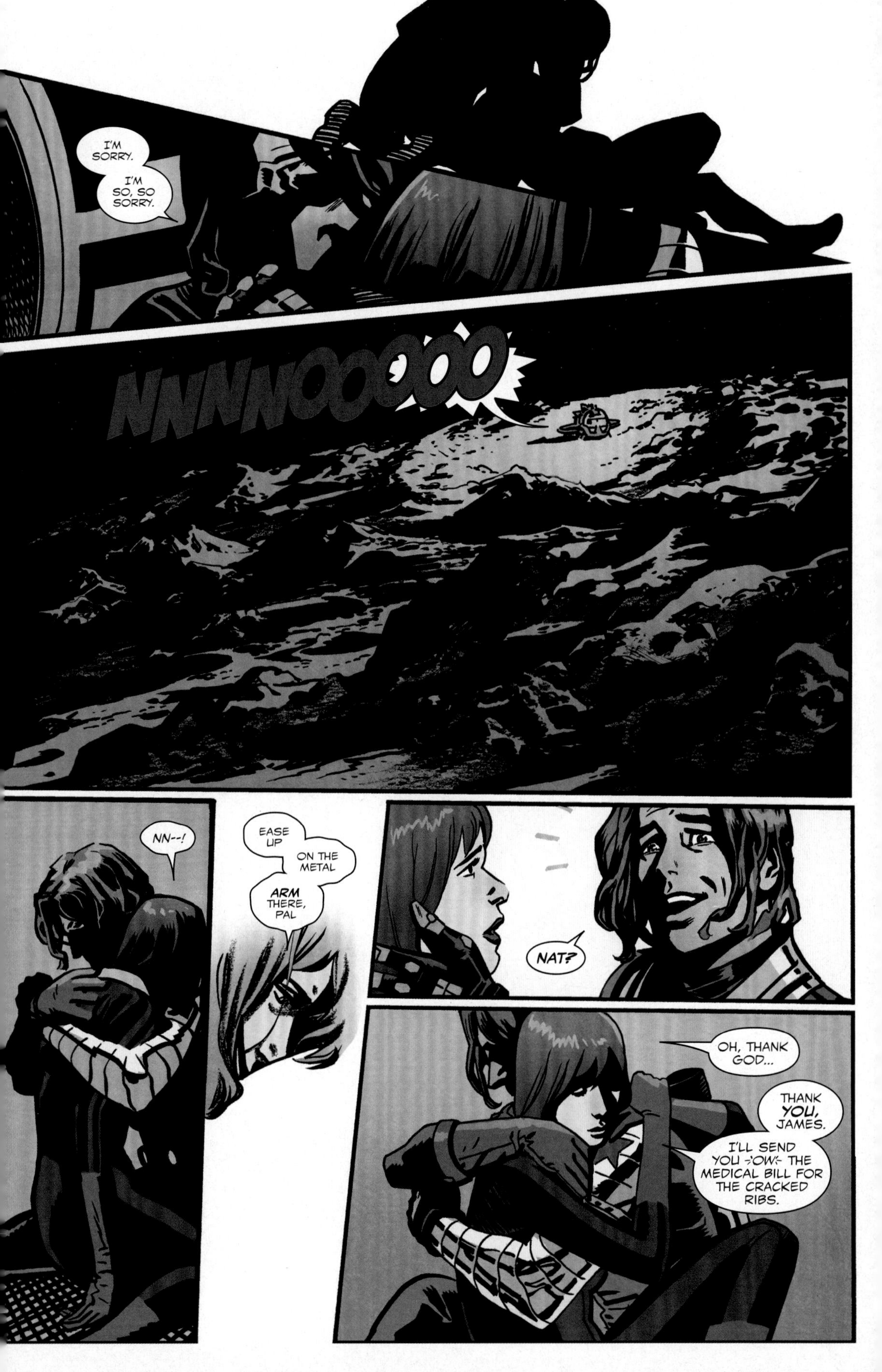
I'M SORRY.
I'M SO, SO SORRY.
NNNNOOOOOO
NN--!
EASE UP
ON THE METAL
ARM THERE, PAL
NAT?
OH, THANK GOD...
THANK YOU, JAMES.
I'LL SEND YOU -OW- THE MEDICAL BILL FOR THE CRACKED RIBS.

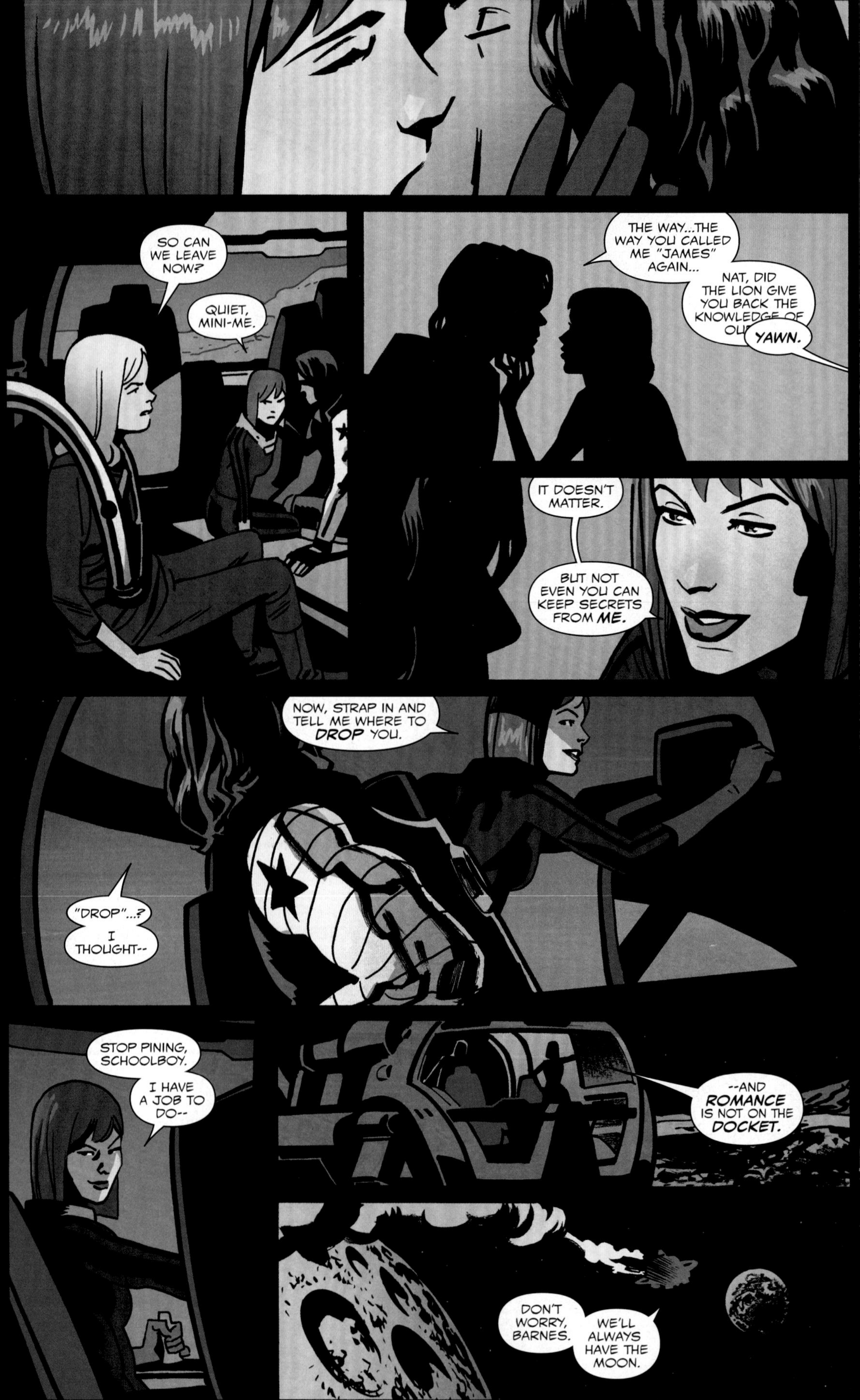
SO CAN WE LEAVE NOW?
QUIET, MINI-ME.
THE WAY...THE WAY YOU CALLED ME "JAMES" AGAIN...
NAT, DID THE LION GIVE YOU BACK THE KNOWLEDGE OF OU
YAWN.
IT DOESN'T MATTER.
BUT NOT EVEN YOU CAN KEEP SECRETS FROM ME.
NOW, STRAP IN AND TELL ME WHERE TO DROP YOU.
"DROP"...? I THOUGHT--
STOP PINING, SCHOOLBOY.
I HAVE A JOB TO DO--
--AND ROMANCE IS NOT ON THE DOCKET.
DON'T WORRY, BARNES.
WE'LL ALWAYS HAVE THE MOON.

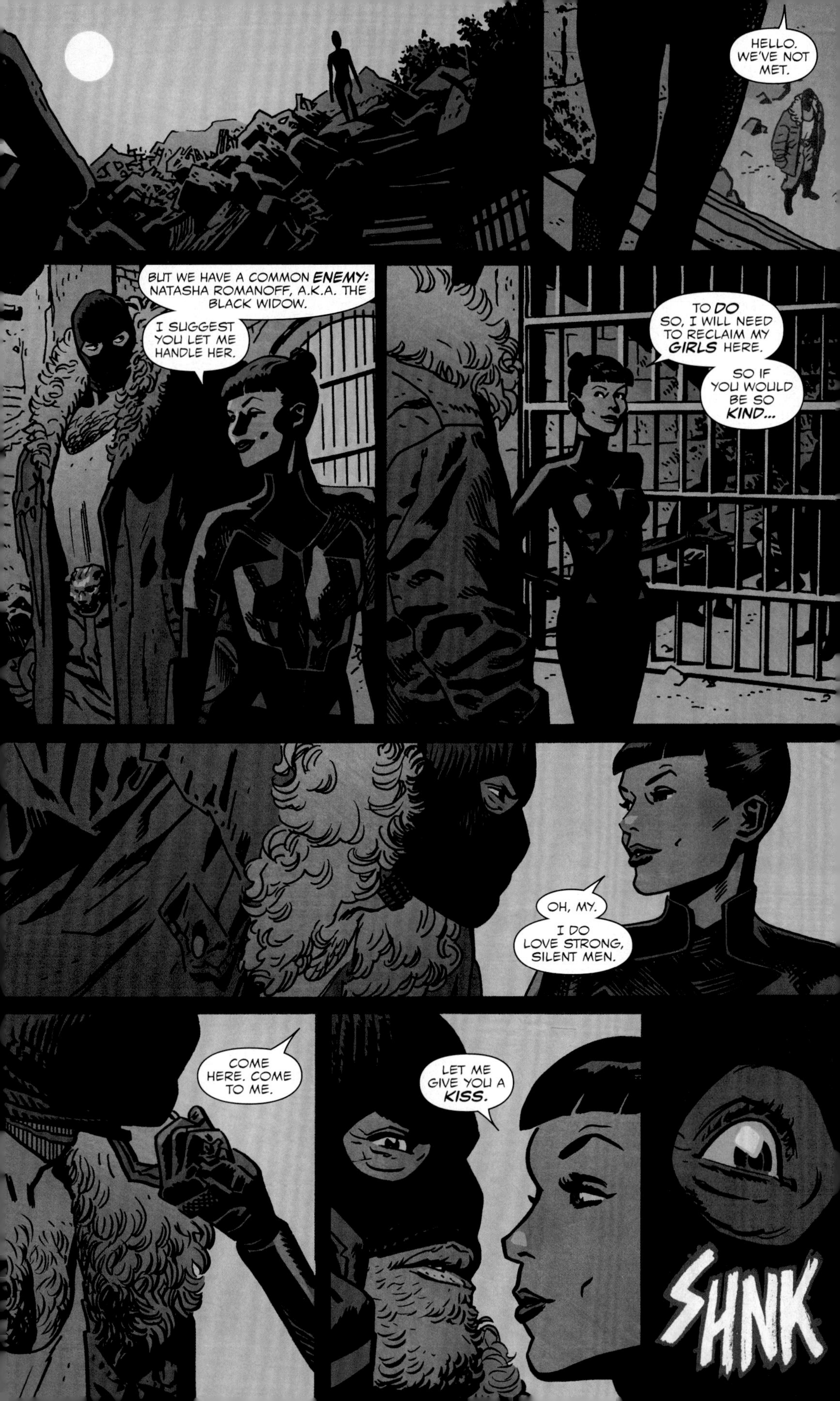
HELLO. WE'VE NOT MET.
BUT WE HAVE A COMMON ENEMY: NATASHA ROMANOFF, A.K.A. THE BLACK WIDOW.
I SUGGEST YOU LET ME HANDLE HER.
TO DO SO, I WILL NEED TO RECLAIM MY GIRLS HERE.
SO IF YOU WOULD BE SO KIND...
OH, MY.
I DO LOVE STRONG, SILENT MEN.
COME HERE. COME TO ME.
LET ME GIVE YOU A KISS.
SHNK

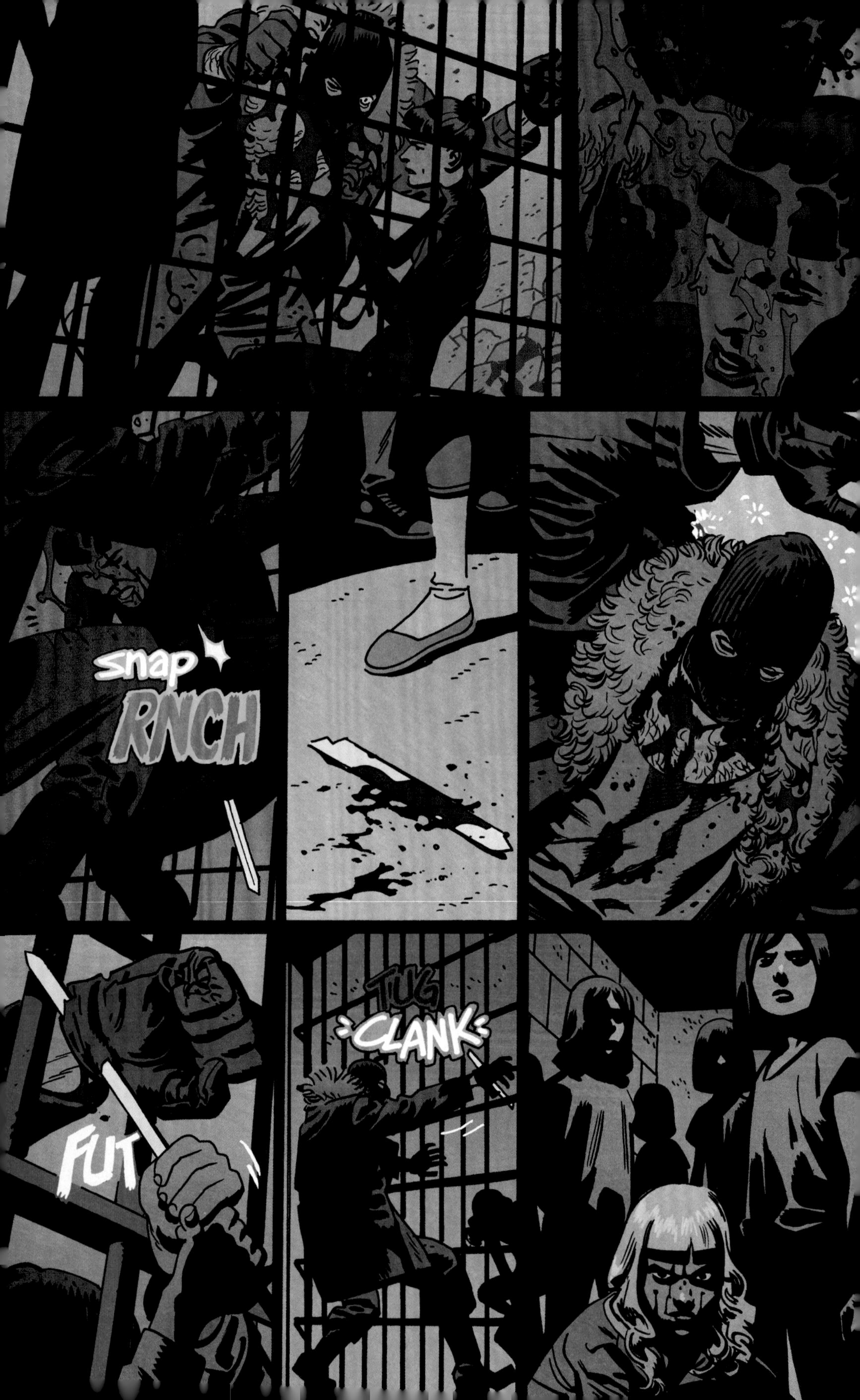
snap
RNCH
FUT
TUG
CLANK

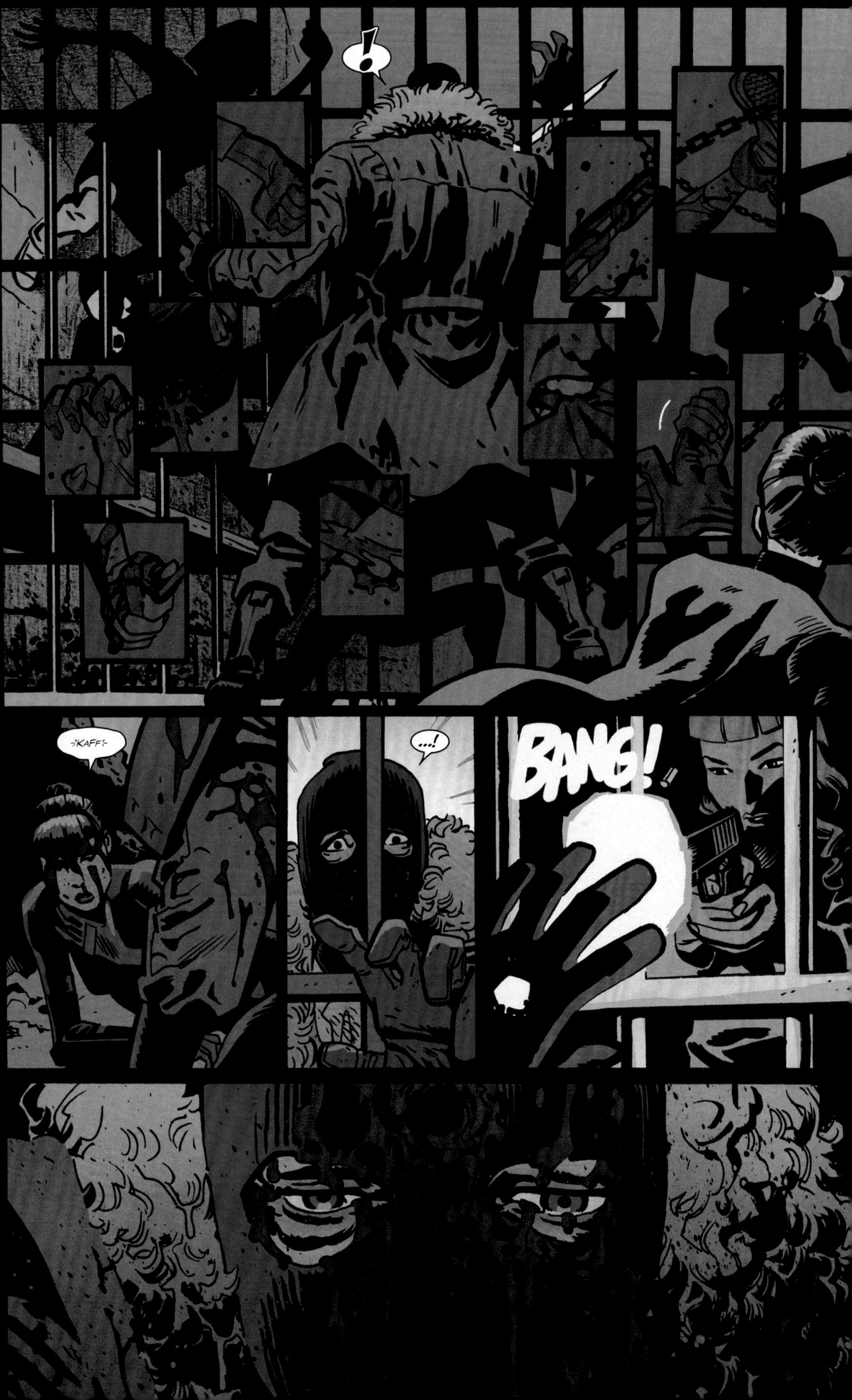
!
-KAFF-
...!
BANG!

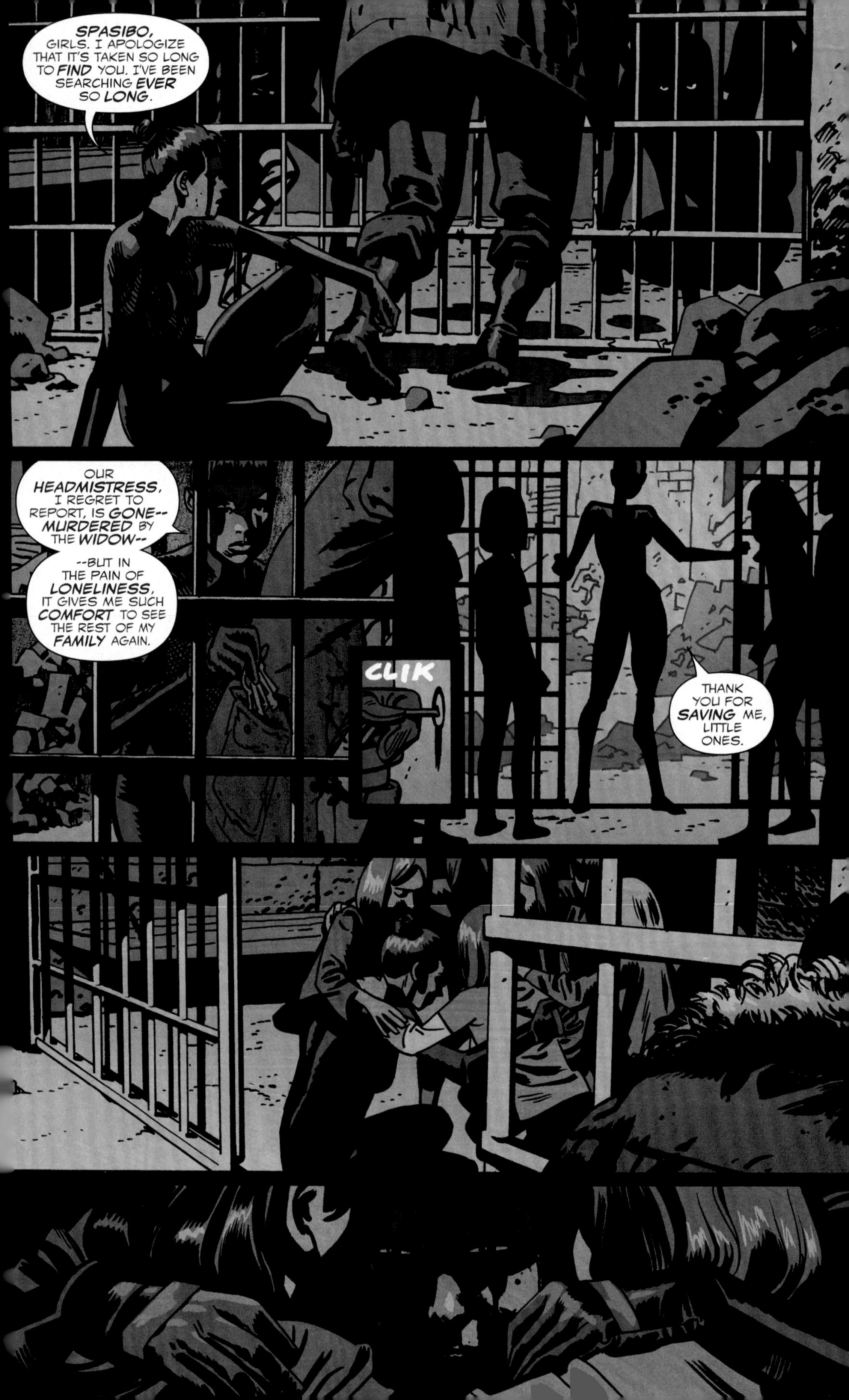
SPASIBO, GIRLS. I APOLOGIZE THAT IT'S TAKEN SO LONG TO FIND YOU. I'VE BEEN SEARCHING EVER SO LONG.
OUR HEADMISTRESS, I REGRET TO REPORT, IS GONE-- MURDERED BY THE WIDOW--
--BUT IN THE PAIN OF LONELINESS, IT GIVES ME SUCH COMFORT TO SEE THE REST OF MY FAMILY AGAIN.
CLIK
THANK YOU FOR SAVING ME, LITTLE ONES.

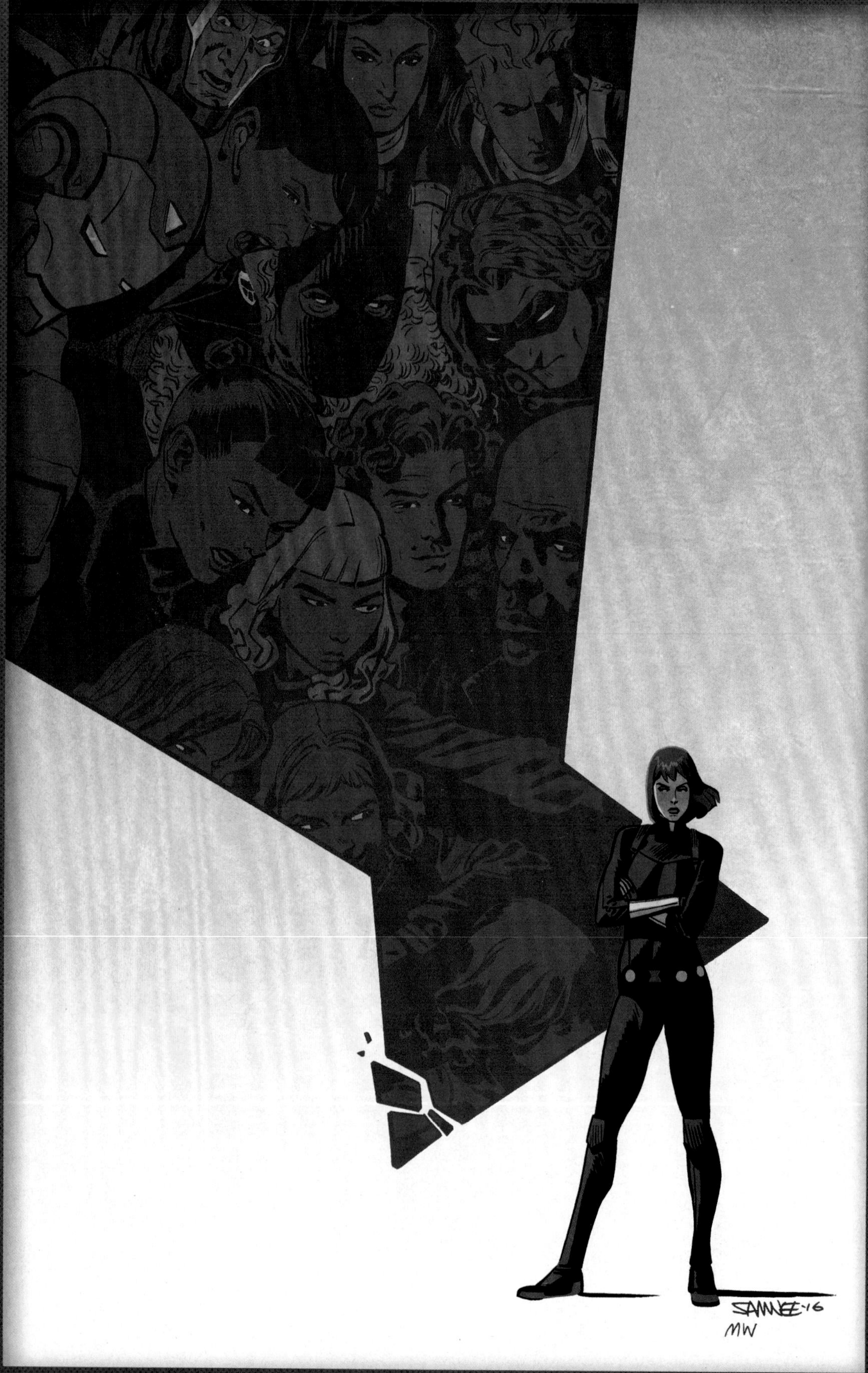
SAMNEE·16
MW

11

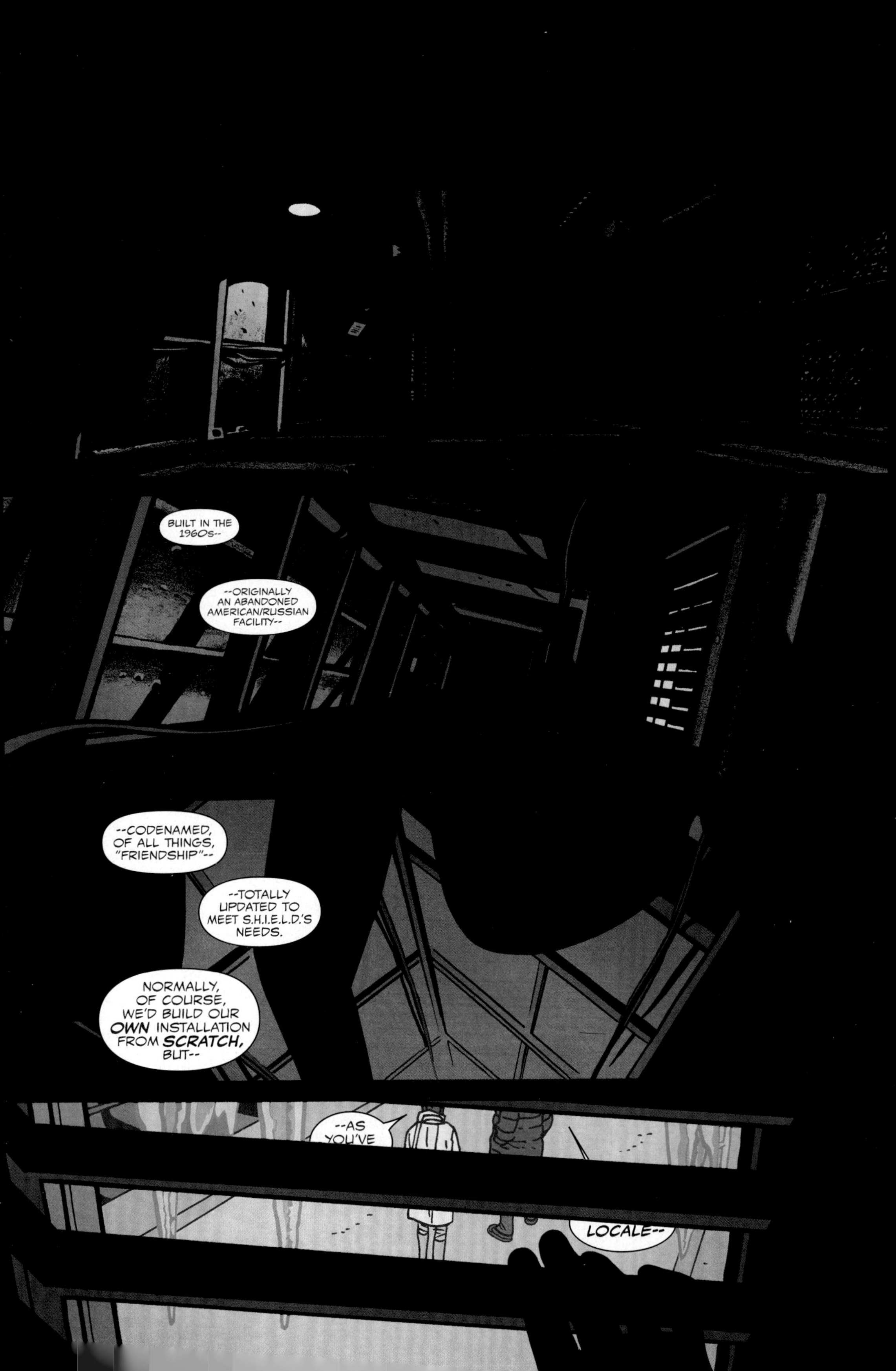
BUILT IN THE 1960s--
--ORIGINALLY AN ABANDONED AMERICAN/RUSSIAN FACILITY--
--CODENAMED, OF ALL THINGS, "FRIENDSHIP"--
--TOTALLY UPDATED TO MEET S.H.I.E.L.D.'S NEEDS.
NORMALLY, OF COURSE, WE'D BUILD OUR OWN INSTALLATION FROM SCRATCH, BUT--
--AS YOU'VE
LOCALE--

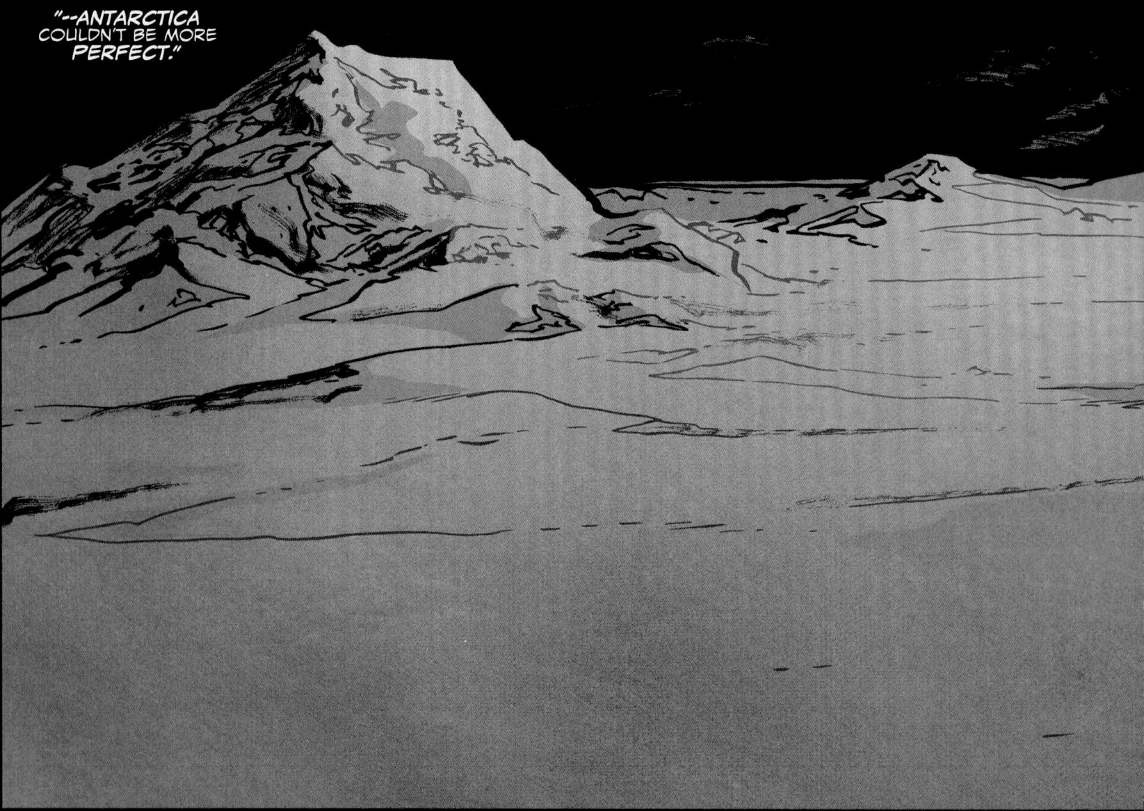
"--ANTARCTICA COULDN'T BE MORE PERFECT."

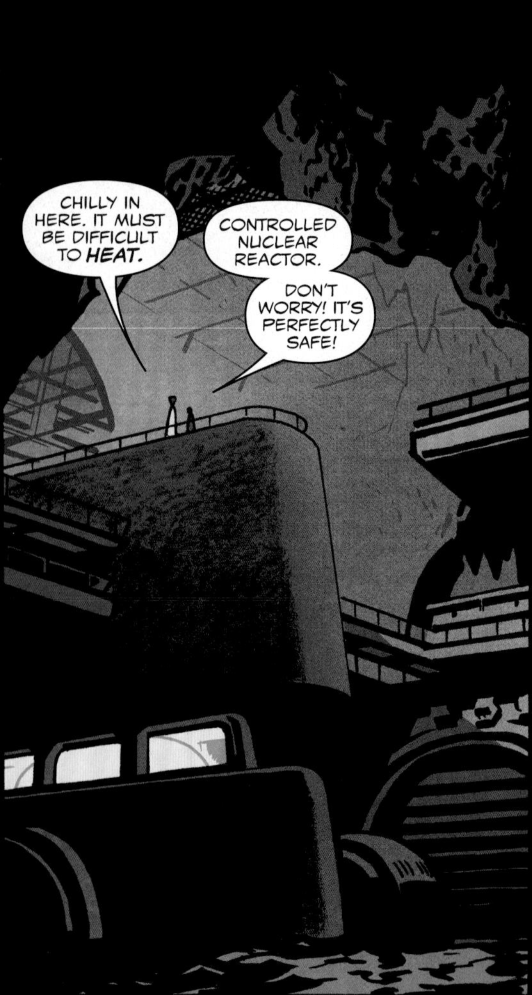
CHILLY IN HERE. IT MUST BE DIFFICULT TO HEAT.
CONTROLLED NUCLEAR REACTOR.
DON'T WORRY! IT'S PERFECTLY SAFE!

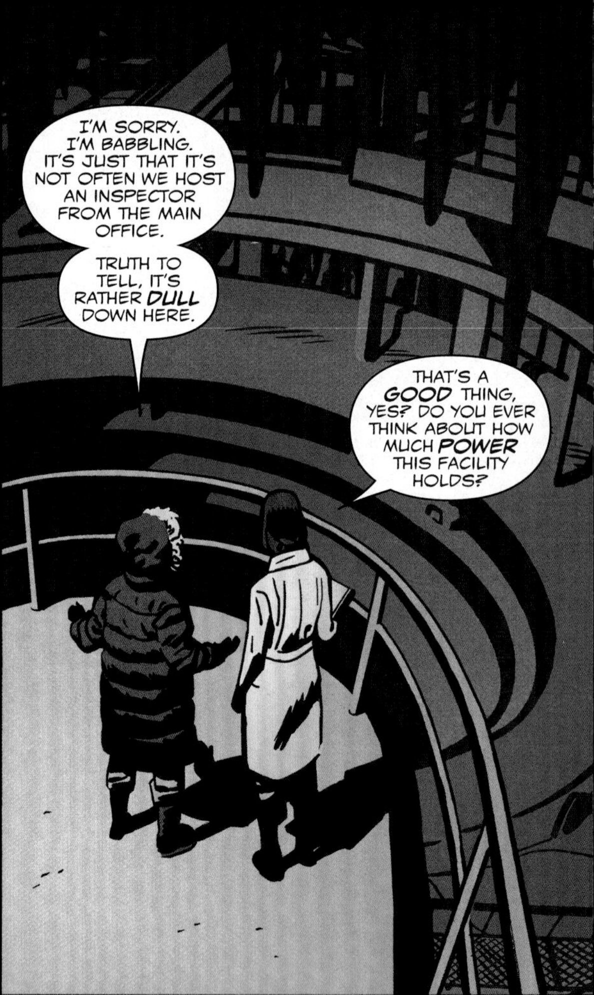
I'M SORRY. I'M BABBLING. IT'S JUST THAT IT'S NOT OFTEN WE HOST AN INSPECTOR FROM THE MAIN OFFICE.
TRUTH TO TELL, IT'S RATHER DULL DOWN HERE.
THAT'S A GOOD THING, YES? DO YOU EVER THINK ABOUT HOW MUCH POWER THIS FACILITY HOLDS?

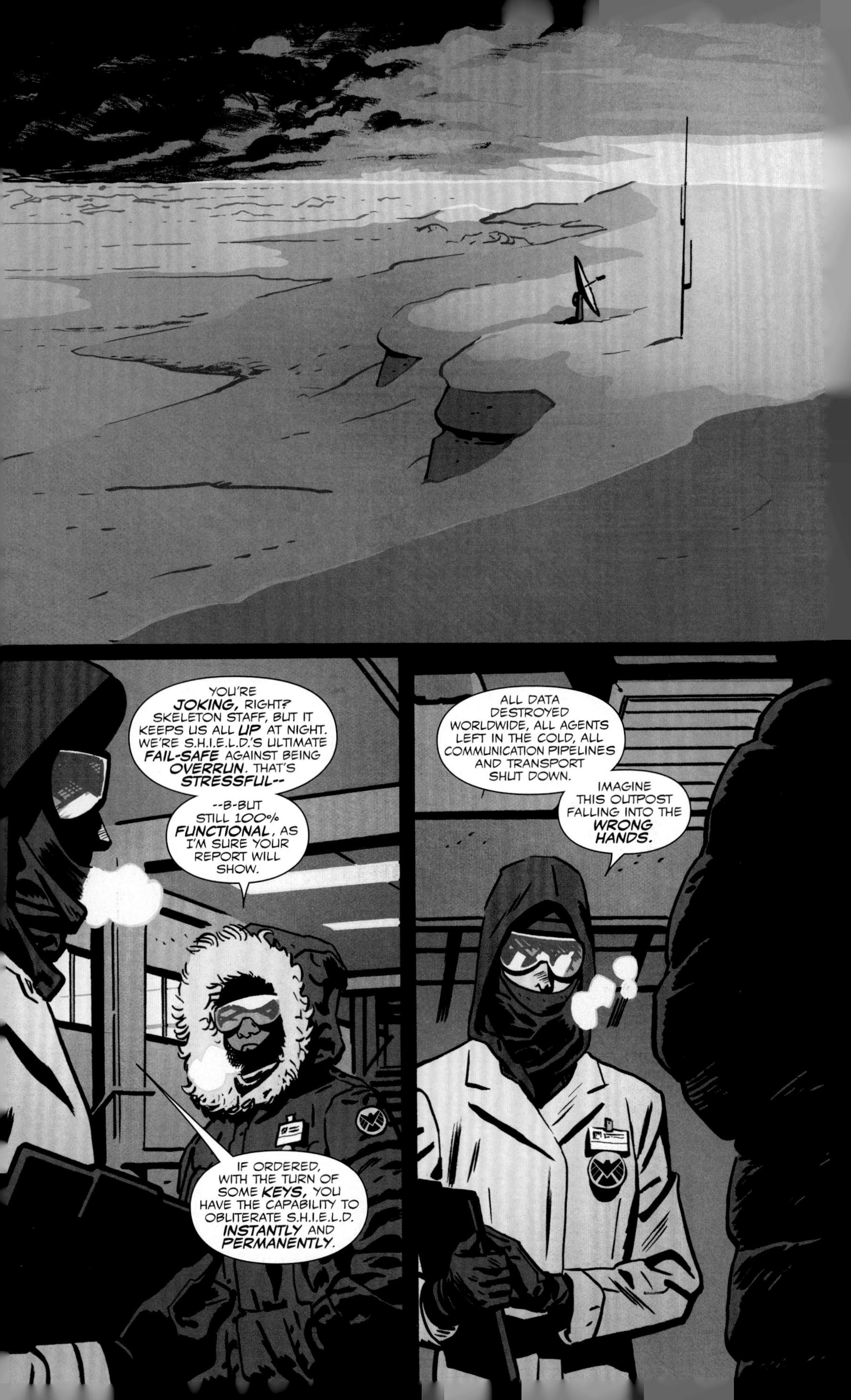
YOU'RE JOKING, RIGHT? SKELETON STAFF, BUT IT KEEPS US ALL UP AT NIGHT. WE'RE S.H.I.E.L.D.'S ULTIMATE FAIL-SAFE AGAINST BEING OVERRUN. THAT'S STRESSFUL--
--B-BUT STILL 100% FUNCTIONAL, AS I'M SURE YOUR REPORT WILL SHOW.
IF ORDERED, WITH THE TURN OF SOME KEYS, YOU HAVE THE CAPABILITY TO OBLITERATE S.H.I.E.L.D. INSTANTLY AND PERMANENTLY.
ALL DATA DESTROYED WORLDWIDE, ALL AGENTS LEFT IN THE COLD, ALL COMMUNICATION PIPELINES AND TRANSPORT SHUT DOWN.
IMAGINE THIS OUTPOST FALLING INTO THE WRONG HANDS.

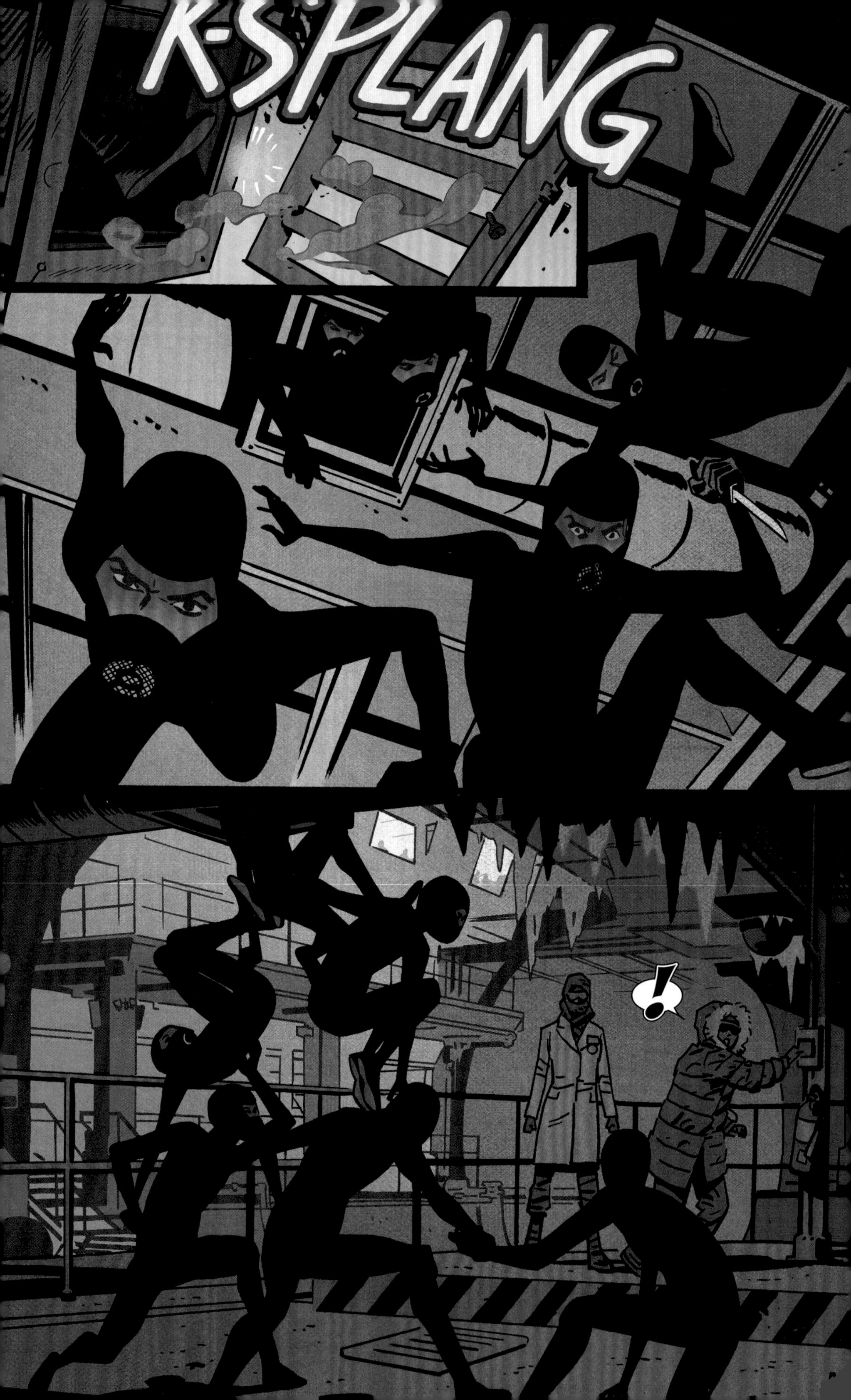
K-SPLANG
!

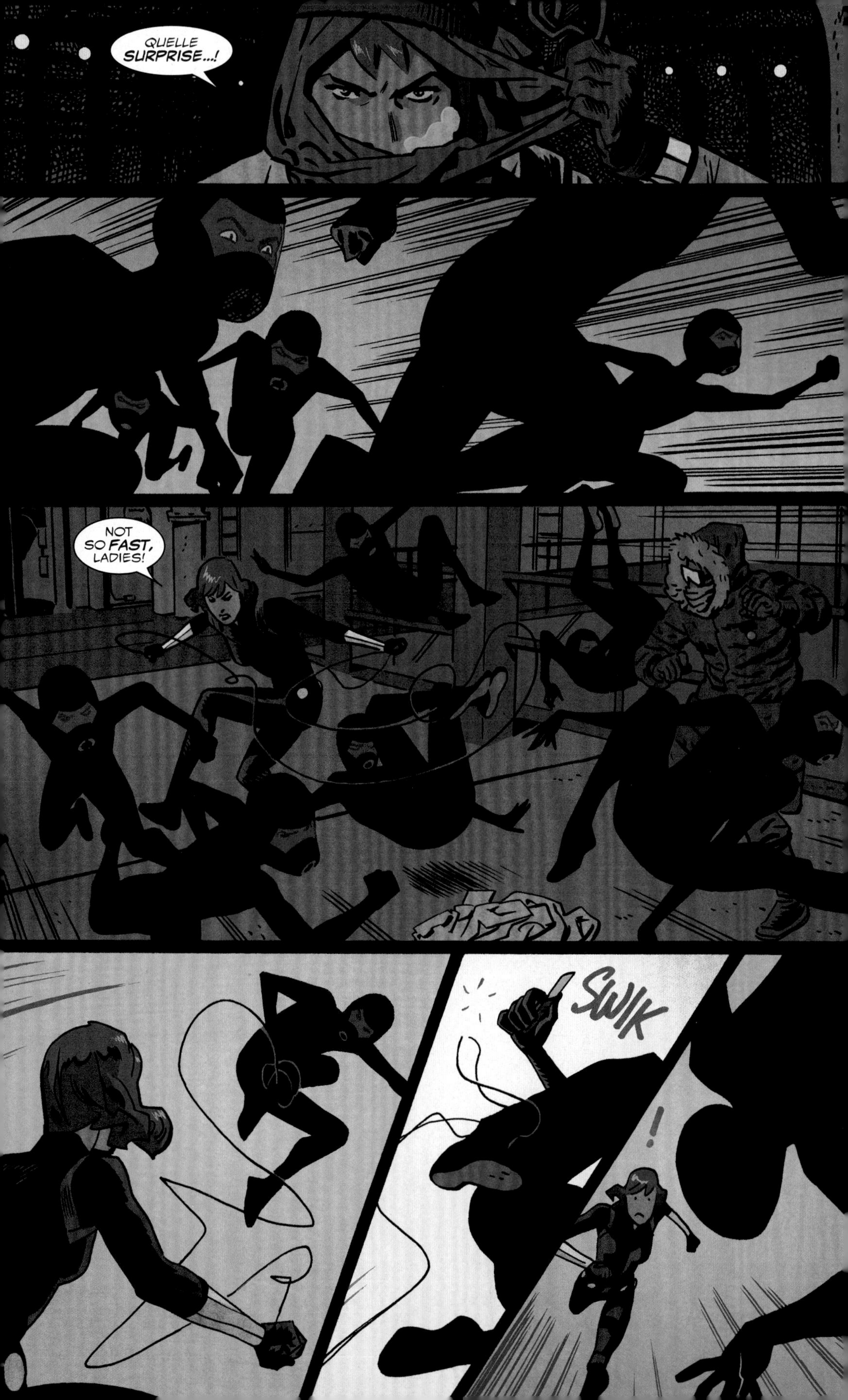
QUELLE SURPRISE...!
NOT SO FAST, LADIES!
SWIK
!

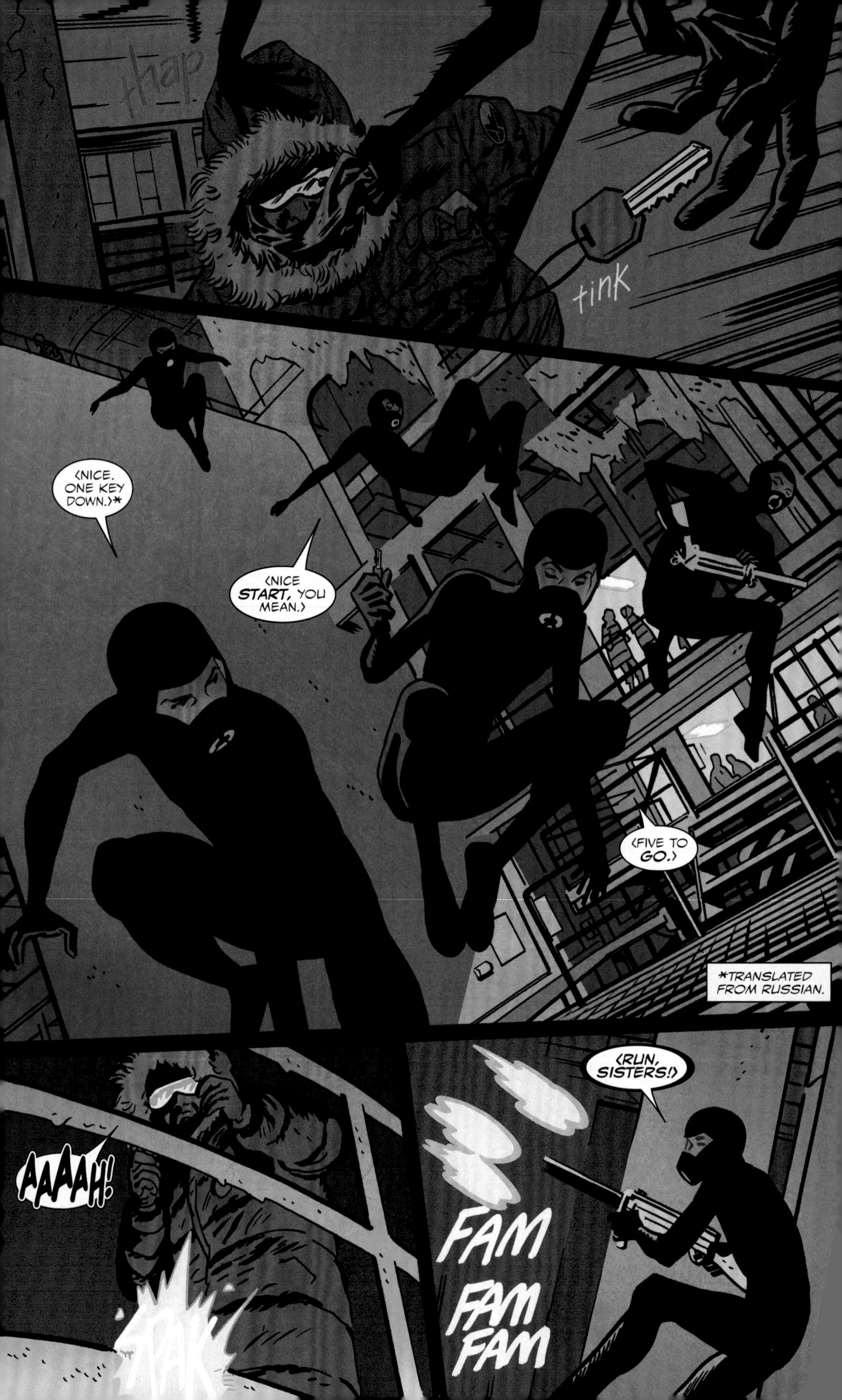
thap
tink
‹NICE. ONE KEY DOWN.›*
‹NICE START, YOU MEAN.›
‹FIVE TO GO.›
*TRANSLATED FROM RUSSIAN.
AAAAH!
SPAK
‹RUN, SISTERS!›
FAM FAM FAM FAM

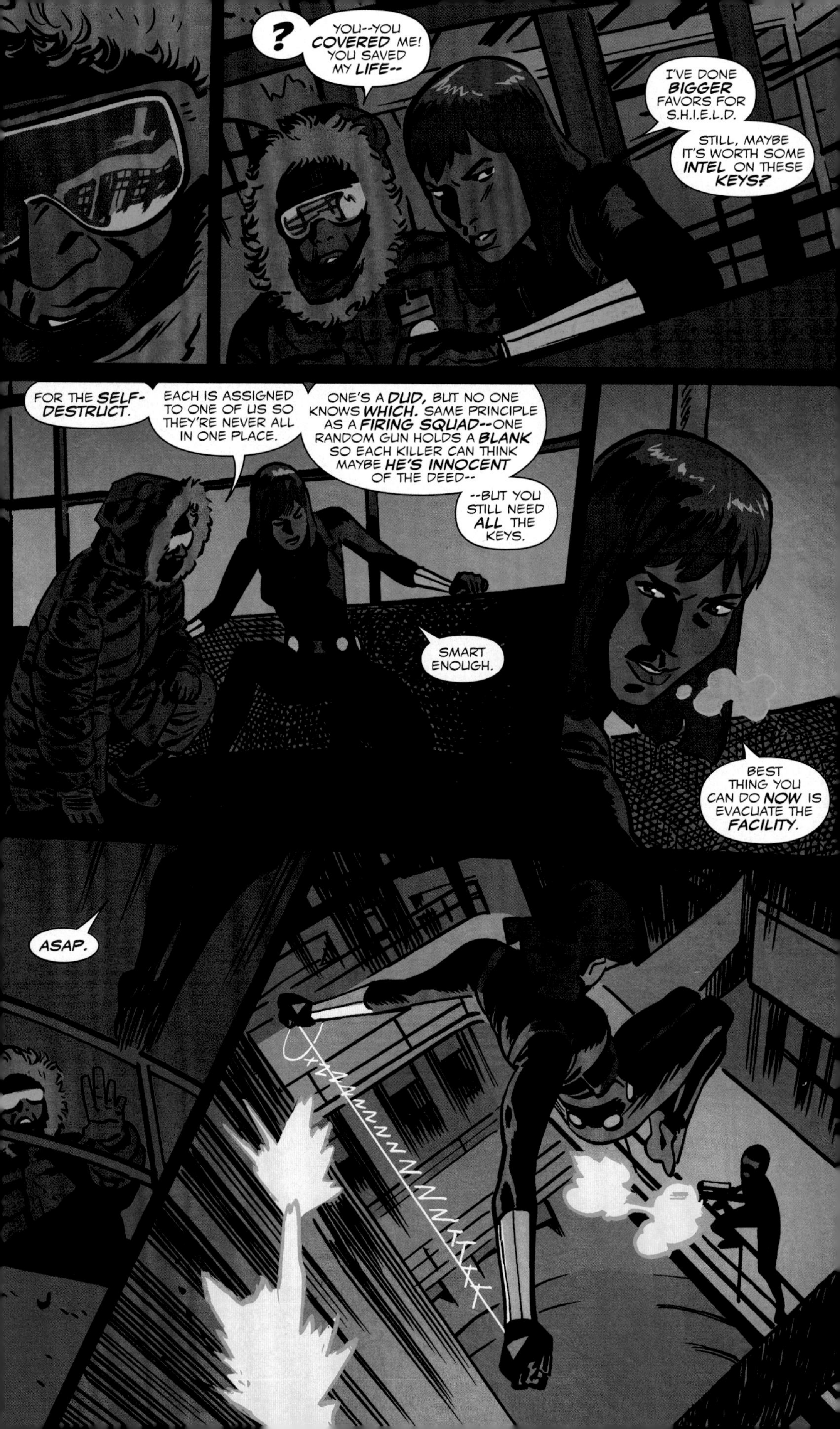
?
YOU--YOU COVERED ME! YOU SAVED MY LIFE--
I'VE DONE BIGGER FAVORS FOR S.H.I.E.L.D.
STILL, MAYBE IT'S WORTH SOME INTEL ON THESE KEYS?
FOR THE SELF-DESTRUCT.
EACH IS ASSIGNED TO ONE OF US SO THEY'RE NEVER ALL IN ONE PLACE.
ONE'S A DUD, BUT NO ONE KNOWS WHICH. SAME PRINCIPLE AS A FIRING SQUAD--ONE RANDOM GUN HOLDS A BLANK SO EACH KILLER CAN THINK MAYBE HE'S INNOCENT OF THE DEED--
--BUT YOU STILL NEED ALL THE KEYS.
SMART ENOUGH.
BEST THING YOU CAN DO NOW IS EVACUATE THE FACILITY.
ASAP.

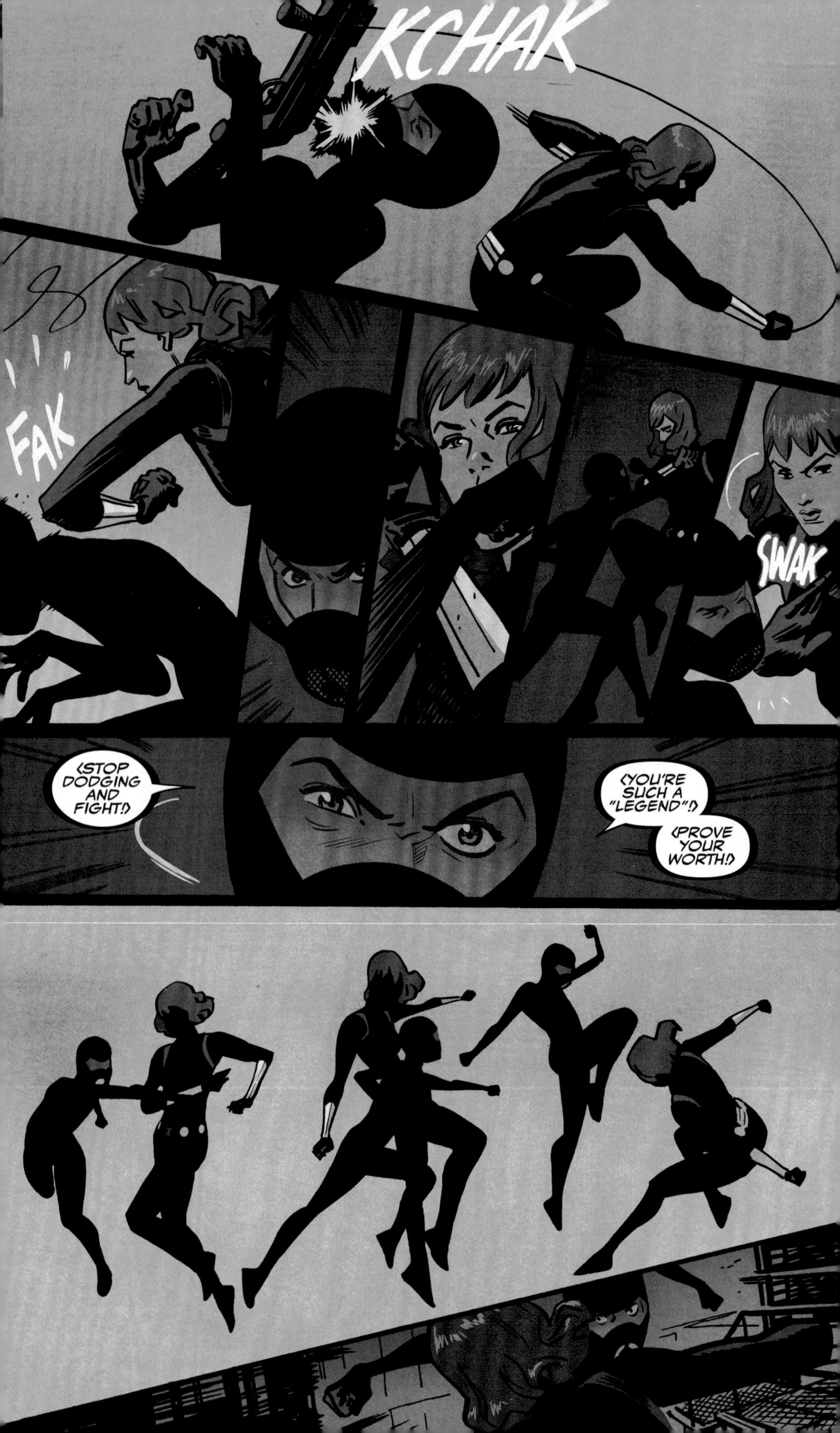
KCHAK
FAK
SWAK
‹STOP DODGING AND FIGHT!›
‹YOU'RE SUCH A "LEGEND"!›
‹PROVE YOUR WORTH!›

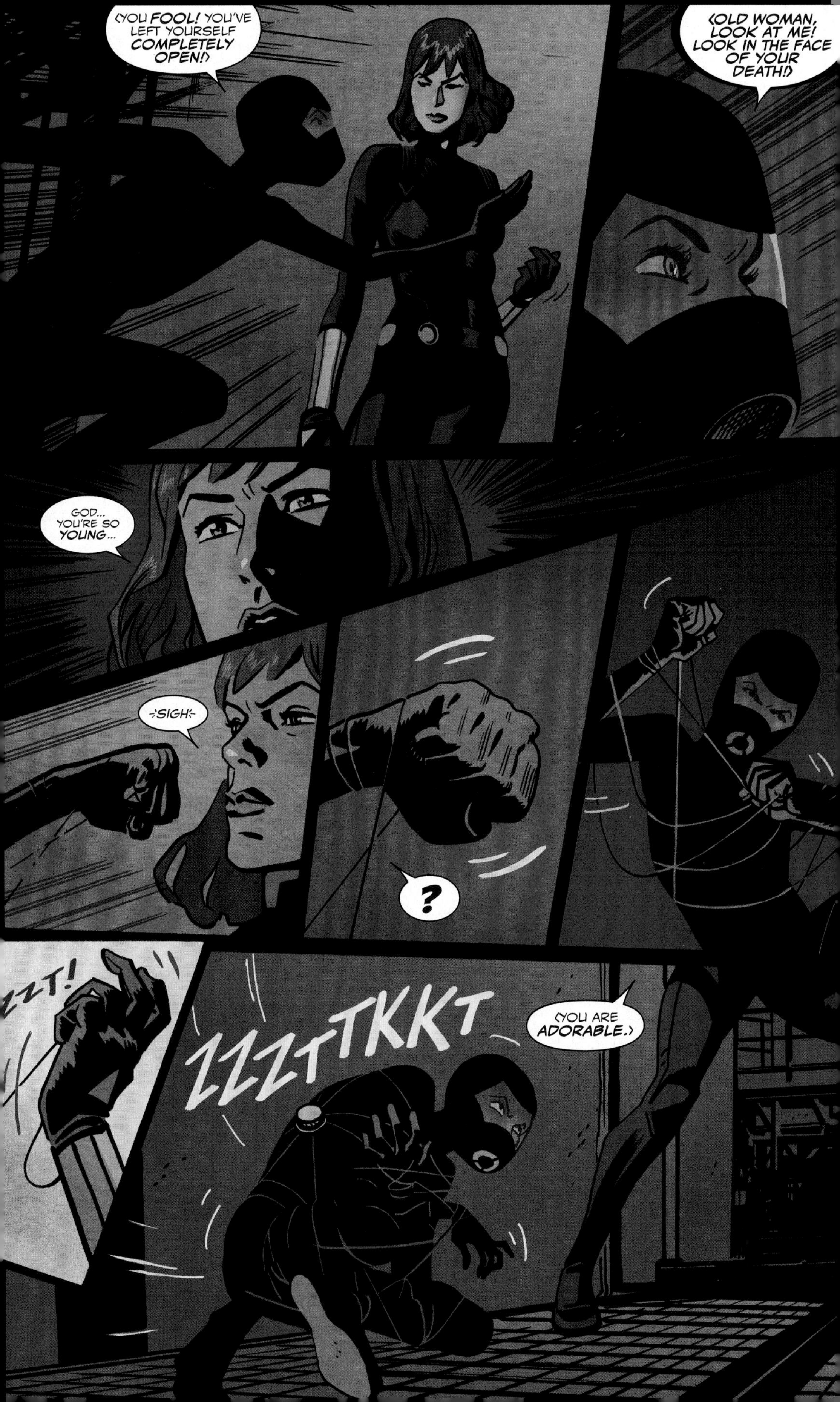

‹YOU FOOL! YOU'VE LEFT YOURSELF COMPLETELY OPEN!›
‹OLD WOMAN, LOOK AT ME! LOOK IN THE FACE OF YOUR DEATH!›
GOD... YOU'RE SO YOUNG...
-SIGH-
?
ZZT!
ZZZTTKKT
‹YOU ARE ADORABLE.›

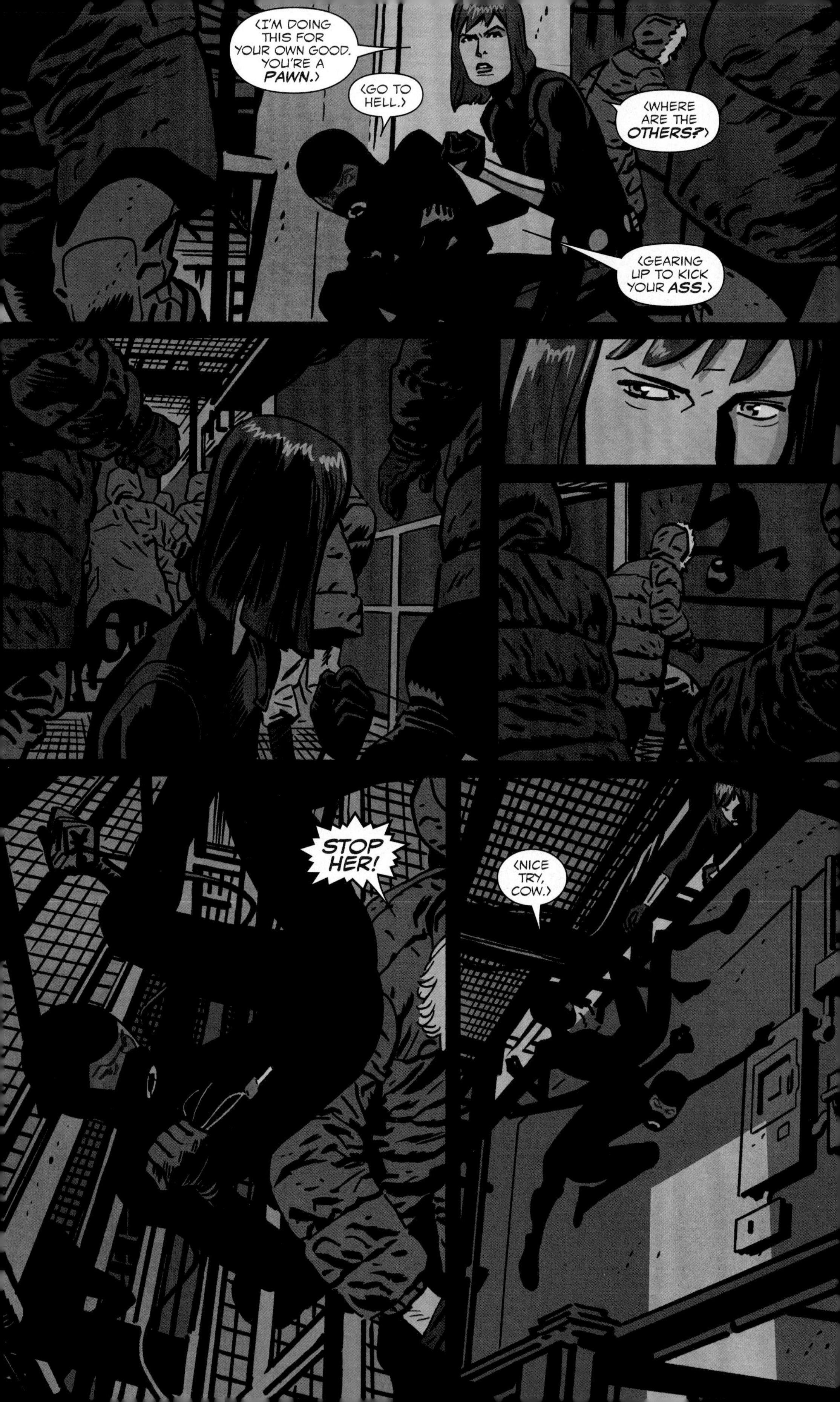

‹I'M DOING THIS FOR YOUR OWN GOOD. YOU'RE A **PAWN.**›
‹GO TO HELL.›
‹WHERE ARE THE **OTHERS?**›
‹GEARING UP TO KICK YOUR **ASS.**›
**STOP HER!**
‹NICE TRY, COW.›

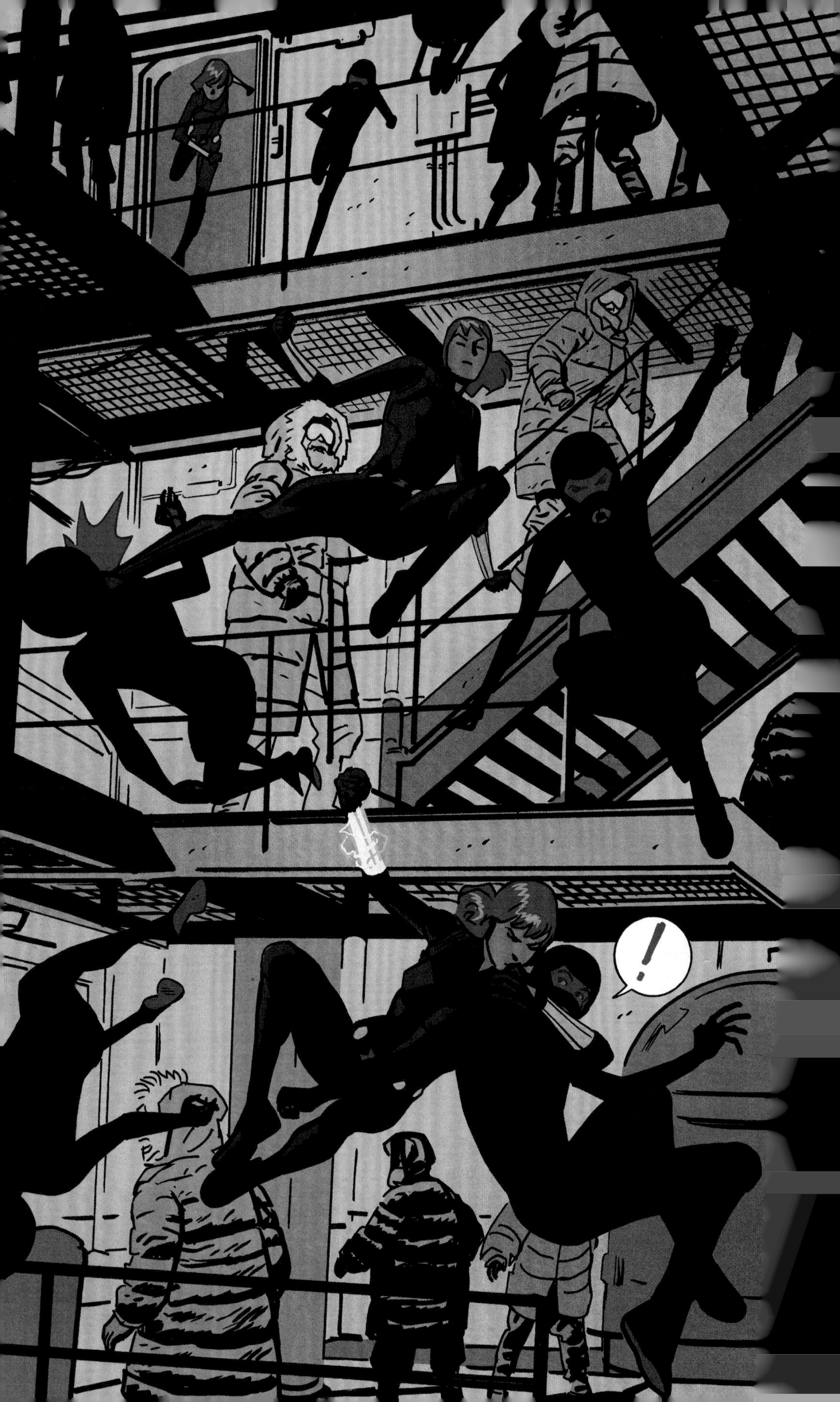
!

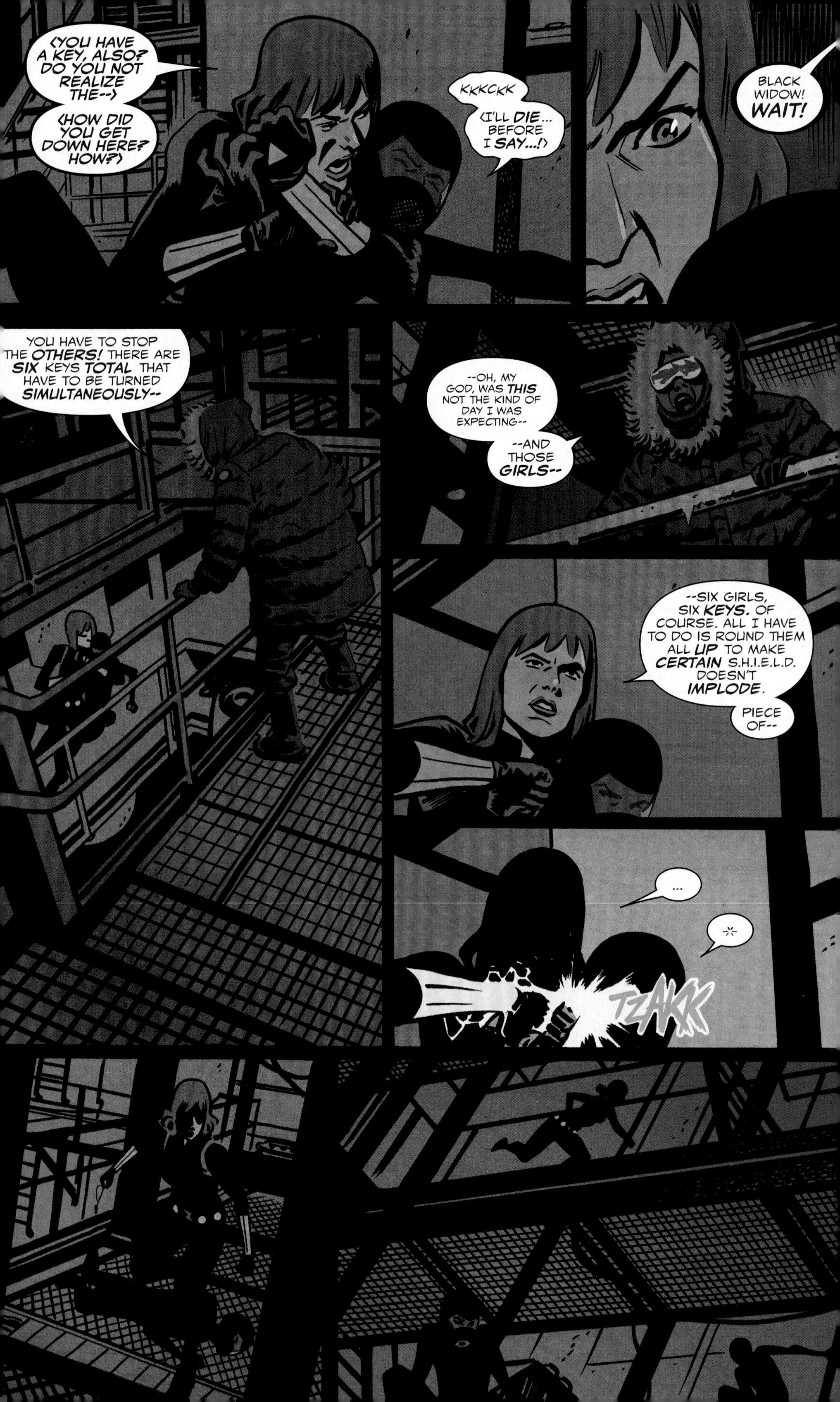

‹YOU HAVE A KEY, ALSO? DO YOU NOT REALIZE THE--›
‹HOW DID YOU GET DOWN HERE? HOW?›
KKKCKK
‹I'LL DIE... BEFORE I SAY...!›
BLACK WIDOW! WAIT!
YOU HAVE TO STOP THE OTHERS! THERE ARE SIX KEYS TOTAL THAT HAVE TO BE TURNED SIMULTANEOUSLY--
--OH, MY GOD, WAS THIS NOT THE KIND OF DAY I WAS EXPECTING--
--AND THOSE GIRLS--
--SIX GIRLS, SIX KEYS. OF COURSE. ALL I HAVE TO DO IS ROUND THEM ALL UP TO MAKE CERTAIN S.H.I.E.L.D. DOESN'T IMPLODE.
PIECE OF--
...
TZAKK

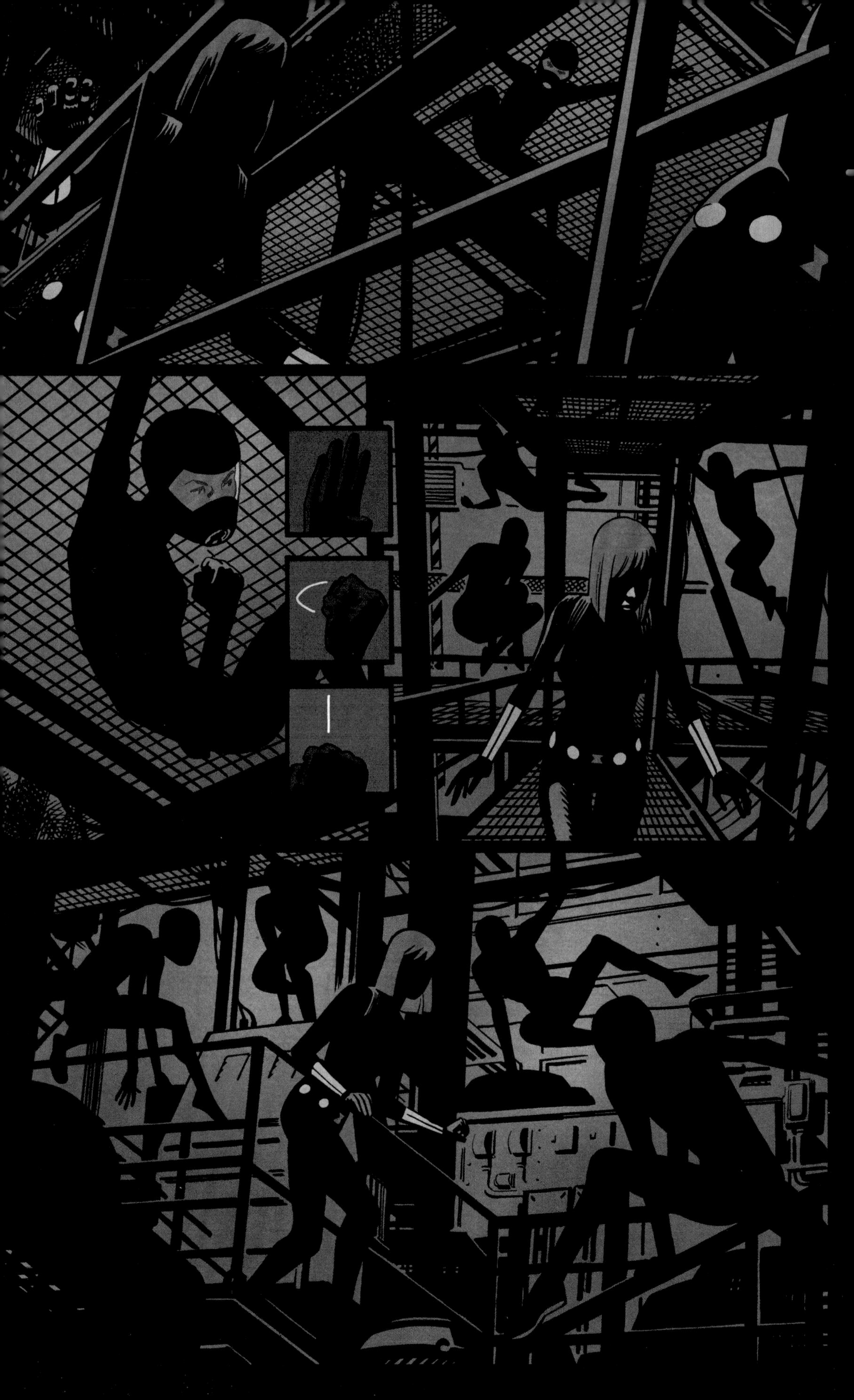

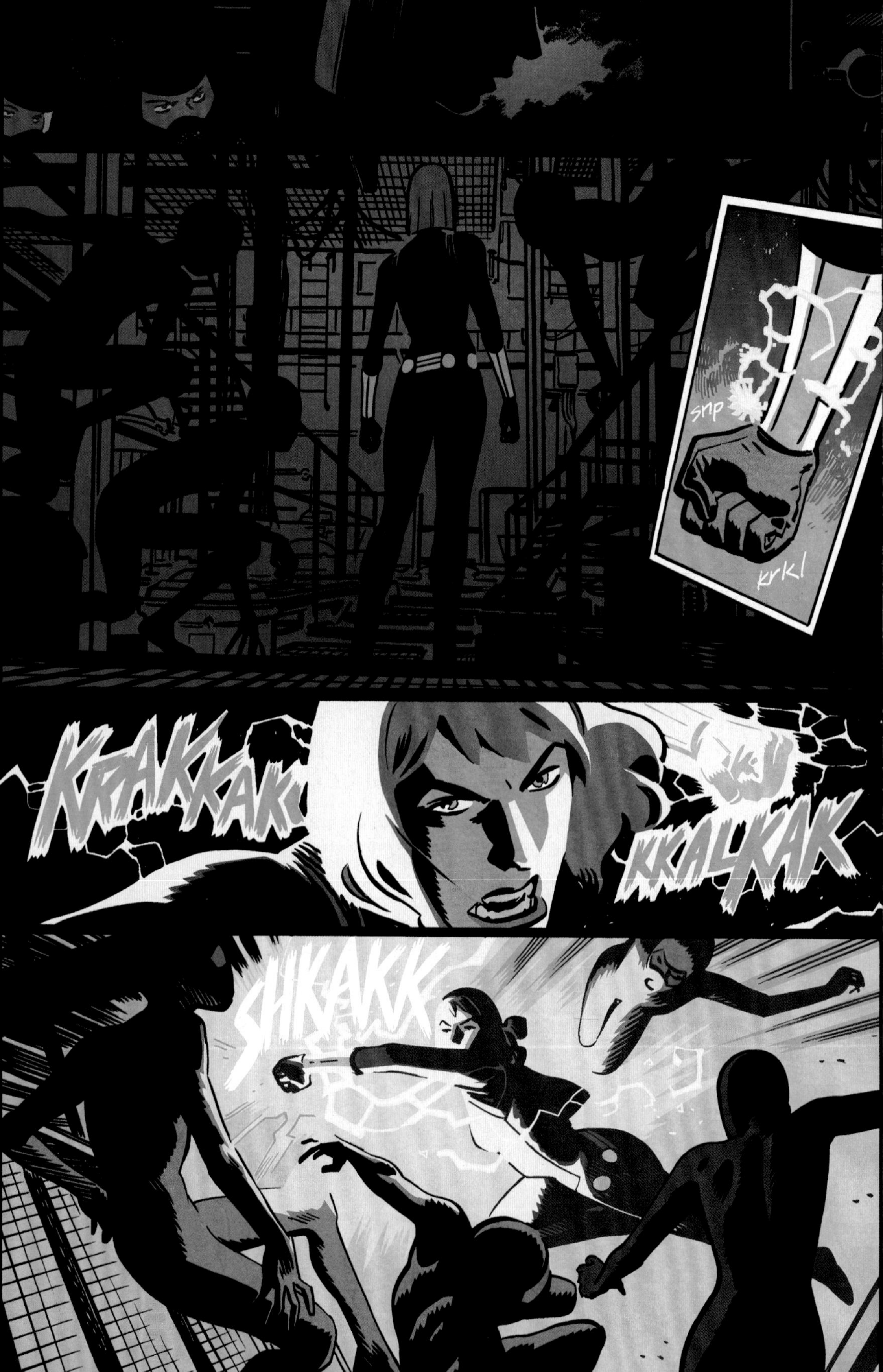
snp
krkl
KRAKKAK
KKALKAK
SHKAKK

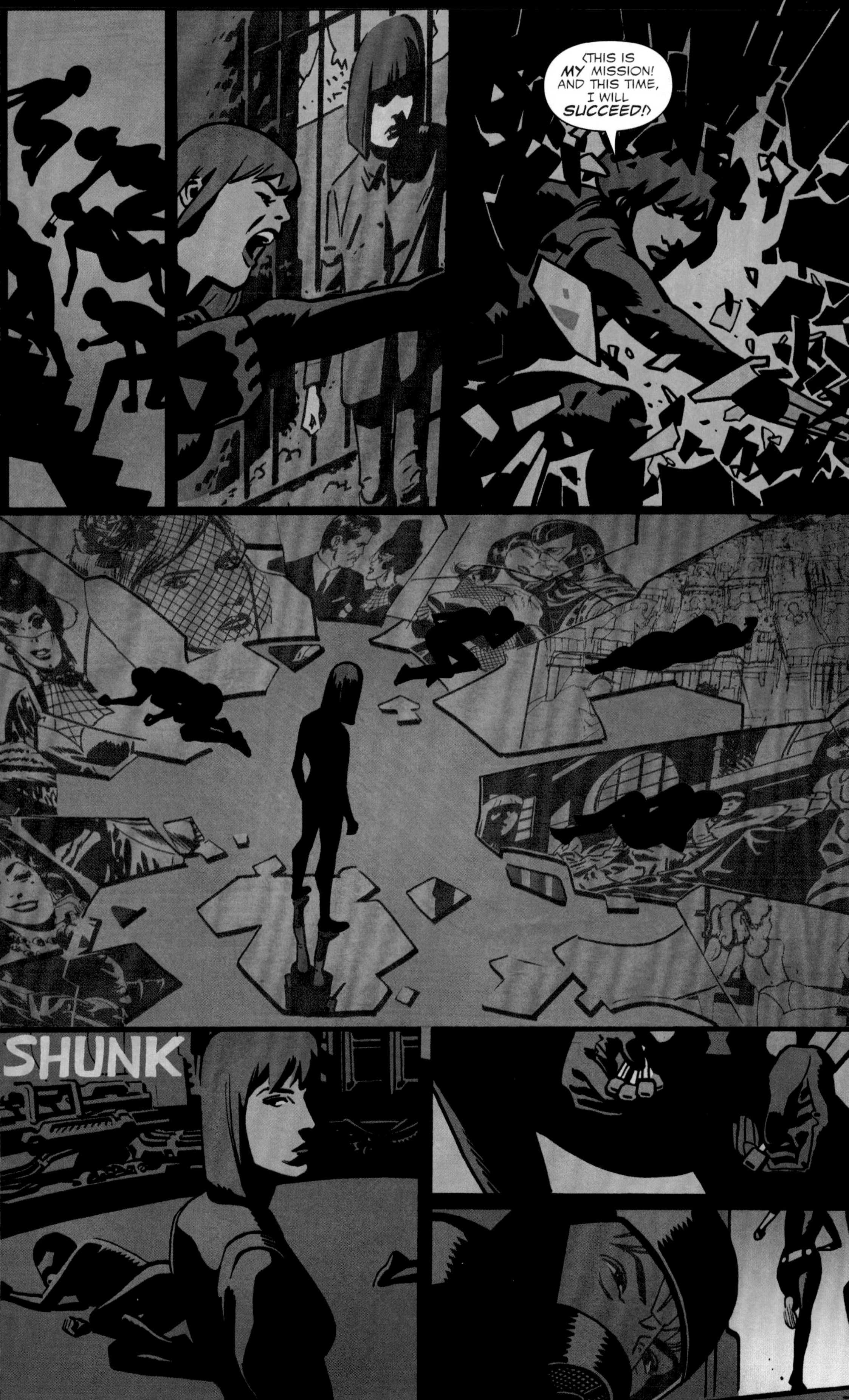
‹THIS IS MY MISSION! AND THIS TIME, I WILL SUCCEED!›
SHUNK

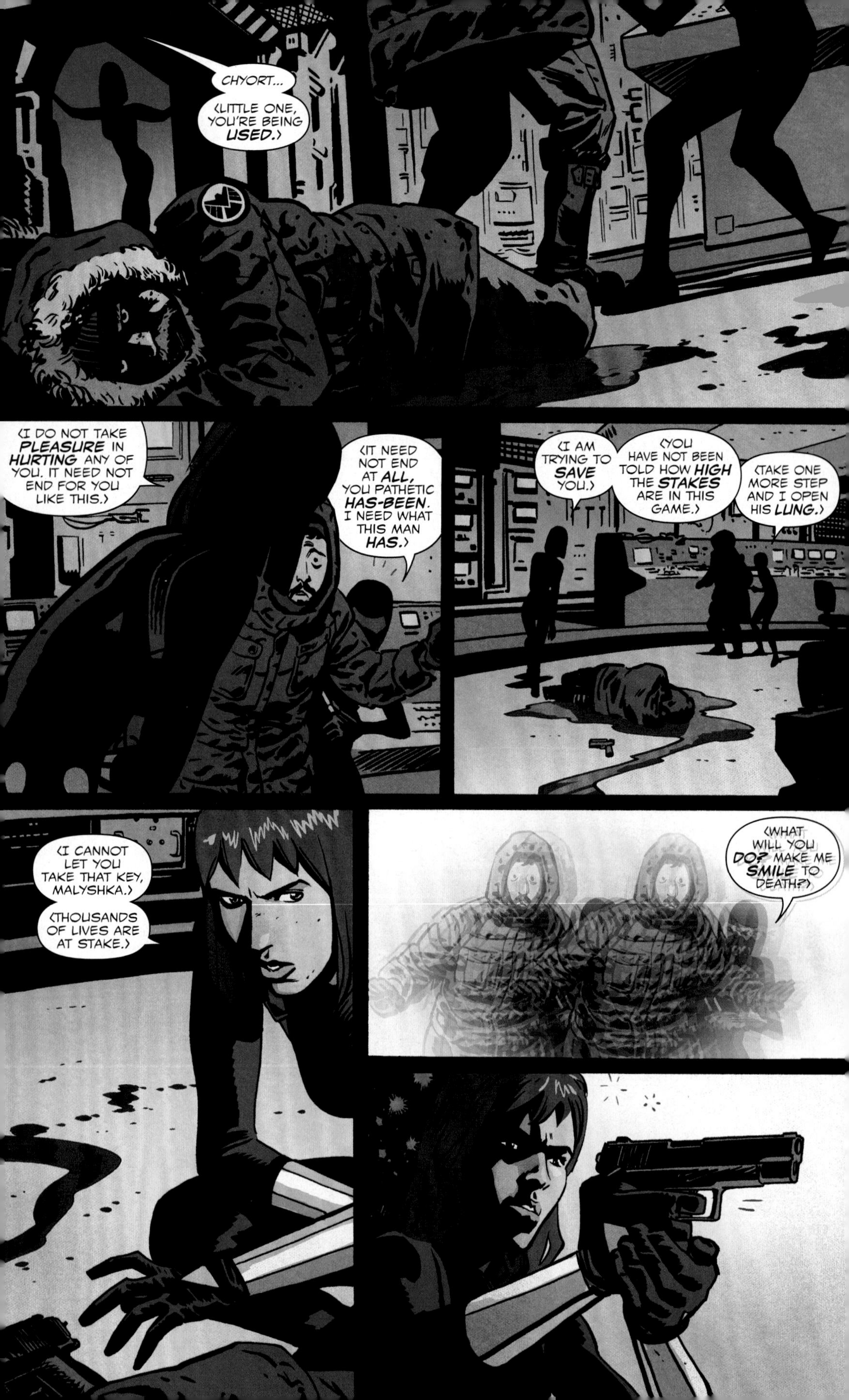
CHYORT...
‹LITTLE ONE, YOU'RE BEING **USED**.›
‹I DO NOT TAKE **PLEASURE** IN **HURTING** ANY OF YOU. IT NEED NOT END FOR YOU LIKE THIS.›
‹IT NEED NOT END AT **ALL**, YOU PATHETIC **HAS-BEEN**. I NEED WHAT THIS MAN **HAS**.›
‹I AM TRYING TO **SAVE** YOU.›
‹YOU HAVE NOT BEEN TOLD HOW **HIGH** THE **STAKES** ARE IN THIS GAME.›
‹TAKE ONE MORE STEP AND I OPEN HIS **LUNG**.›
‹I CANNOT LET YOU TAKE THAT KEY, MALYSHKA.›
‹THOUSANDS OF LIVES ARE AT STAKE.›
‹WHAT WILL YOU **DO?** MAKE ME **SMILE** TO DEATH?›

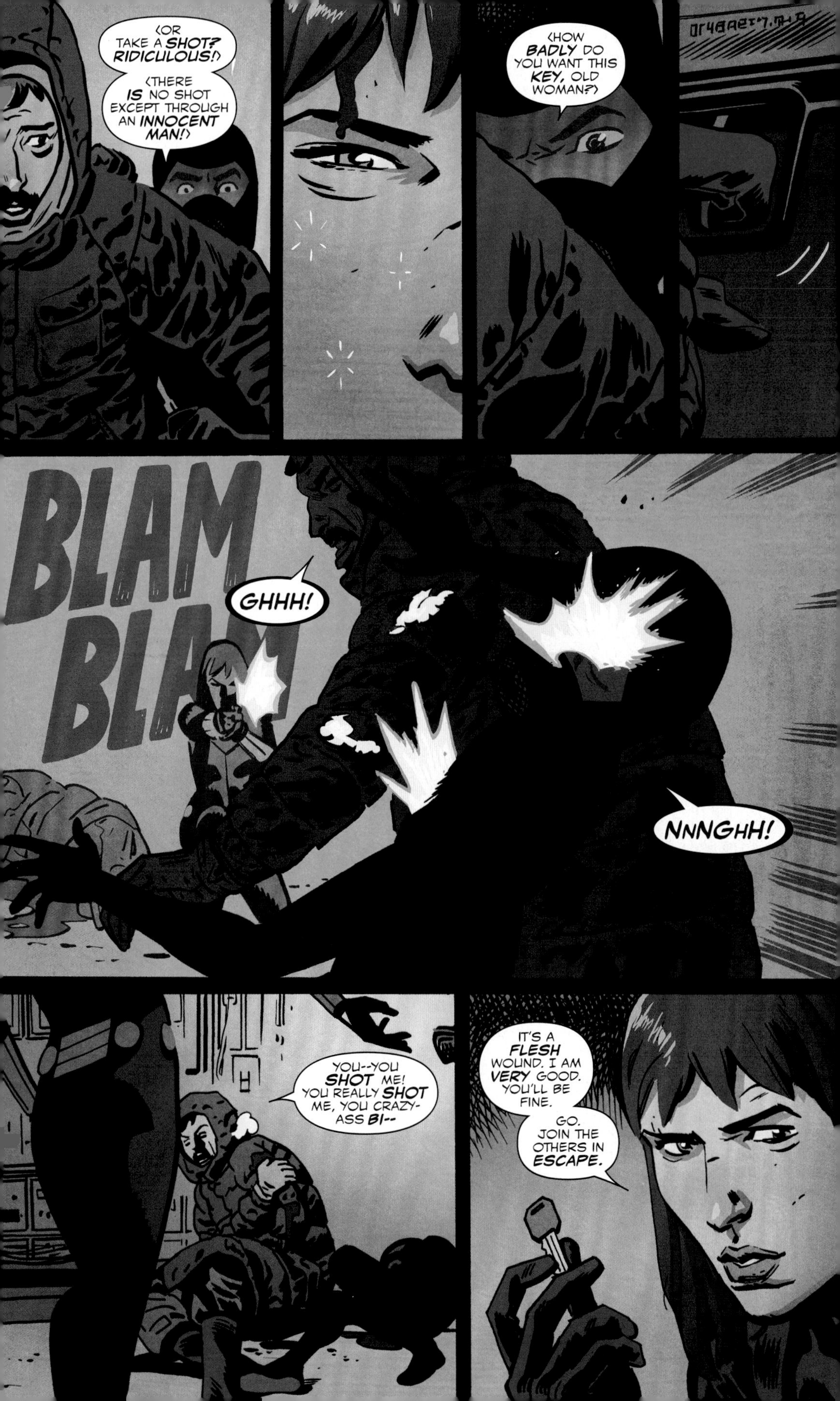

‹OR TAKE A SHOT? RIDICULOUS!›
‹THERE IS NO SHOT EXCEPT THROUGH AN INNOCENT MAN!›
‹HOW BADLY DO YOU WANT THIS KEY, OLD WOMAN?›
BLAM
BLAM
GHHH!
NNNGHH!
YOU--YOU SHOT ME! YOU REALLY SHOT ME, YOU CRAZY-ASS BI--
IT'S A FLESH WOUND. I AM VERY GOOD. YOU'LL BE FINE.
GO. JOIN THE OTHERS IN ESCAPE.

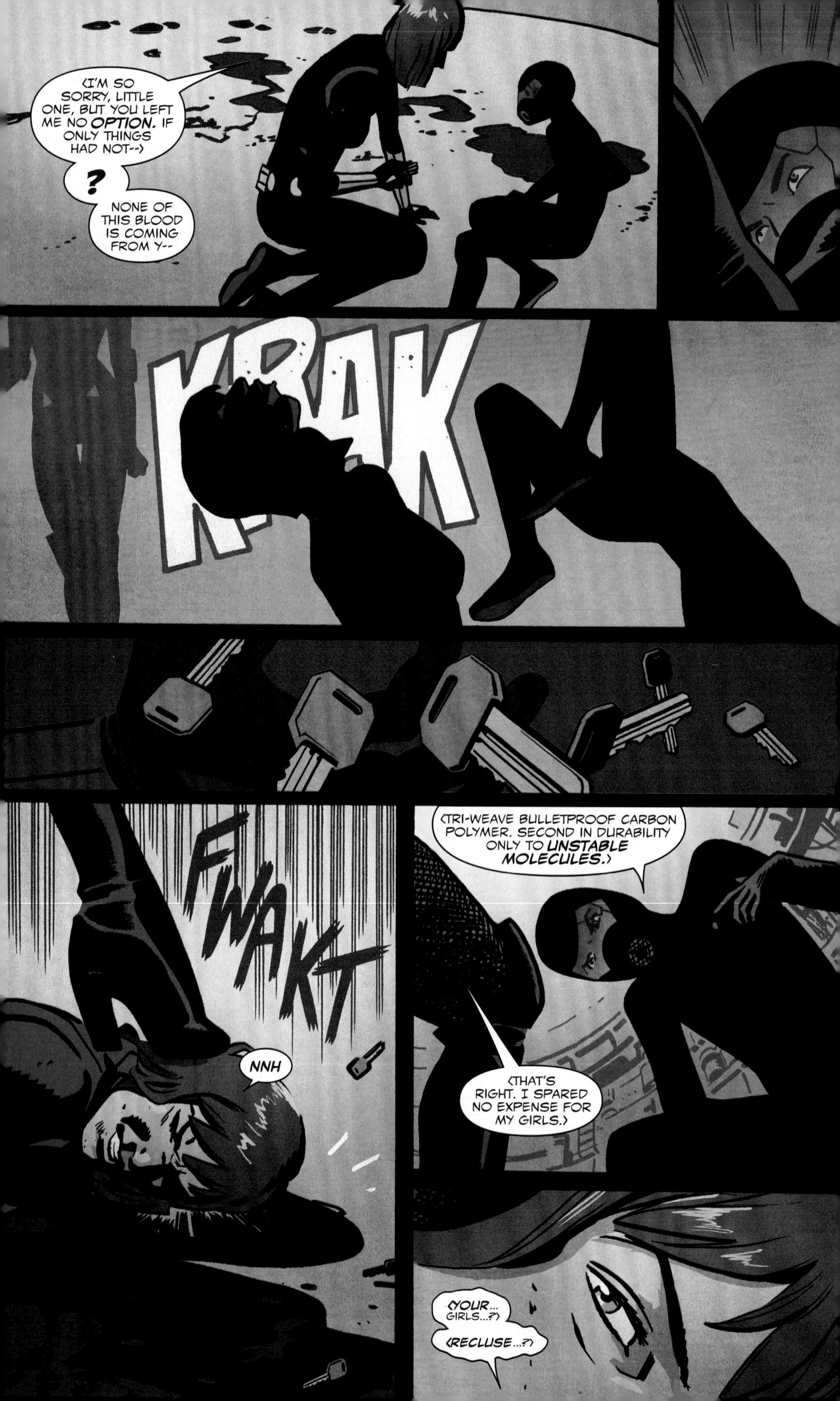

‹I'M SO SORRY, LITTLE ONE, BUT YOU LEFT ME NO OPTION. IF ONLY THINGS HAD NOT--›
?
NONE OF THIS BLOOD IS COMING FROM Y--
KRAK
FWAKT
NNH
‹TRI-WEAVE BULLETPROOF CARBON POLYMER. SECOND IN DURABILITY ONLY TO UNSTABLE MOLECULES.›
‹THAT'S RIGHT. I SPARED NO EXPENSE FOR MY GIRLS.›
‹YOUR... GIRLS...?›
‹RECLUSE...?›

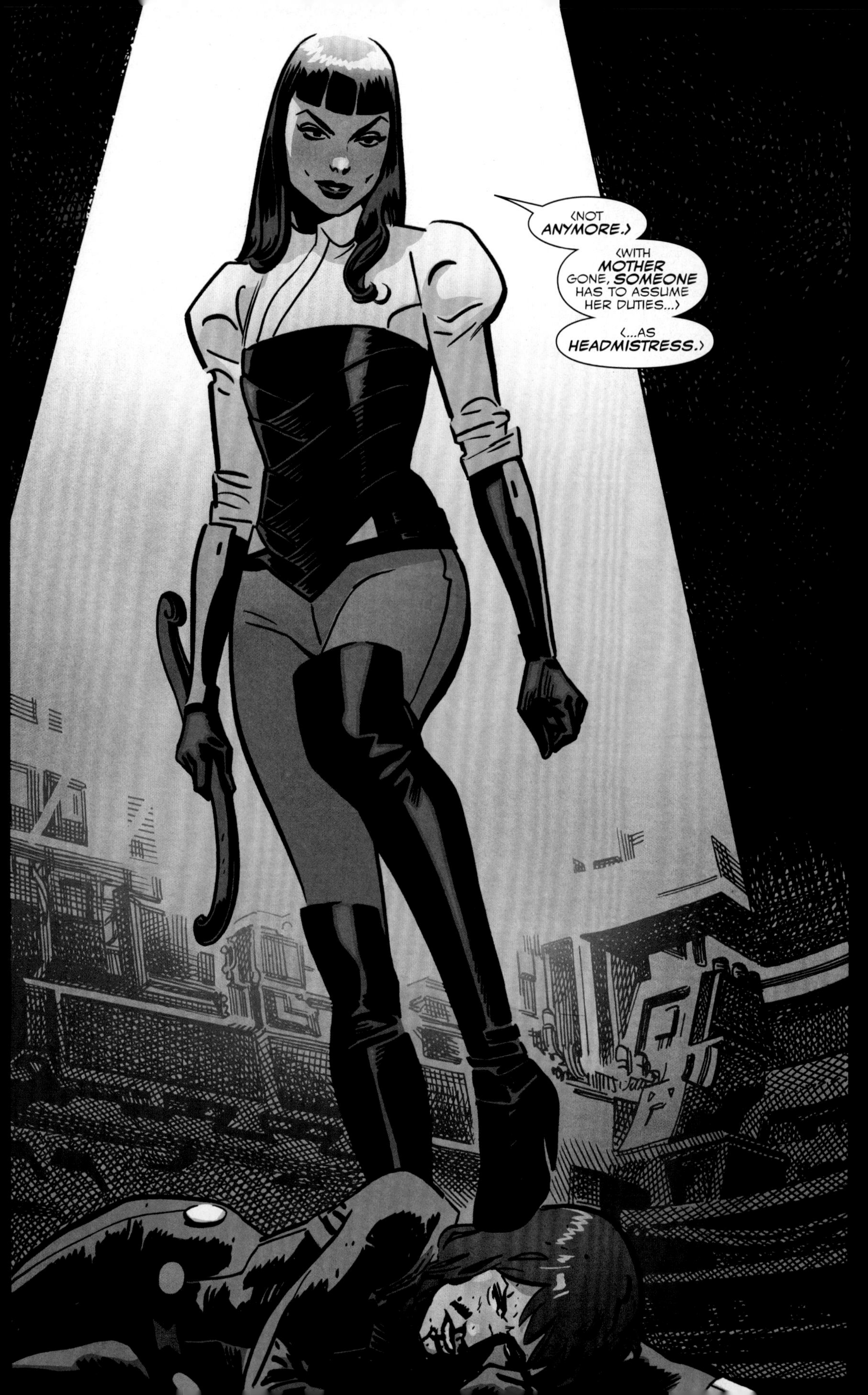
‹NOT ANYMORE.›
‹WITH MOTHER GONE, SOMEONE HAS TO ASSUME HER DUTIES...›
‹...AS HEADMISTRESS.›

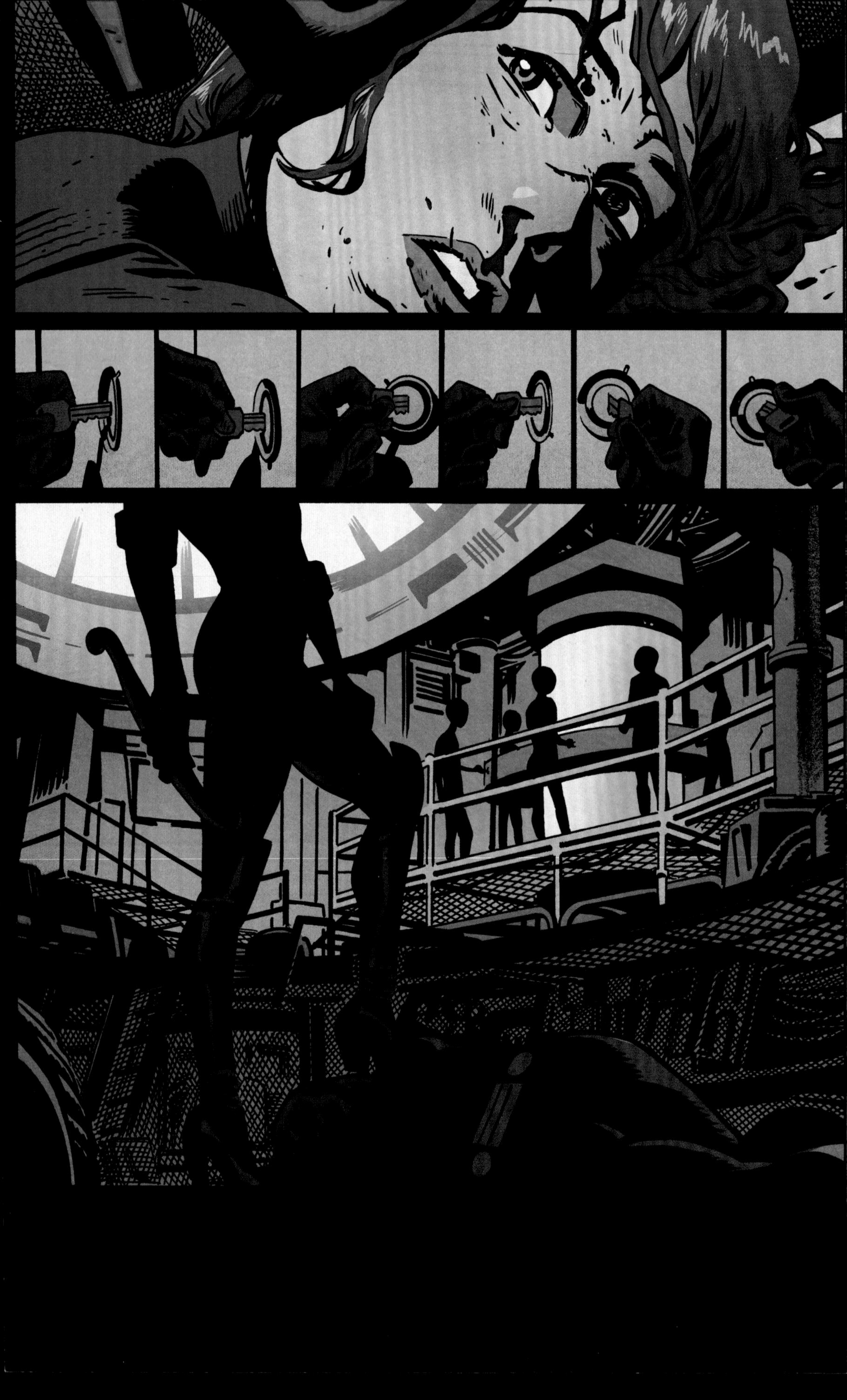

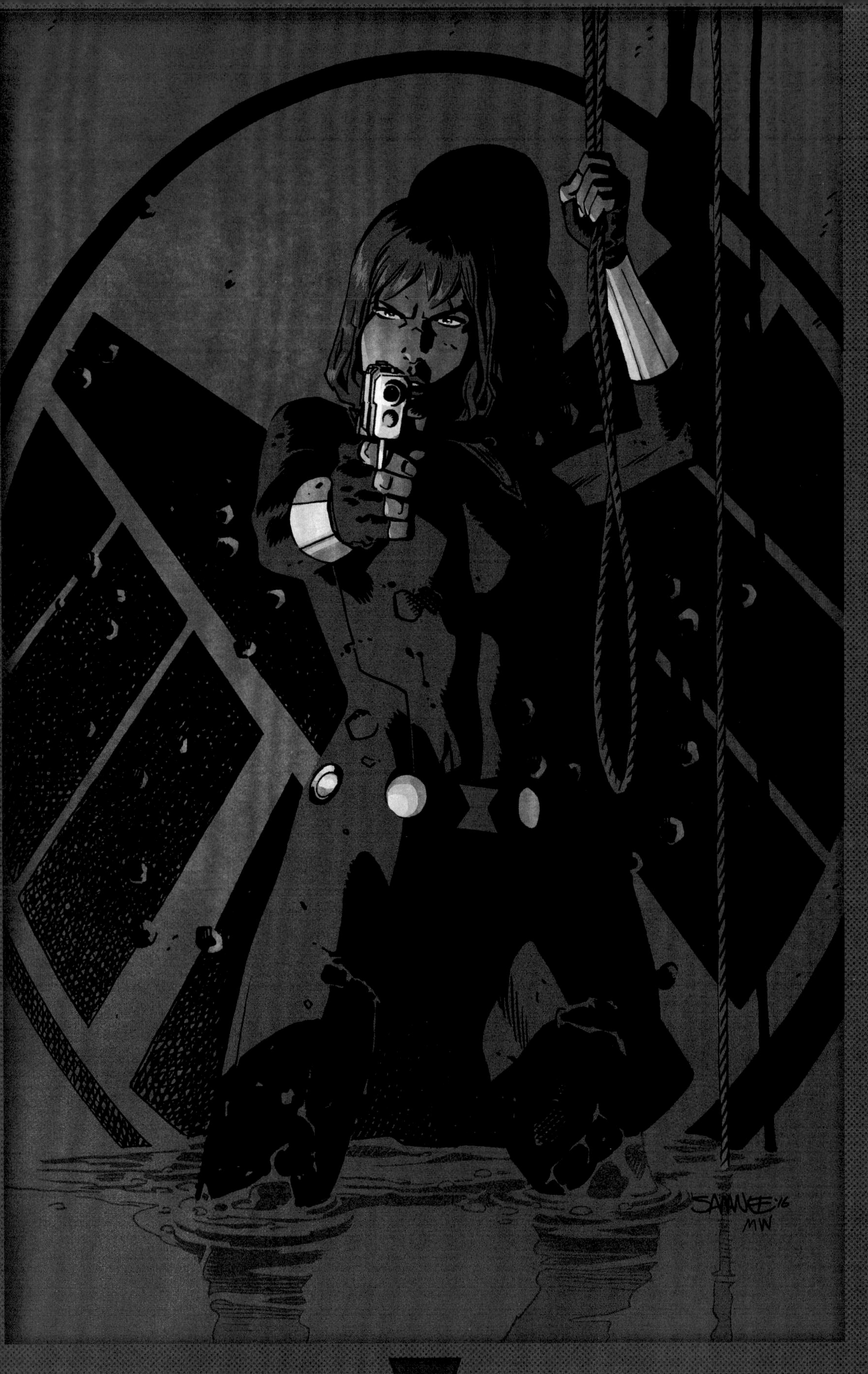
SAMNEE '16
MW

12

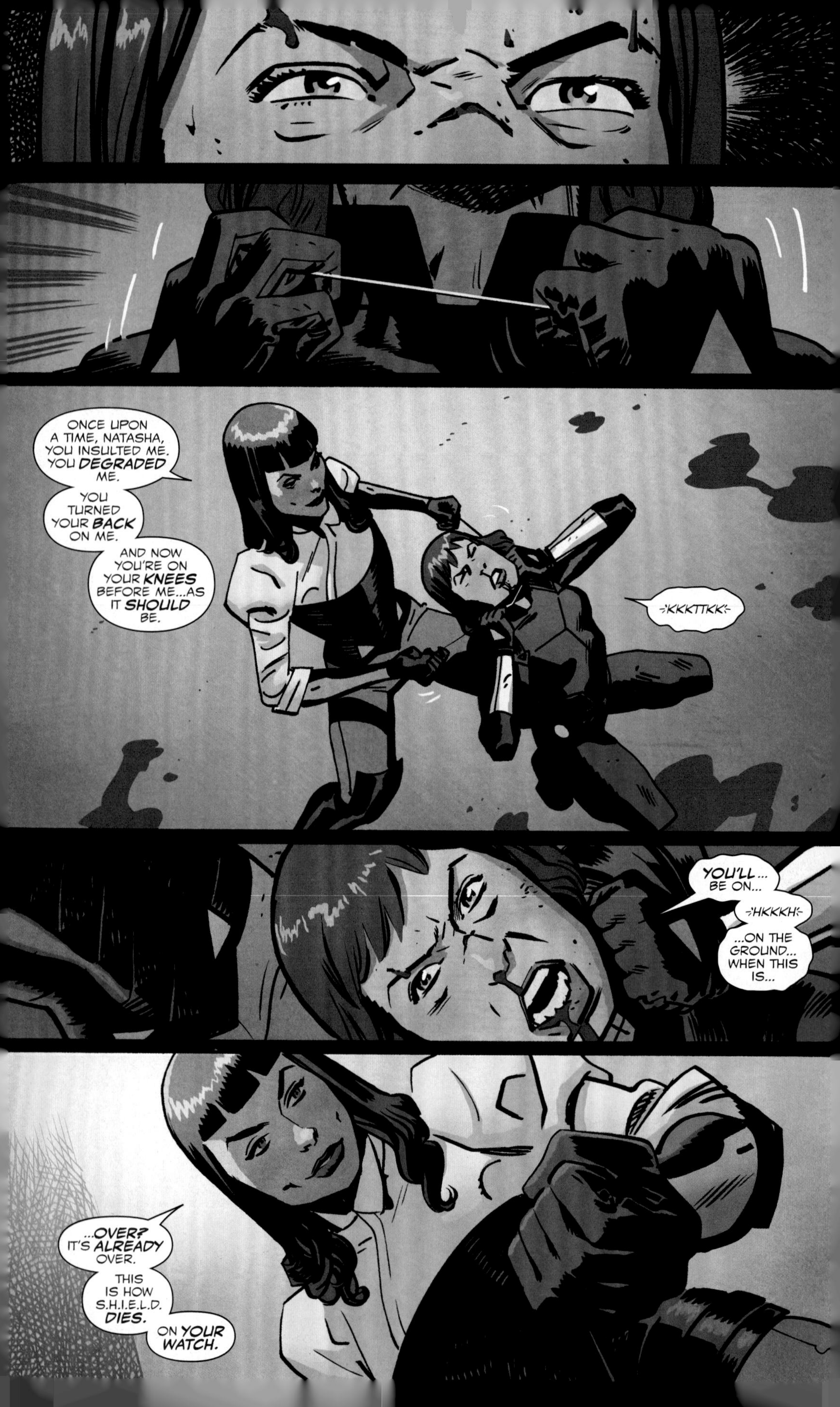

ONCE UPON A TIME, NATASHA, YOU INSULTED ME. YOU DEGRADED ME.
YOU TURNED YOUR BACK ON ME.
AND NOW YOU'RE ON YOUR KNEES BEFORE ME...AS IT SHOULD BE.
-KKKTTKK-
YOU'LL... BE ON...
-HKKKH-
...ON THE GROUND... WHEN THIS IS...
...OVER? IT'S ALREADY OVER.
THIS IS HOW S.H.I.E.L.D. DIES.
ON YOUR WATCH.

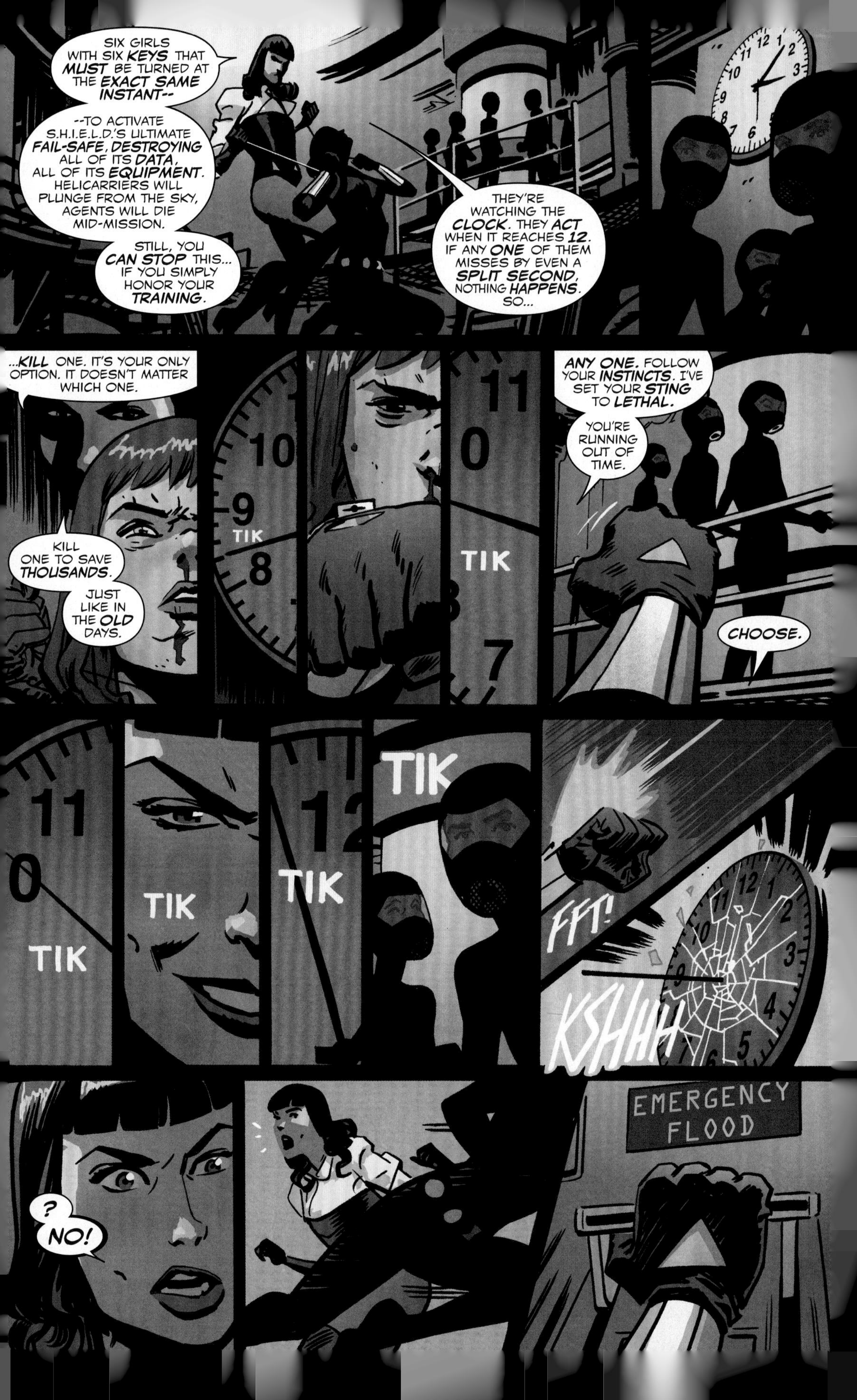
SIX GIRLS WITH SIX KEYS THAT MUST BE TURNED AT THE EXACT SAME INSTANT--
--TO ACTIVATE S.H.I.E.L.D.'S ULTIMATE FAIL-SAFE, DESTROYING ALL OF ITS DATA, ALL OF ITS EQUIPMENT. HELICARRIERS WILL PLUNGE FROM THE SKY, AGENTS WILL DIE MID-MISSION.
STILL, YOU CAN STOP THIS... IF YOU SIMPLY HONOR YOUR TRAINING.
THEY'RE WATCHING THE CLOCK. THEY ACT WHEN IT REACHES 12. IF ANY ONE OF THEM MISSES BY EVEN A SPLIT SECOND, NOTHING HAPPENS. SO...
...KILL ONE. IT'S YOUR ONLY OPTION. IT DOESN'T MATTER WHICH ONE.
KILL ONE TO SAVE THOUSANDS.
JUST LIKE IN THE OLD DAYS.
TIK
TIK
ANY ONE. FOLLOW YOUR INSTINCTS. I'VE SET YOUR STING TO LETHAL.
YOU'RE RUNNING OUT OF TIME.
CHOOSE.
TIK
TIK
TIK
TIK
FFT!
KSHHH
EMERGENCY FLOOD
?
NO!

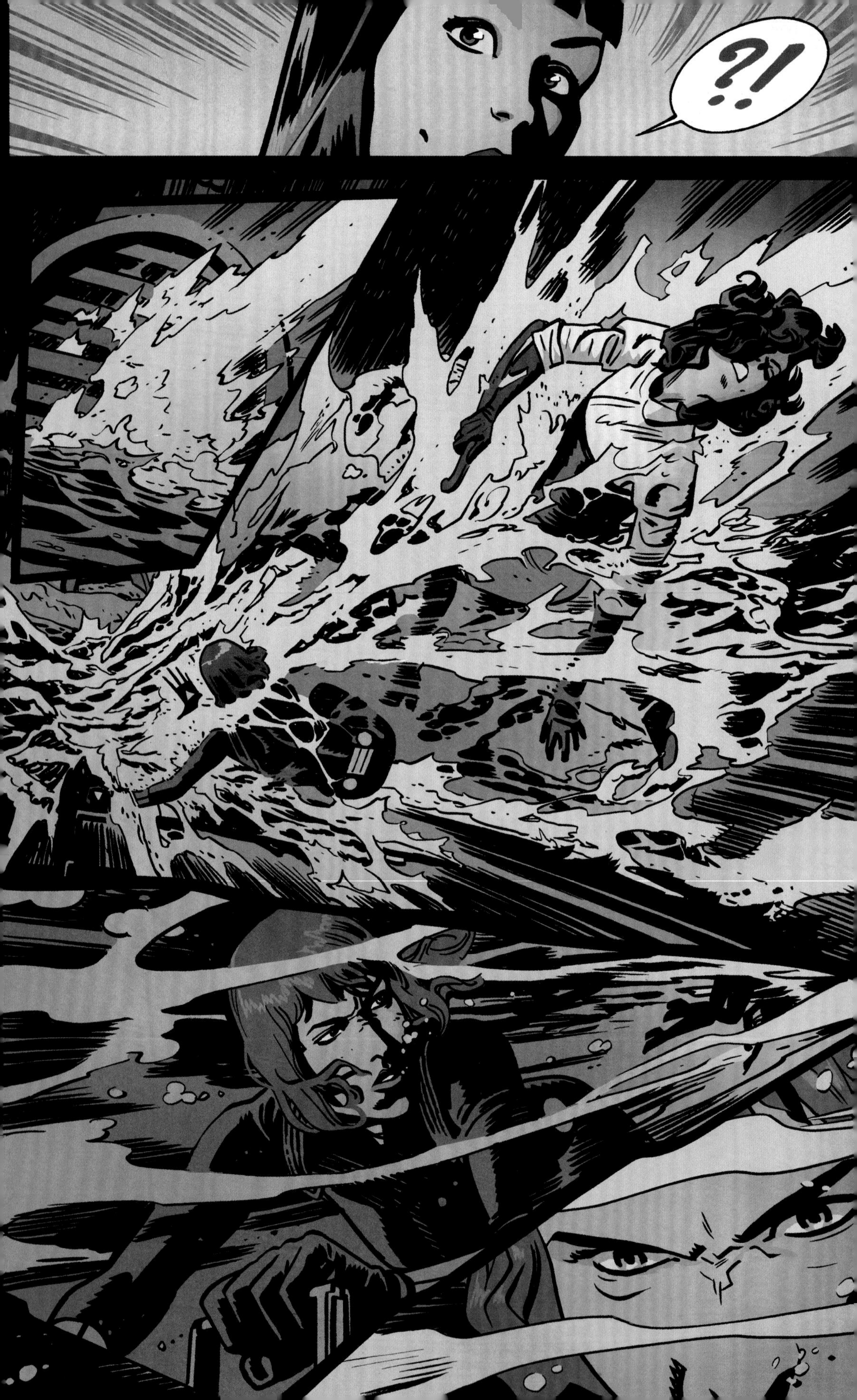
?!

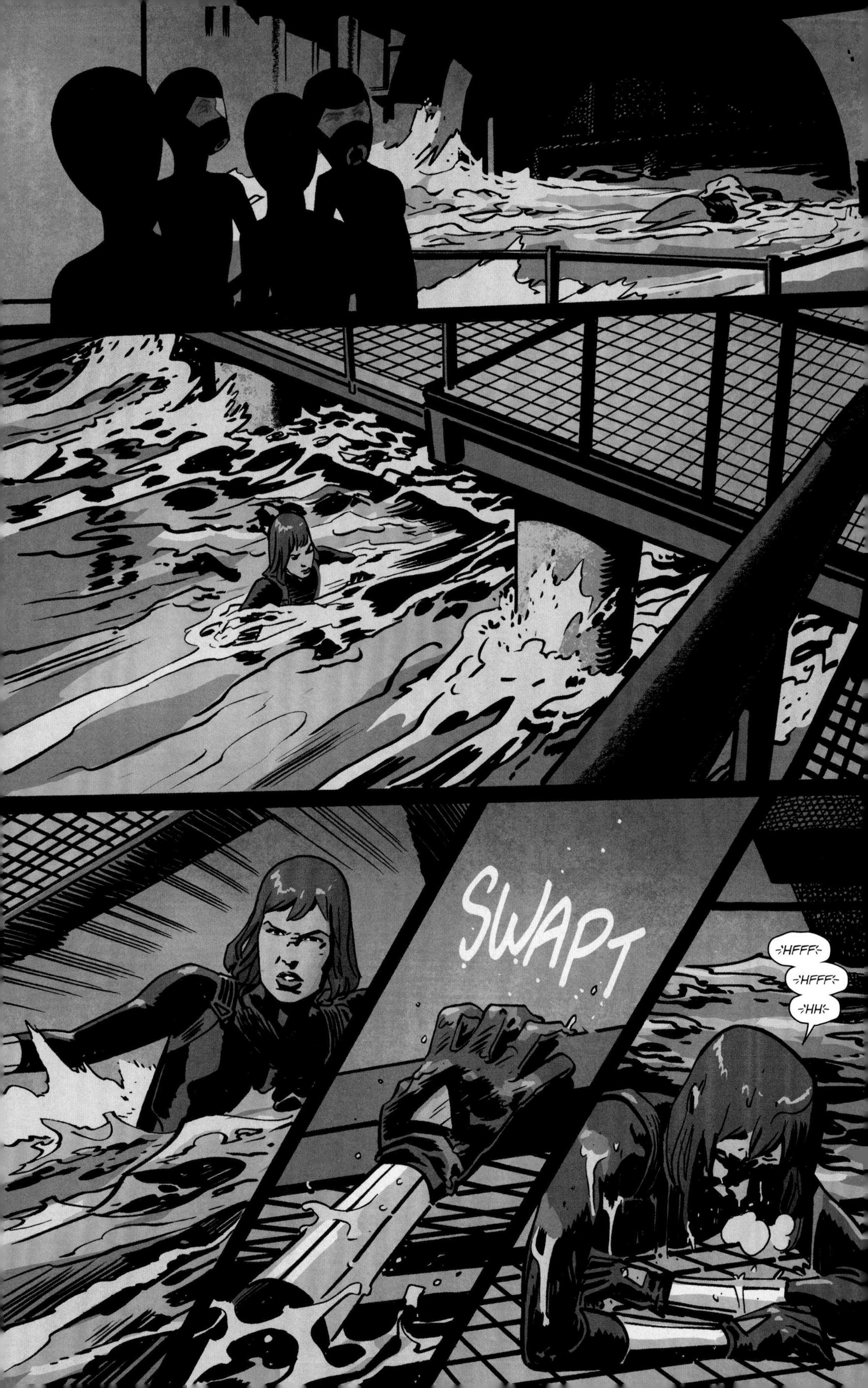
SWAPT
-HFFF-
-HFFF-
-HH-

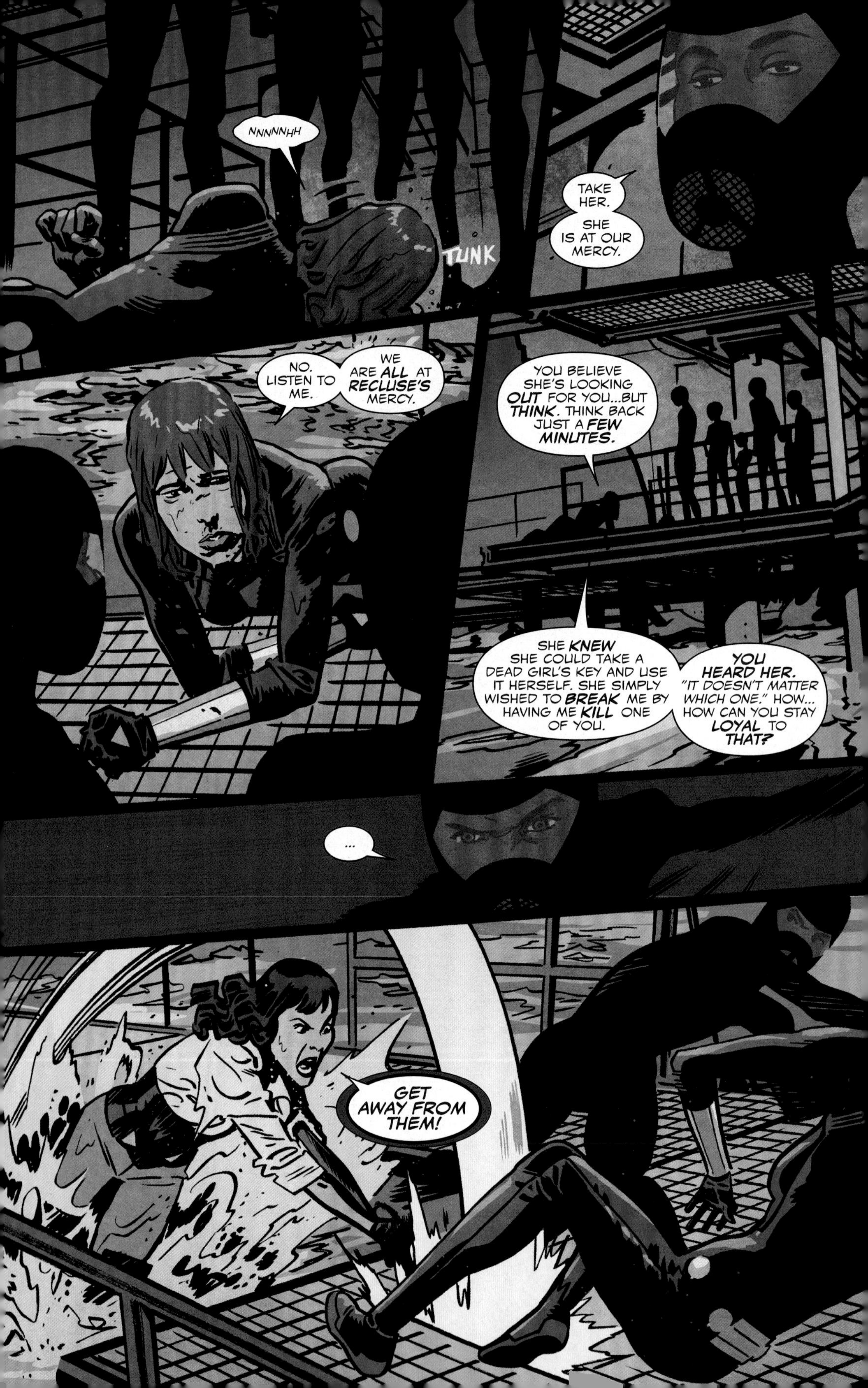
NNNNNHH
TUNK
TAKE HER.
SHE IS AT OUR MERCY.
NO. LISTEN TO ME.
WE ARE ALL AT RECLUSE'S MERCY.
YOU BELIEVE SHE'S LOOKING OUT FOR YOU...BUT THINK. THINK BACK JUST A FEW MINUTES.
SHE KNEW SHE COULD TAKE A DEAD GIRL'S KEY AND USE IT HERSELF. SHE SIMPLY WISHED TO BREAK ME BY HAVING ME KILL ONE OF YOU.
YOU HEARD HER. "IT DOESN'T MATTER WHICH ONE." HOW... HOW CAN YOU STAY LOYAL TO THAT?
...
GET AWAY FROM THEM!

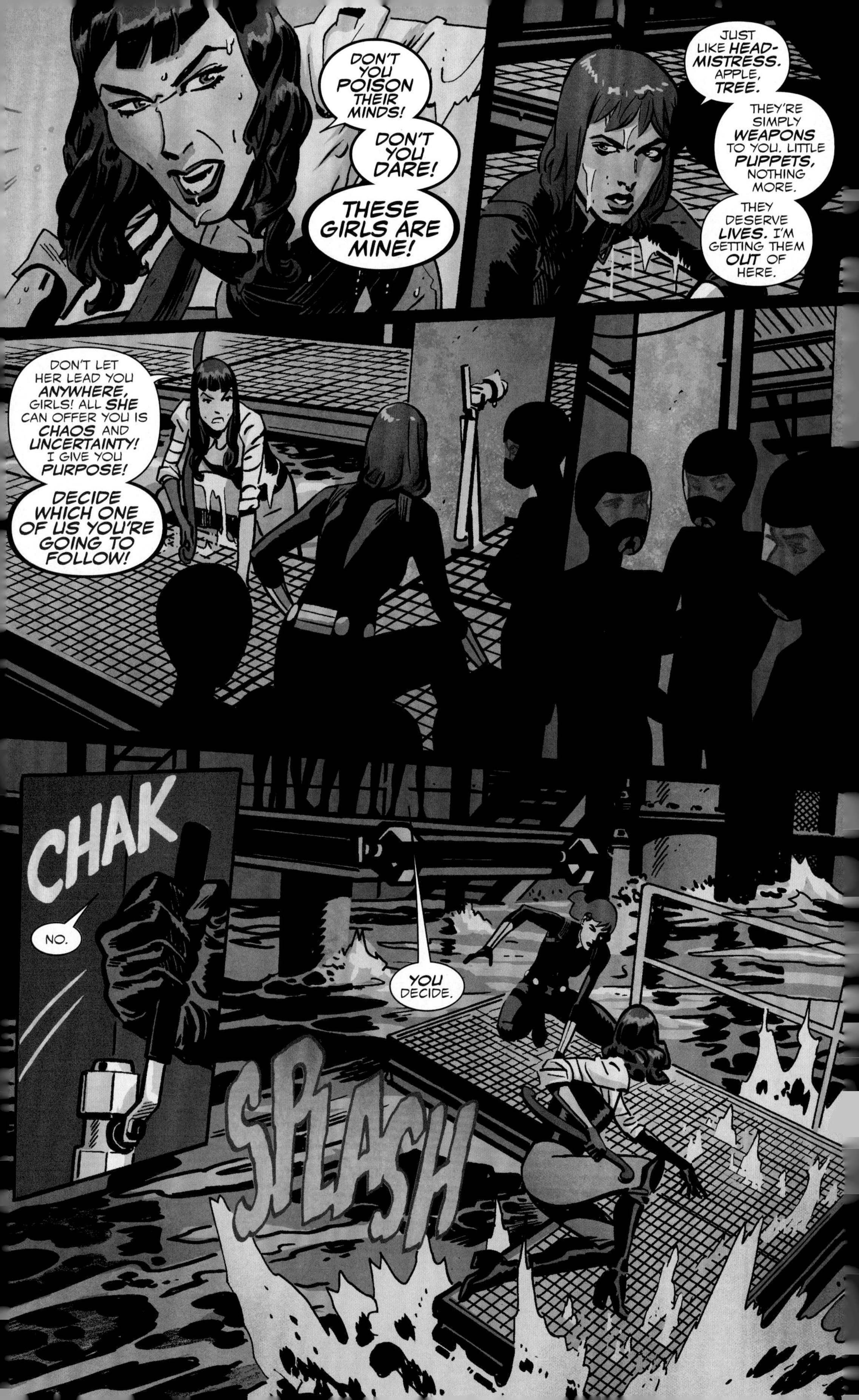
DON'T YOU POISON THEIR MINDS!
DON'T YOU DARE!
THESE GIRLS ARE MINE!
JUST LIKE HEADMISTRESS. APPLE, TREE.
THEY'RE SIMPLY WEAPONS TO YOU. LITTLE PUPPETS, NOTHING MORE.
THEY DESERVE LIVES. I'M GETTING THEM OUT OF HERE.
DON'T LET HER LEAD YOU ANYWHERE, GIRLS! ALL SHE CAN OFFER YOU IS CHAOS AND UNCERTAINTY! I GIVE YOU PURPOSE!
DECIDE WHICH ONE OF US YOU'RE GOING TO FOLLOW!
CHAK
NO.
YOU DECIDE.
SPLASH

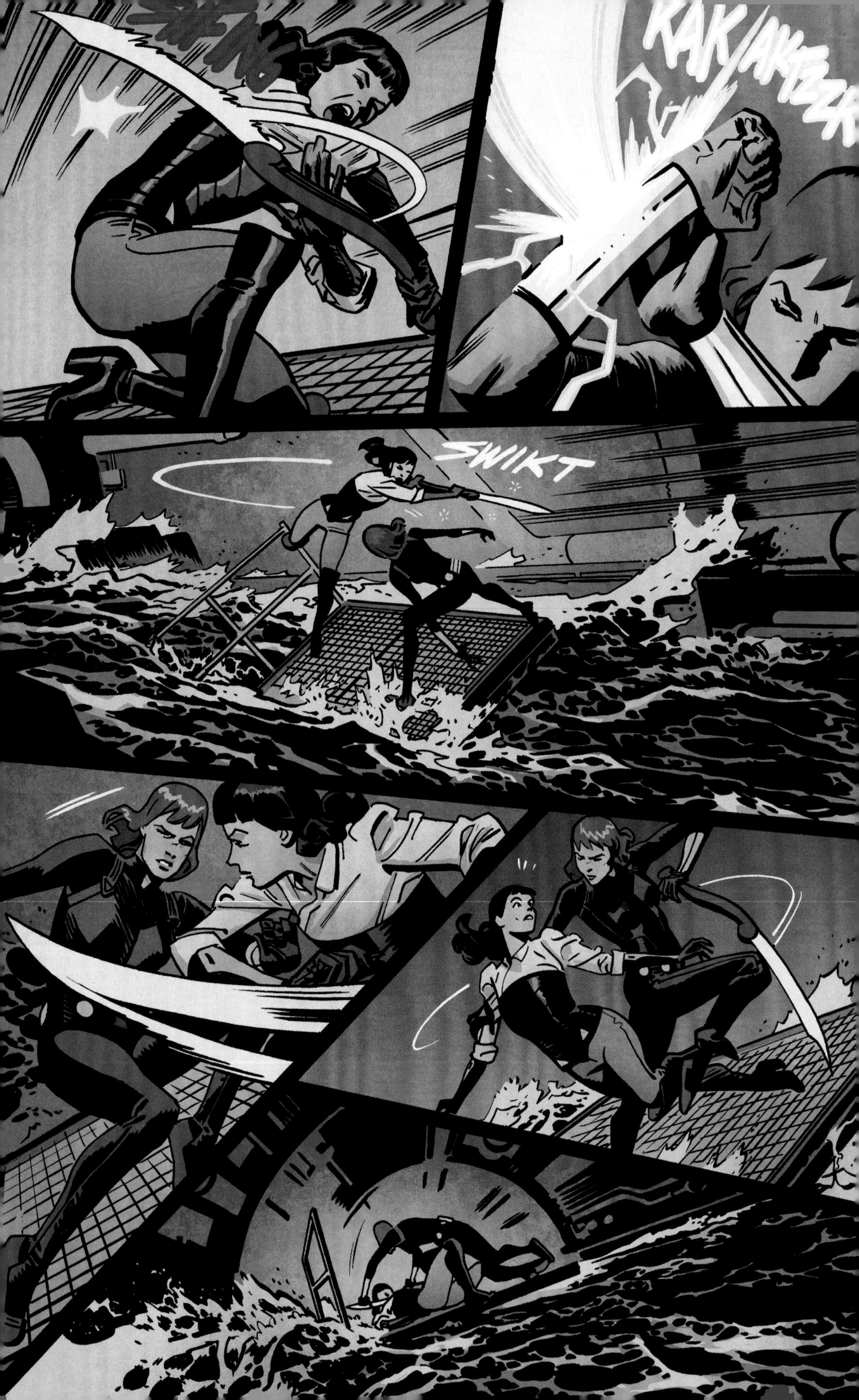
KAKAKTZZK
SWIKT

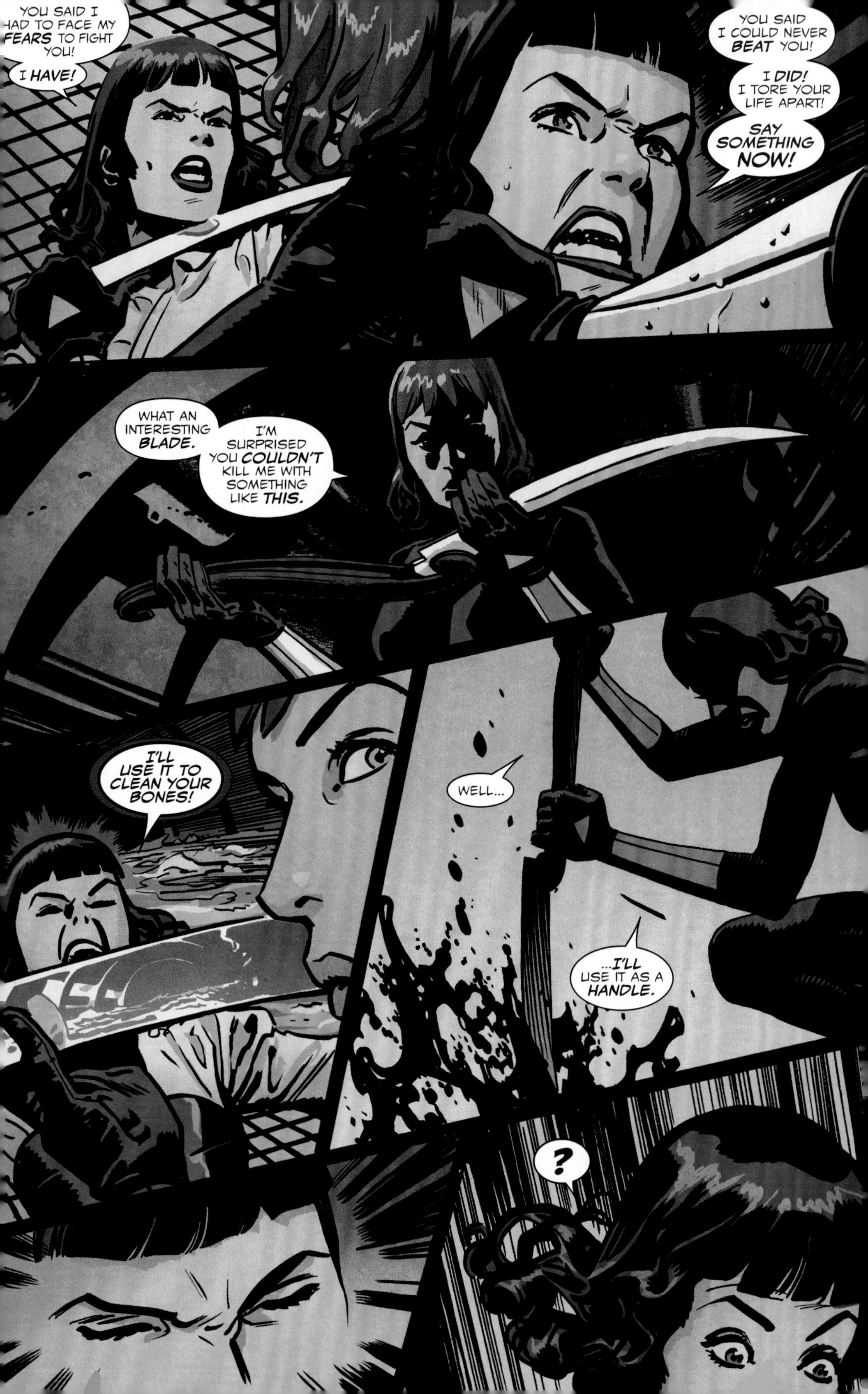
YOU SAID I HAD TO FACE MY FEARS TO FIGHT YOU!
I HAVE!
YOU SAID I COULD NEVER BEAT YOU!
I DID! I TORE YOUR LIFE APART!
SAY SOMETHING NOW!
WHAT AN INTERESTING BLADE.
I'M SURPRISED YOU COULDN'T KILL ME WITH SOMETHING LIKE THIS.
I'LL USE IT TO CLEAN YOUR BONES!
WELL...
...I'LL USE IT AS A HANDLE.
?

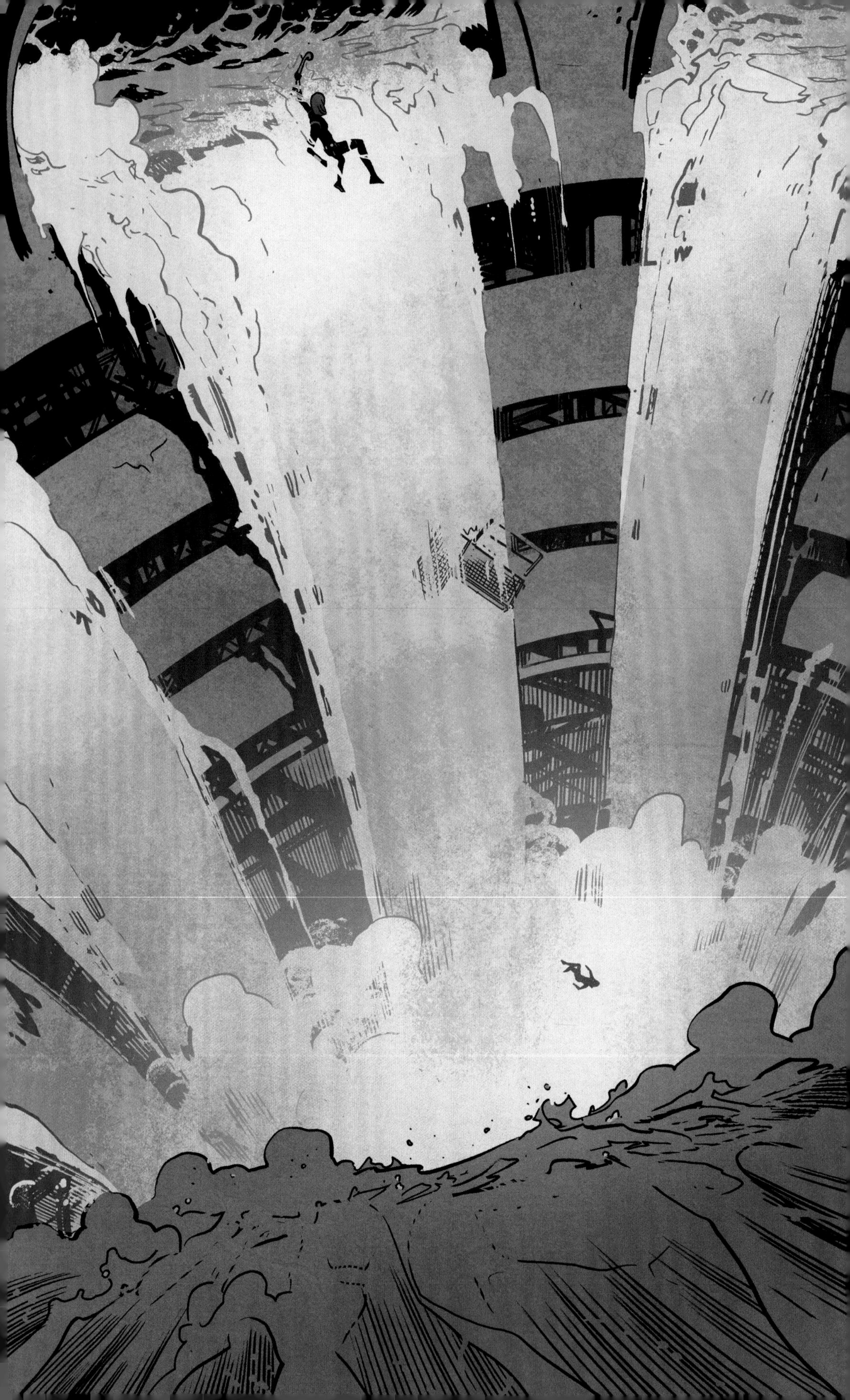

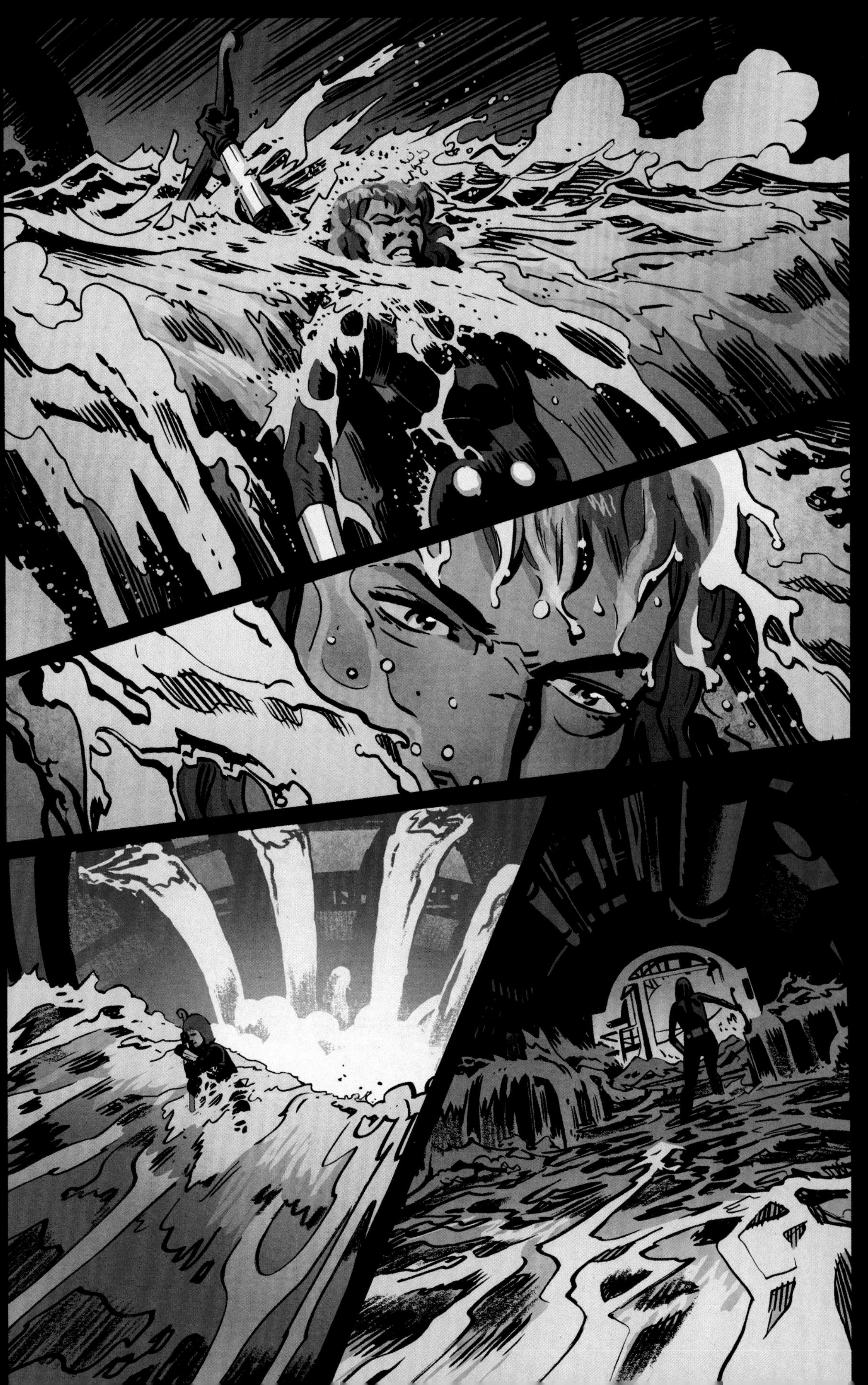

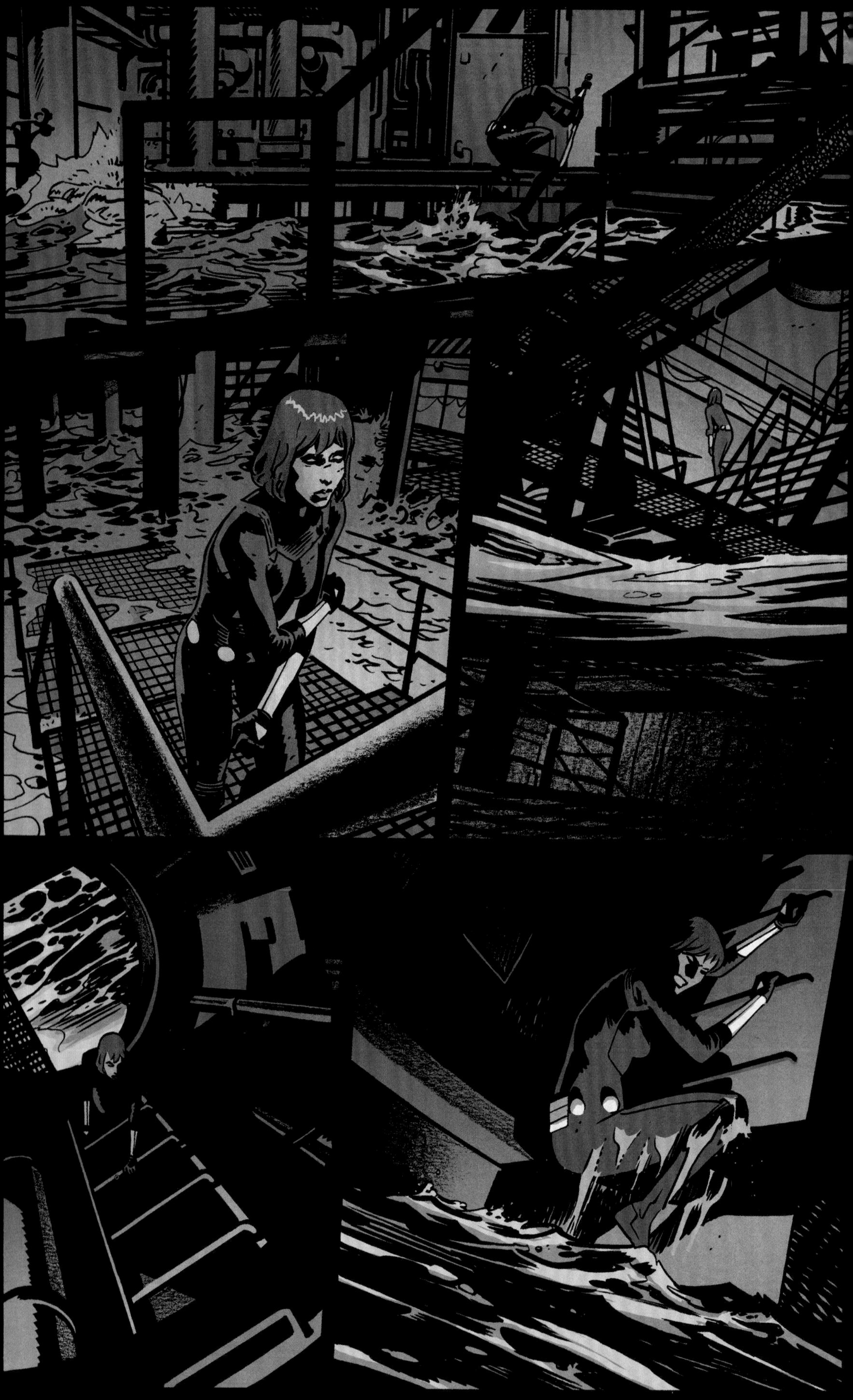

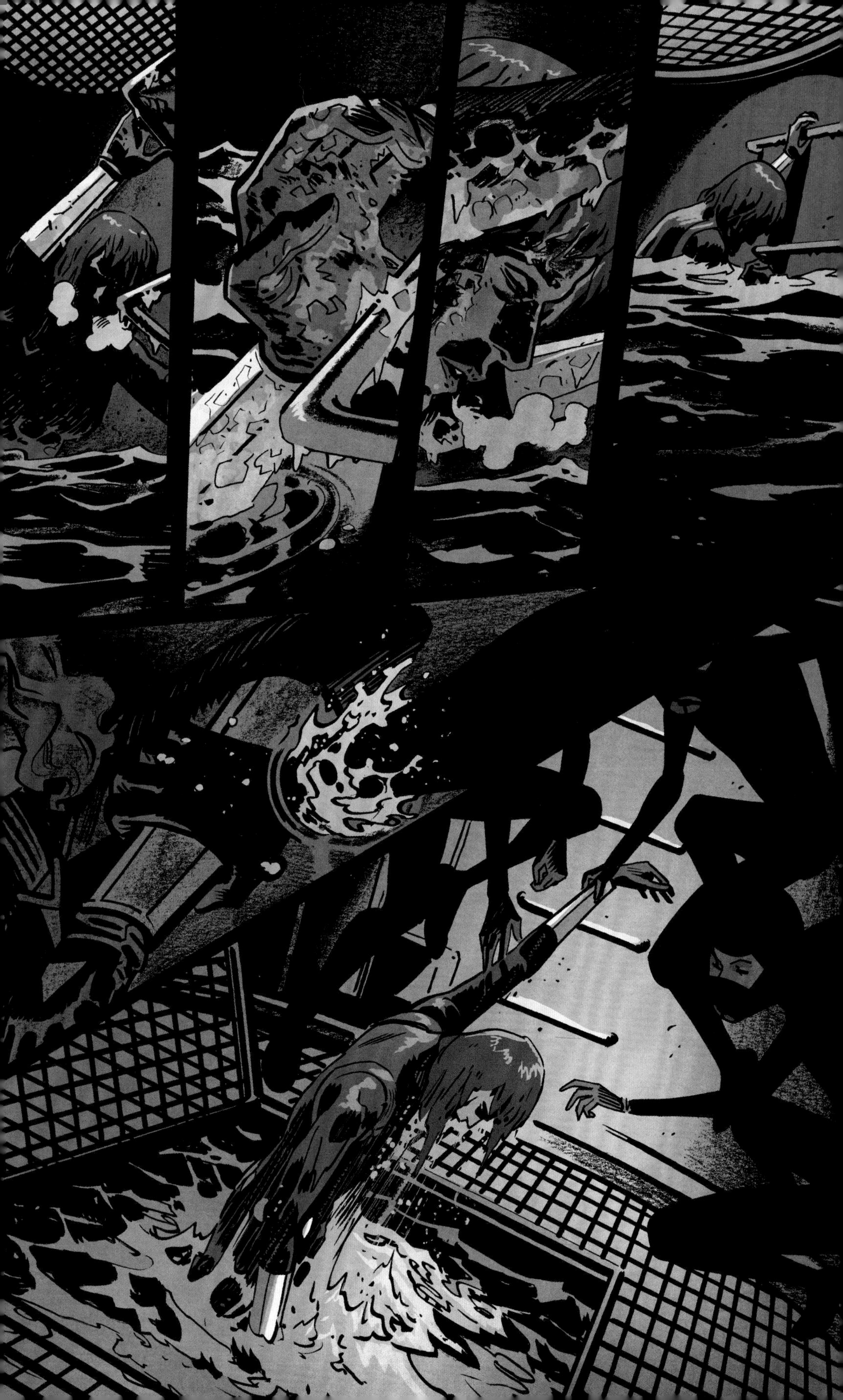

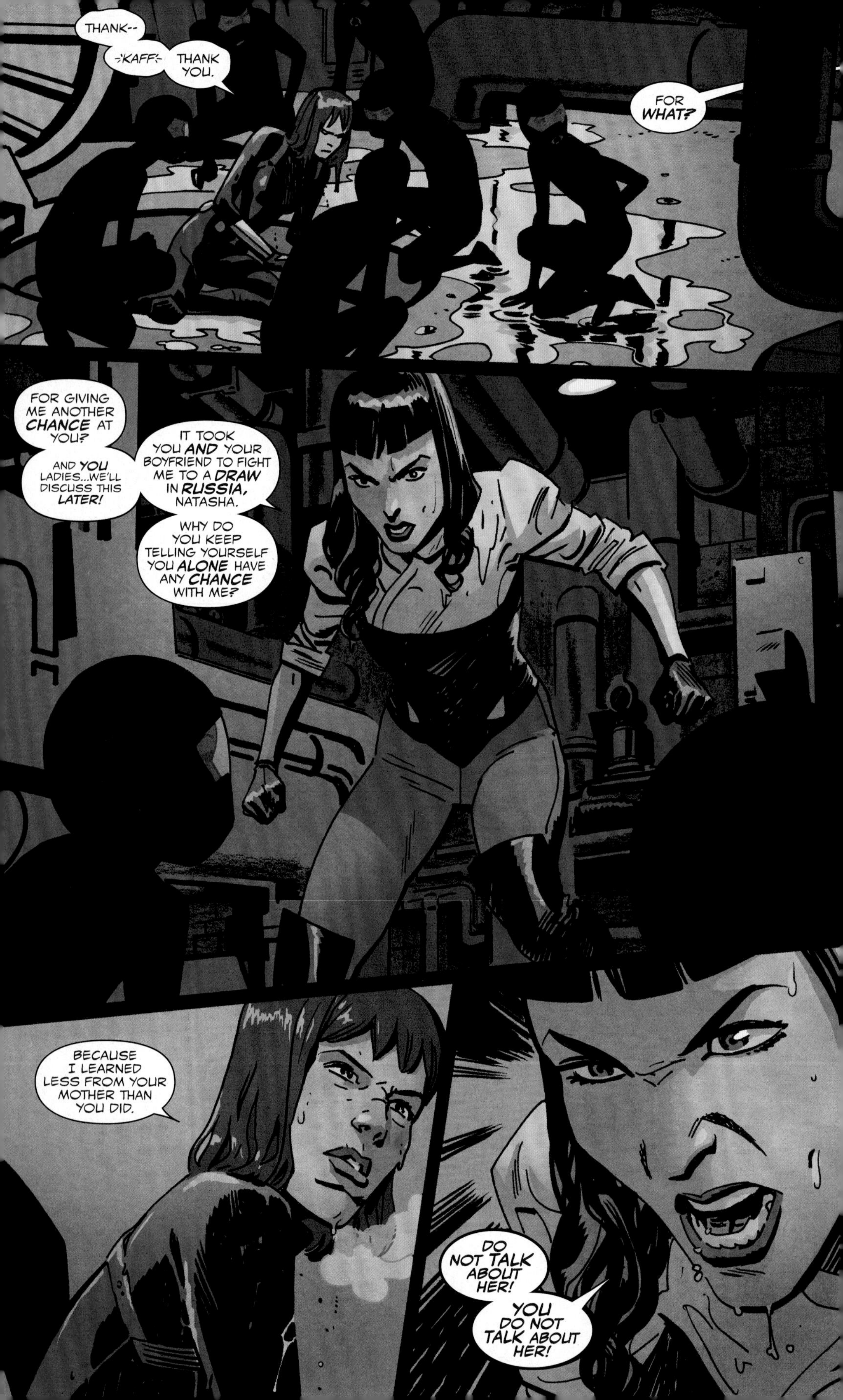
THANK--
-KAFF- THANK YOU.
FOR WHAT?
FOR GIVING ME ANOTHER CHANCE AT YOU?
AND YOU LADIES...WE'LL DISCUSS THIS LATER!
IT TOOK YOU AND YOUR BOYFRIEND TO FIGHT ME TO A DRAW IN RUSSIA, NATASHA.
WHY DO YOU KEEP TELLING YOURSELF YOU ALONE HAVE ANY CHANCE WITH ME?
BECAUSE I LEARNED LESS FROM YOUR MOTHER THAN YOU DID.
DO NOT TALK ABOUT HER!
YOU DO NOT TALK ABOUT HER!

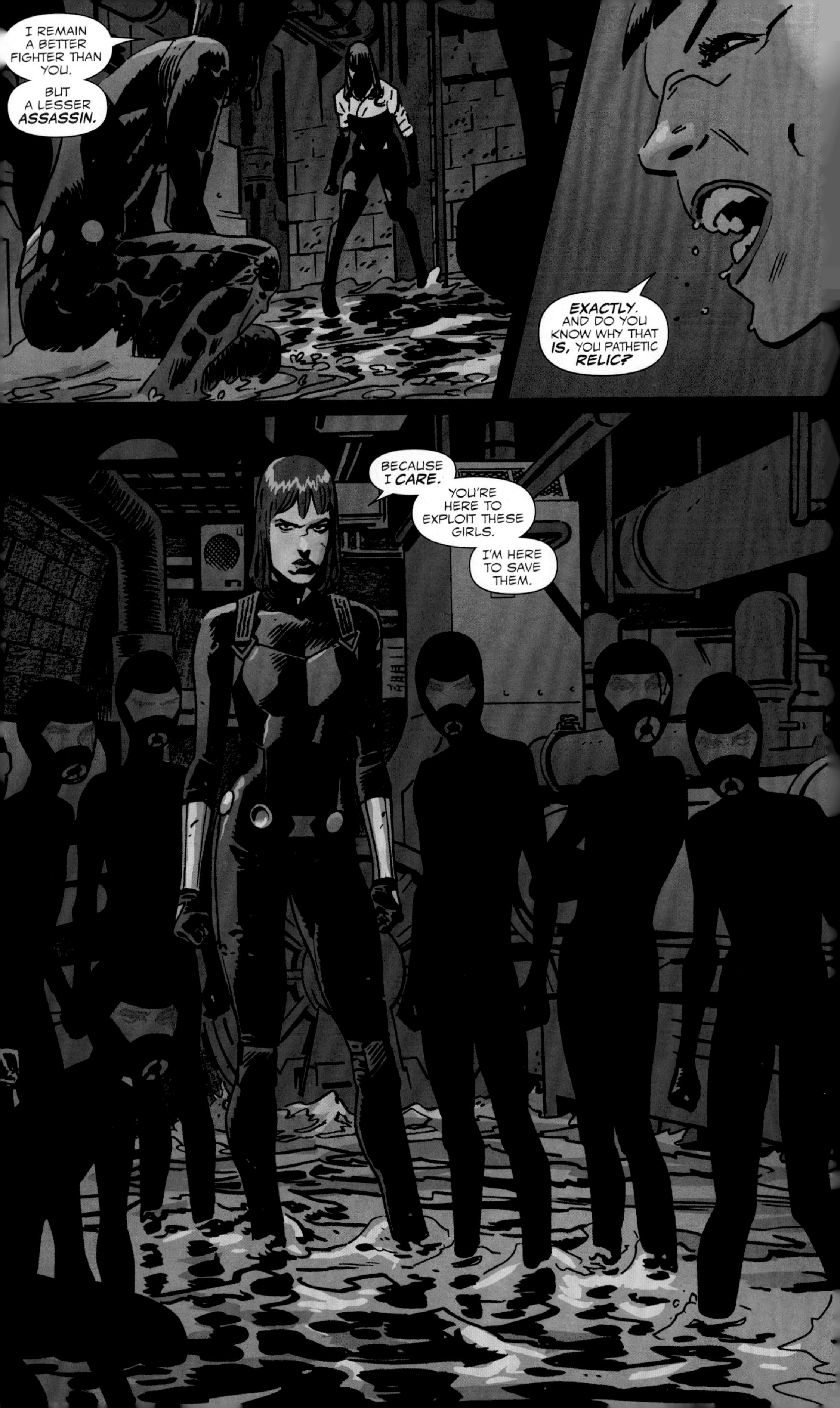
I REMAIN A BETTER FIGHTER THAN YOU.
BUT A LESSER **ASSASSIN.**
**EXACTLY.** AND DO YOU KNOW WHY THAT **IS,** YOU PATHETIC **RELIC?**
BECAUSE I **CARE.**
YOU'RE HERE TO EXPLOIT THESE GIRLS.
I'M HERE TO SAVE THEM.

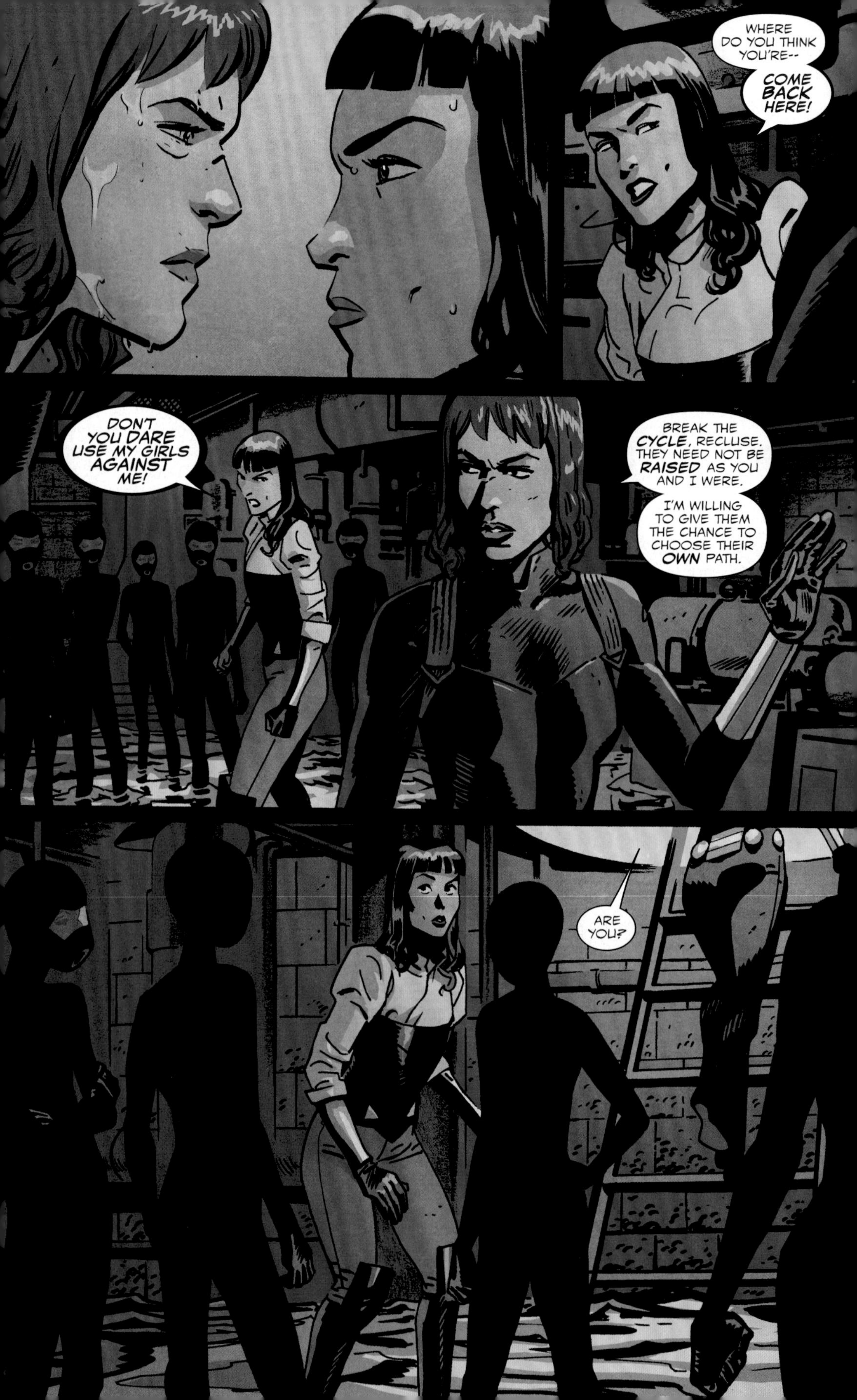
WHERE DO YOU THINK YOU'RE--
COME BACK HERE!
DON'T YOU DARE USE MY GIRLS AGAINST ME!
BREAK THE CYCLE, RECLUSE. THEY NEED NOT BE RAISED AS YOU AND I WERE.
I'M WILLING TO GIVE THEM THE CHANCE TO CHOOSE THEIR OWN PATH.
ARE YOU?

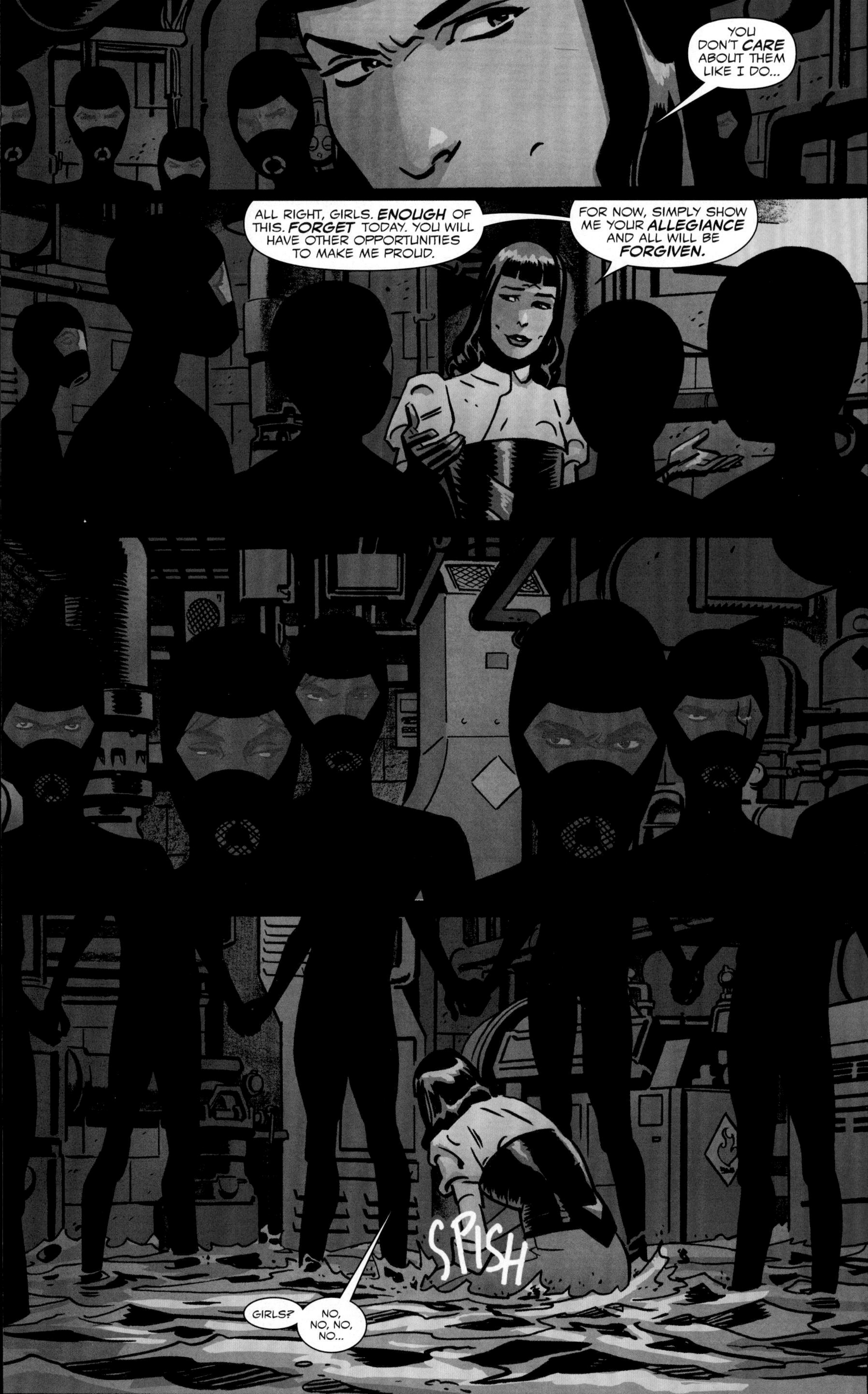
YOU DON'T CARE ABOUT THEM LIKE I DO...
ALL RIGHT, GIRLS. ENOUGH OF THIS. FORGET TODAY. YOU WILL HAVE OTHER OPPORTUNITIES TO MAKE ME PROUD.
FOR NOW, SIMPLY SHOW ME YOUR ALLEGIANCE AND ALL WILL BE FORGIVEN.
SPISH
GIRLS?
NO, NO, NO, NO...

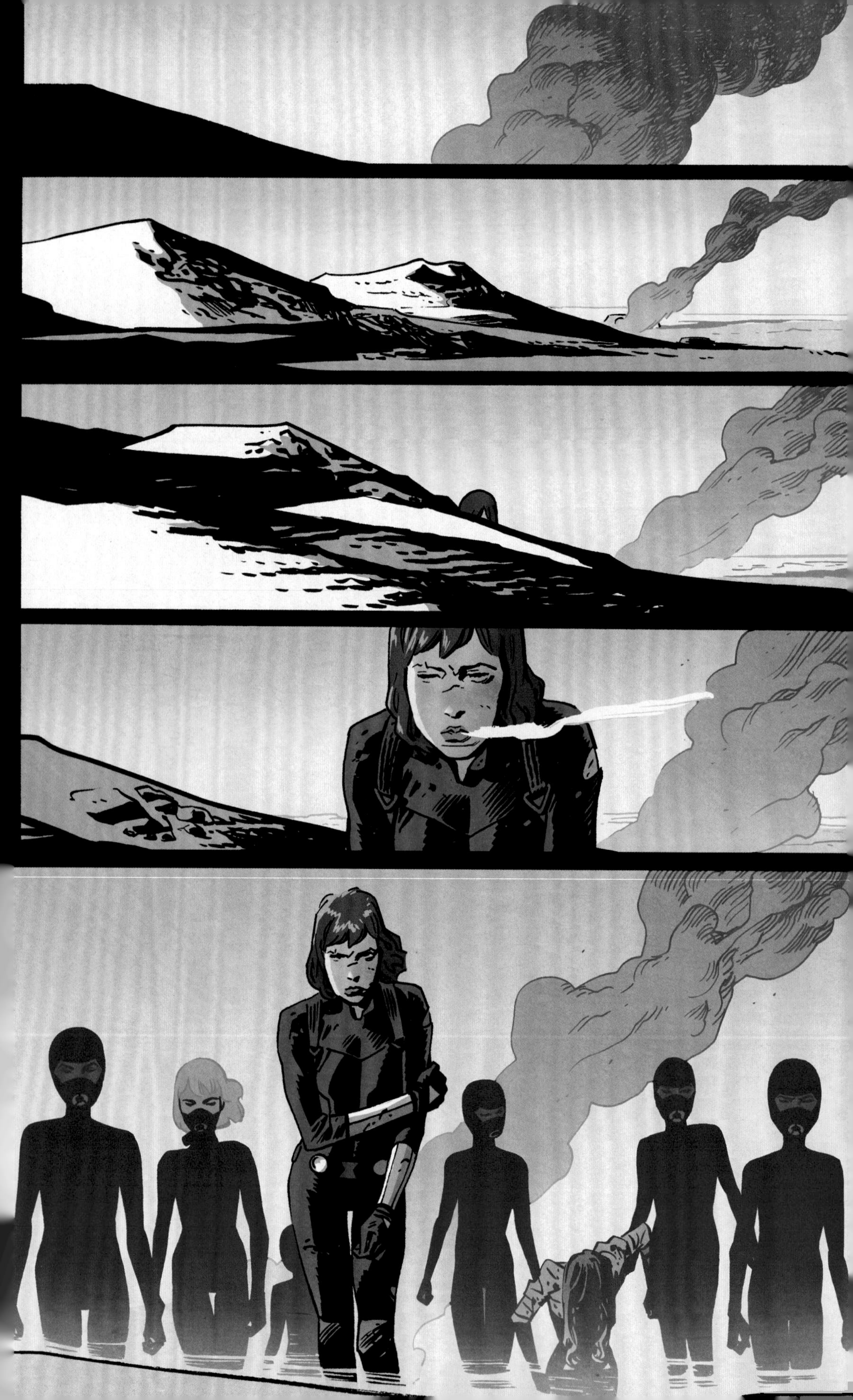

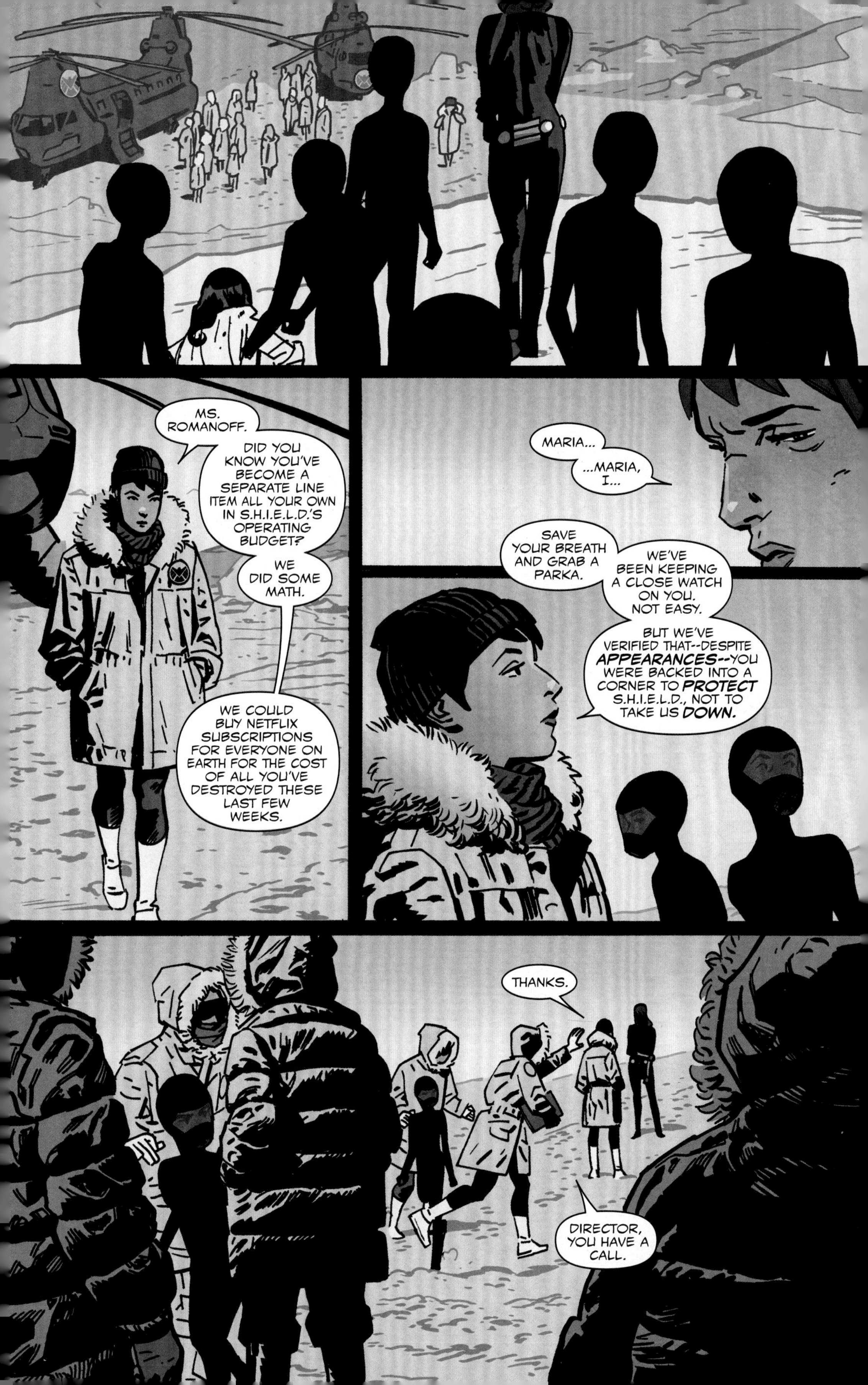
MS. ROMANOFF.
DID YOU KNOW YOU'VE BECOME A SEPARATE LINE ITEM ALL YOUR OWN IN S.H.I.E.L.D.'S OPERATING BUDGET?
WE DID SOME MATH.
WE COULD BUY NETFLIX SUBSCRIPTIONS FOR EVERYONE ON EARTH FOR THE COST OF ALL YOU'VE DESTROYED THESE LAST FEW WEEKS.
MARIA...
...MARIA, I...
SAVE YOUR BREATH AND GRAB A PARKA.
WE'VE BEEN KEEPING A CLOSE WATCH ON YOU. NOT EASY.
BUT WE'VE VERIFIED THAT--DESPITE **APPEARANCES**--YOU WERE BACKED INTO A CORNER TO **PROTECT** S.H.I.E.L.D., NOT TO TAKE US **DOWN.**
THANKS.
DIRECTOR, YOU HAVE A CALL.

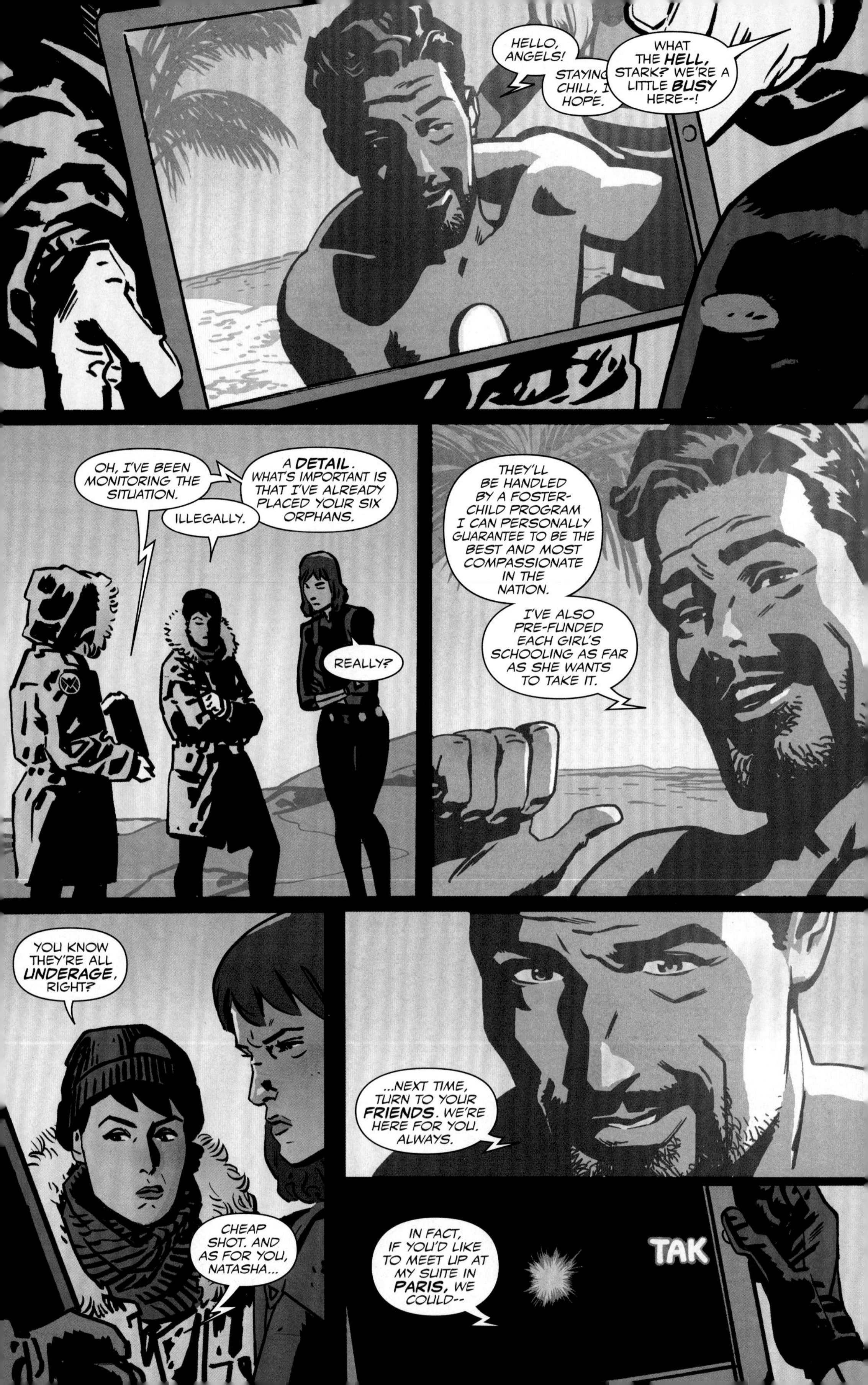
HELLO, ANGELS!
STAYING CHILL, I HOPE.
WHAT THE HELL, STARK? WE'RE A LITTLE BUSY HERE--!
OH, I'VE BEEN MONITORING THE SITUATION.
ILLEGALLY.
A DETAIL. WHAT'S IMPORTANT IS THAT I'VE ALREADY PLACED YOUR SIX ORPHANS.
REALLY?
THEY'LL BE HANDLED BY A FOSTER-CHILD PROGRAM I CAN PERSONALLY GUARANTEE TO BE THE BEST AND MOST COMPASSIONATE IN THE NATION.
I'VE ALSO PRE-FUNDED EACH GIRL'S SCHOOLING AS FAR AS SHE WANTS TO TAKE IT.
YOU KNOW THEY'RE ALL UNDERAGE, RIGHT?
CHEAP SHOT. AND AS FOR YOU, NATASHA...
...NEXT TIME, TURN TO YOUR FRIENDS. WE'RE HERE FOR YOU. ALWAYS.
IN FACT, IF YOU'D LIKE TO MEET UP AT MY SUITE IN PARIS, WE COULD--
TAK

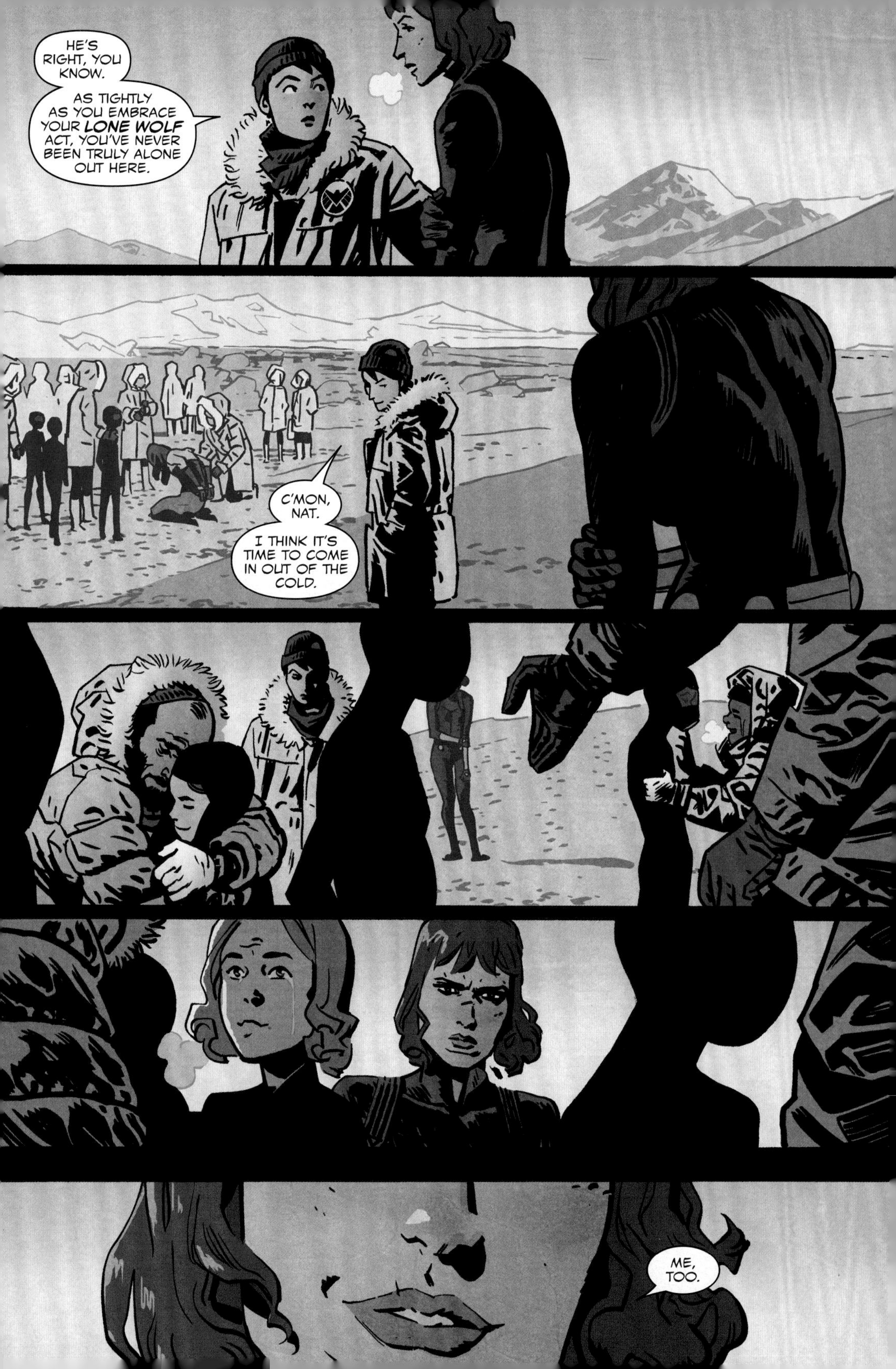
HE'S RIGHT, YOU KNOW.
AS TIGHTLY AS YOU EMBRACE YOUR **LONE WOLF** ACT, YOU'VE NEVER BEEN TRULY ALONE OUT HERE.
C'MON, NAT.
I THINK IT'S TIME TO COME IN OUT OF THE COLD.
ME, TOO.

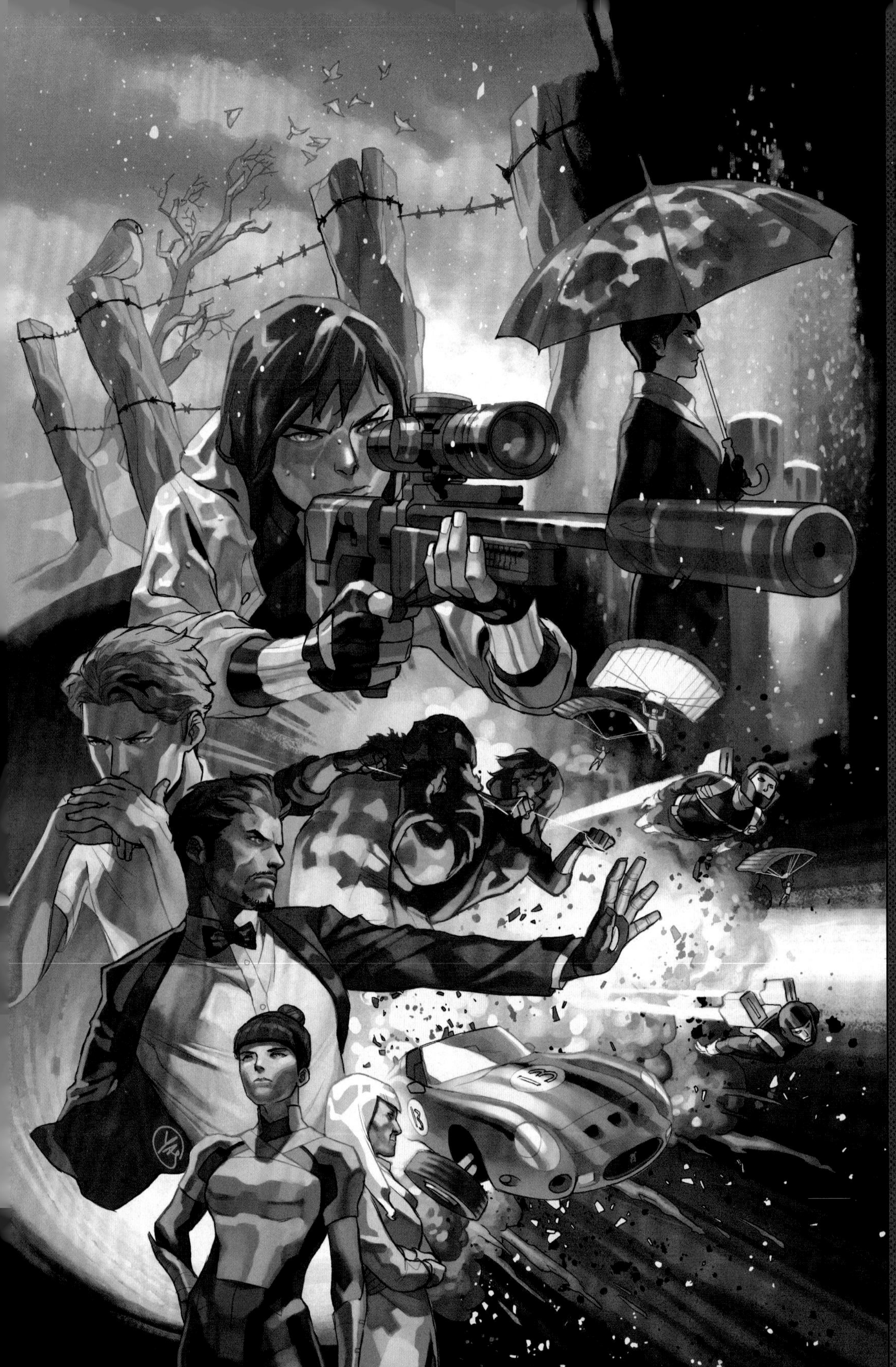

YASMINE PUTRI

NO. 7 STORY THUS FAR VARIANT

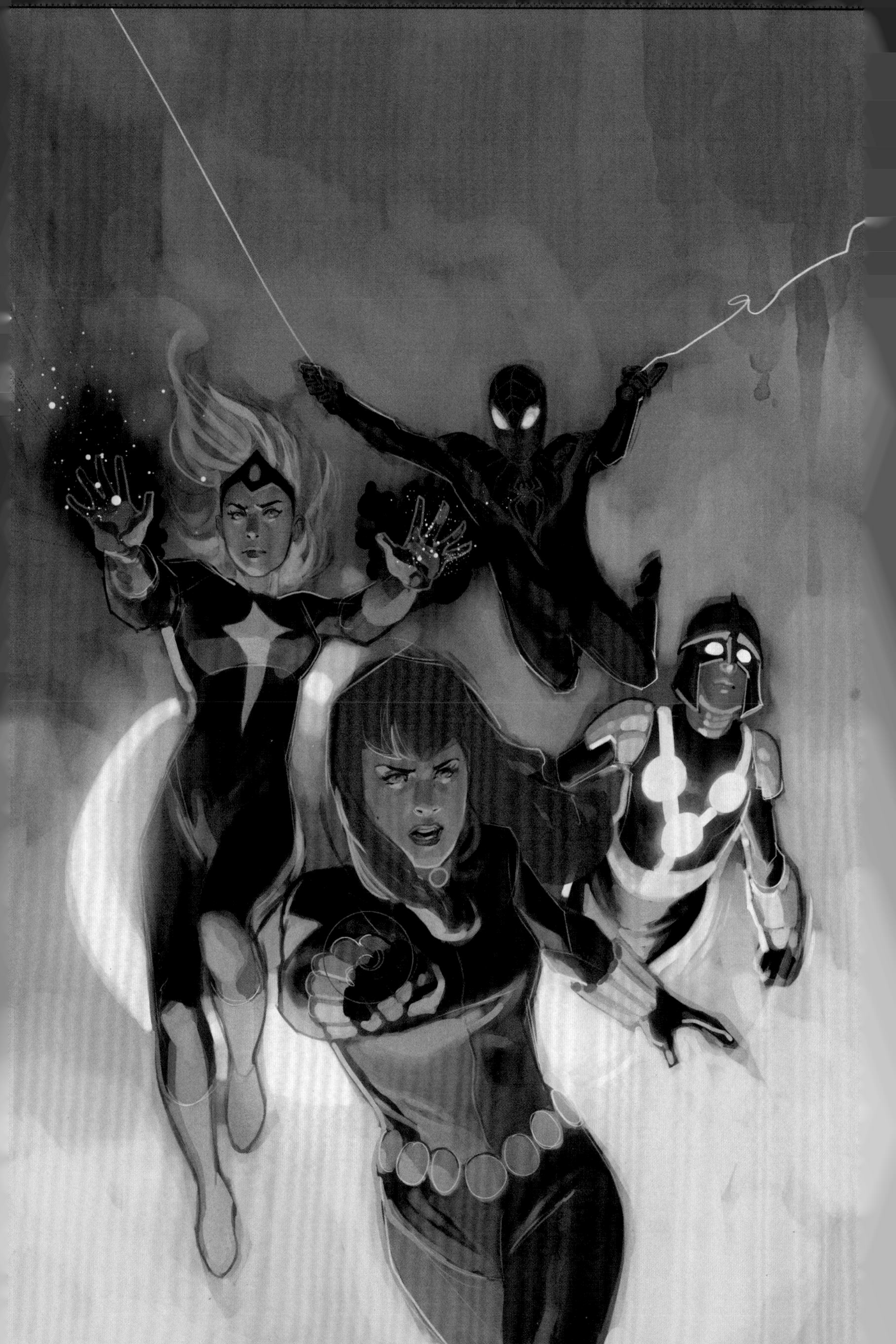

**PHIL NOTO**
**NO. 7 CHAMPIONS VARIANT**

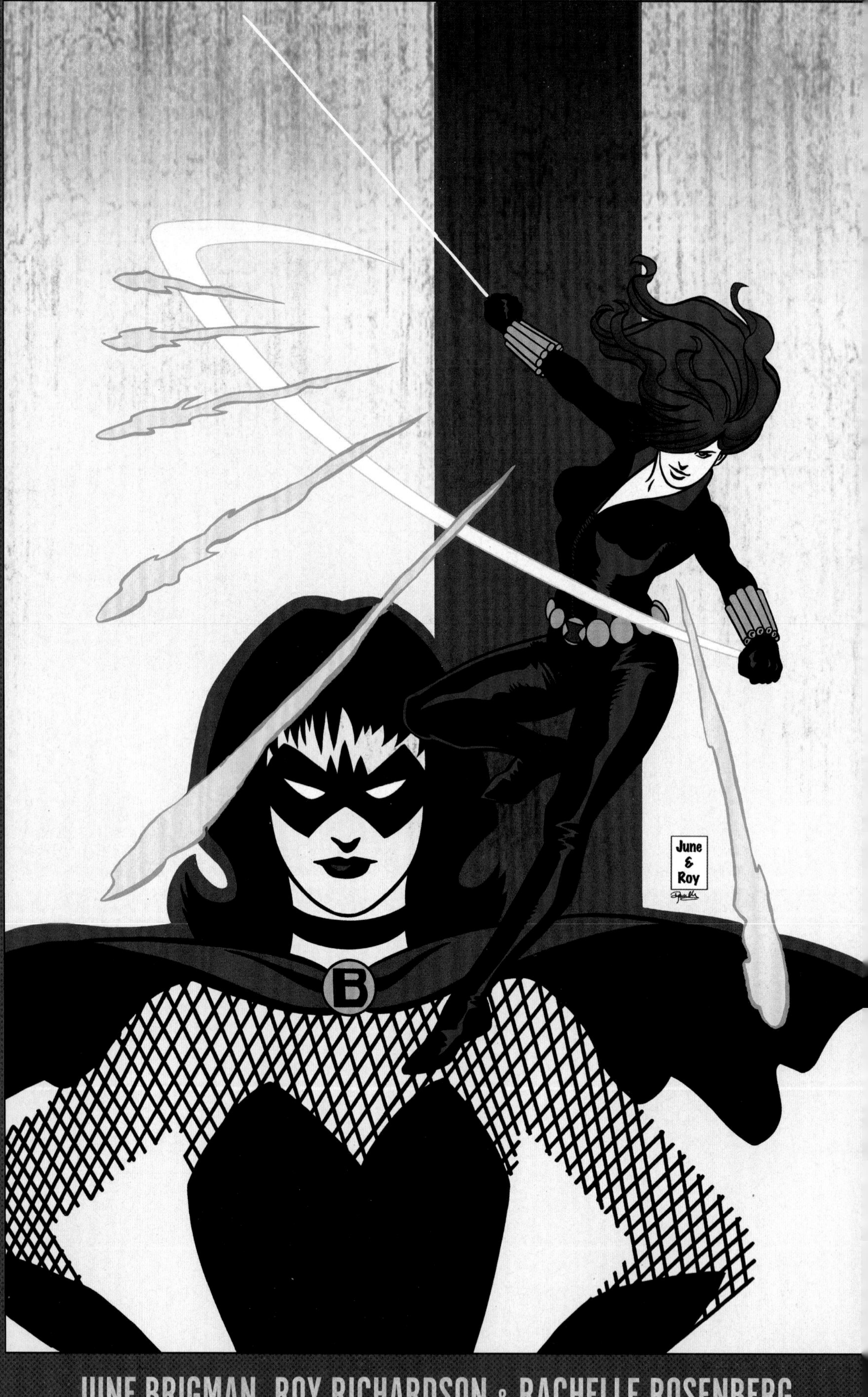
June
&
Roy

JUNE BRIGMAN, ROY RICHARDSON & RACHELLE ROSENBERG

NO. 7 CLASSIC VARIANT